THE EVERYTHING BRIDGE BOOK

Dear Reader,

I just love to go to work each day, because my job and my avocation—bridge—are one and the same. I have been playing this great game—mostly in the duplicate format—for nearly forty years.

My outlook has changed over the years. I play for the love of it, and winning is a nice bonus but not essential. Still, I strive each time to do my best—and I still want to tell everyone how great the game can be. I am an experienced player, but I have tons and tons yet to learn, and that's one of the elements of the game that keeps me coming back.

Join me in a most wonderful journey. There is no sport in the world except bridge where you can compete against the best simply by buying an entry in the same game. I have never played in a world championship, but I have sat at the table with world champions many times. It's very exciting.

You won't regret your decision to learn a game that will take you around the world and that you can play for a lifetime.

Brent Manley

Welcome to the EVERYTHING® Series!

These handy, accessible books give you all you need to tackle a difficult project, gain a new hobby, comprehend a fascinating topic, prepare for an exam, or even brush up on something you learned back in school but have since forgotten.

You can choose to read an *Everything*® book from cover to cover or just pick out the information you want from our four useful boxes: e-questions, e-facts, e-alerts, and e-ssentials.

We give you everything you need to know on the subject, but throw in a lot of fun stuff along the way, too.

We now have more than 400 *Everything*® books in print, spanning such wide-ranging categories as weddings, pregnancy, cooking, music instruction, foreign language, crafts, pets, New Age, and so much more. When you're done reading them all, you can finally say you know *Everything*®!

E-QUESTION

Answers to
common questions

FACTS

Important snippets
of information

ALERTS!

Urgent
warnings

ESSENTIALS

Quick
handy tips

PUBLISHER Karen Cooper

DIRECTOR OF ACQUISITIONS AND INNOVATION Paula Munier

MANAGING EDITOR, EVERYTHING SERIES Lisa Laing

COPY CHIEF Casey Ebert

ACQUISITIONS EDITOR Lisa Laing

DEVELOPMENT EDITOR Brett Palana-Shanahan

EDITORIAL ASSISTANT Hillary Thompson

Visit the entire Everything® series at *www.everything.com*

THE EVERYTHING®

BRIDGE BOOK

2nd Edition

Easy-to-follow instructions
to have you playing in no time!

Brent Manley

Avon, Massachusetts

Dedication

To Donna, the light of my life

An Everything® Series Book.
Everything® and everything.com® are registered trademarks of F+W Media, Inc.

Published by Adams Media, a division of F+W Media, Inc.
57 Littlefield Street, Avon, MA 02322 U.S.A.
www.adamsmedia.com

ISBN 10: 1-60550-123-9
ISBN 13: 978-1-60550-123-9

Printed in the United States of America.

J   I   H   G   F   E   D   C   B   A

Library of Congress Cataloging-in-Publication Data
is available from the publisher.

This book is available at quantity discounts for bulk purchases.
For information, please call 1-800-289-0963.

Contents

Acknowledgments

Much of what you will find in this book is the product of my experience in nearly four decades of playing bridge, making errors and slowly but surely learning from them. I would like to thank all the opponents over the years who have made me pay for my bridge "sins." I have found that the best way to learn is the hard way—playing against good opponents.

I have also learned a lot from reading, and although I have not taken any material directly from their books and articles, much of the wisdom of Eddie Kantar, Mike Lawrence, Larry Cohen, and Bobby Wolff can be found in these pages.

The World Bridge Federation has afforded me the opportunity to observe firsthand how world champions play, and I thank in particular WBF President Jose Damiani for his faith in me to do the job of chief editor of the Daily Bulletin at world championships.

Top Ten Reasons to Play Bridge

1. You'll use your mind and stay mentally sharp.

2. You'll find new friends at bridge games wherever you travel in the world.

3. You can associate with bright, inquisitive people.

4. Bridge will keep you away from the television and the refrigerator.

5. You can enjoy a bridge cruise with a celebrity host.

6. You'll feel a bond with people from all walks of life who also love the game.

7. You'll be able to play in the same tournaments as national and world champions.

8. You'll feel the thrill of executing an advanced play and enjoy the confidence it brings.

9. As you get better, you'll be able to measure your progress.

10. But most of all—you'll have fun!

Introduction

▶ A COMMON MISCONCEPTION about the game of bridge is that it is too tough, too complicated. Only experts can really enjoy playing—or so the story goes. Nothing could be further from the truth.

The vast majority of the estimated 100 million people who play bridge around the world do so for its social aspects—and just for fun. That doesn't mean you can't aspire to expert status or that you can't strive for greatness. Who knows, you might be the next prodigy laying claim to a world championship in just a few short years. None of that is necessary, however, for you to find a lifetime of enjoyment in what many consider to be the world's greatest card game.

Consider that only a miniscule percentage of the world's golfers have a legitimate shot at a major championship such as the Masters. That doesn't keep them from hitting the links and having a great time doing it. Similarly, you can have fun at bridge without threatening a reigning world champion.

The big problem with golf—and most other physical sports—is that at some point your body is going to interfere with your desire to keep playing. With bridge, as long as your mind works, you can keep going practically your entire life.

Many people take up bridge semi-seriously at retirement, but there are thousands of young people learning bridge in schools all over North America as you read this passage. Most bridge clubs now use bidding boxes for silent bidding, making bridge the ideal game for the hearing-impaired. There is almost no physical handicap that could prevent a person from enjoying bridge.

The long and the short of it is that if you can count to thirteen, you are a hot prospect for learning the best card game there is. The language of the game, the bidding, can be quite complex if that is your cup of tea. If not, you can reap hours and hours of pleasure from bridge in its simplest forms.

If you enjoy a more competitive but still friendly environment, you may venture out into the world of duplicate bridge, where there are regular games at bridge clubs and tournaments every week of the year. If you become familiar with duplicate, you will be welcome at clubs all over the world, from Europe to the Far East to South America. You won't even have to speak the native language to play—the language of the bidding is truly universal.

With the advent of bridge play on the Internet, you can play day and night from the comfort of your home. You can sit in on world championships from all over the world—or watch experts as they practice online. Spectators, known in the bridge world as kibitzers, are always welcome.

You can use the Internet yourself to practice with your partner before you meet at a tournament. You can find new partners online, visit any of the dozens of websites with teaching and information about the game, most of them free.

Every bridge hand is new. You could play bridge all day every day for 1,000 years and still never see the same deal twice. Experience will help you make the right choices in familiar situations, but the cards change every time you pick up a new hand.

As you advance, plays you thought were only for experts will become clear, and you will know the exhilaration of days when it seems you can do no wrong at the table. Lest you get too cocky, the game also has a way of bringing you back down to earth, but if you approach bridge with the attitude that it's wonderful to lose yourself in a session of strategy and mental acuity, you will always know that you are getting the most from an incredibly interesting form of recreation.

This is your starting point. You are about to take up a sport you can play the same at ninety as you did at twenty-five, maybe even better.

CHAPTER 1

Welcome to the Game of Bridge!

Playing bridge provides a wonderful opportunity to meet people in a recreational environment where you can socialize and use your intellect. Among all card games, bridge is unique. Your imagination and deductive reasoning will take you far if you let them.

Modern Bridge

When Harold Vanderbilt made the scoring change that revolutionized bridge, the game became far more challenging and allowed for the introduction of new insights and possibilities.

At this stage of your understanding of the game, all you need to know is that the situation and the scoring in bridge will change as you progress in a session. Bonus points are available, but the penalties for failure (or folly) also increase. These variables make the game more challenging and give you the chance to take risks, even bluff on occasion.

Bridge enjoyed its heyday in the 1940s and 1950s, reaching its peak of popularity in the 1960s, when it was *the* pastime on college campuses.

Although facing competition today from many other forms of leisure activity, bridge is still played worldwide and still has millions of fans who play regularly. It is estimated there are 20 million bridge players in North America alone. The World Bridge Federation has approximately 100 member countries.

The Many Benefits of Bridge

Bridge has enjoyed a renaissance in the past decade as an increasing number of young professionals, empty nesters, baby boomers, and seniors have discovered the challenges and pleasures of the game. Bridge is attractive to so many players nowadays in part because it's not necessary to play at the expert level to enjoy the game. New players quickly learn the social aspects of organized games.

FACT

There are more than 3,200 bridge clubs in North America, and with a bit of advance notice, most are very welcoming to visitors and often provide partners. For a list of clubs, visit *www.acbl.org*.

From your own home, to the Internet, to the bridge club, to cruise ships, to organized tournaments on the local, regional, and national level, you will find bridge to be the vehicle for meeting new friends who share your growing interest in this fascinating game.

Develop Your Communication Skills

As you learn from this book and develop your skills at bridge, you will find your communication and social skills advancing. The game of bridge may seem daunting at first, but you will soon become quite at ease with the buzz-words of bridge. You will find yourself fascinated with the endless possibilities, the excitement of your triumphs and, believe it or not, even some of your failures. Just about every aspect of bridge has something interesting about it.

Learn a New Language

The jargon of bridge is as unique as the game. Don't be discouraged if you don't know all the terminology right away. If you don't know, ask (or keep reading in this chapter). You will find that experienced players are pleased to help you learn, and most can remember when they started out and needed a bit of mentoring.

One of the special wonders of bridge is that it offers you the opportunity to communicate with your partner in a limited language of only fifteen words. When you have an opportunity to speak, or "bid," you can use the words of bridge to tell the other players about the cards that you hold.

ALERT!

Many aspects of bridge are not intuitive, so don't give up if one or more parts of the game come to you more slowly than you would like. Always keep a positive attitude and accept that lack of success is not failure. It is just a critical part of learning.

Meet New People

As you learn to play, bridge will provide many opportunities for you to find new friends. You will find that those who share a passion for the game have a special bond that is easily recognized. Bridge is played all over the world, and you can find new friends at clubs, tournaments, and cruises.

On the Internet, you can meet and play with people from distant lands who share your common interest in the game. With dozens of free and pay sites, you can choose when to play at a moment's notice. If you want to play for only a few rounds, you can. Often you will find yourself engrossed in the game and play for hours at a time.

A social bridge game is inexpensive to host. You need nothing more than three friends, a couple of decks of cards, a table and comfortable chairs, a pencil, a pad of paper, and, of course, some snacks. You can hold a bridge game that lasts an hour or two, or an entire afternoon or evening.

If you prefer a more organized setting and the face-to-face bridge experience, try one of the more than 3,000 bridge clubs affiliated with the American Contract Bridge League. These clubs are run by friendly, welcoming people who are excited each time they encounter a prospective new member or out-of-town visitor.

Use Your Intellect and Sharpen Your Memory

You and your partner will experience different situations with each round of bridge. The multitasking skills that are required to play bridge successfully are excellent ways to exercise your mind and keep your intellect nimble and quick. You will learn methods for winning in this book and with each hand you will apply those methods to win more points than your opponents. That is what bridge is all about.

The very best resource for bridge players is the American Contract Bridge League, located in Memphis, Tennessee (*www.acbl.org*, or 1-800-467-1623). The ACBL staff can answer your questions, help you find bridge clubs or tournaments, inform you how to contact a bridge teacher, send a sample of the monthly magazine if you are not a member, and sign you up on the spot if you want to join.

Bridge is great exercise for the mind. You must train yourself to follow the cards, keeping track of who played what, who showed out of a suit and how many cards in that suit the other players hold. You will become a bridge detective, putting together clues from the bidding and play that can lead you to the right line of play. Getting it right through a process of logic is one of the most rewarding aspects of the game.

Getting Started: Bridge Basics

There are two phases of bridge. In the first phase one card is dealt to each of the four players in turn until all the cards are dealt. Each player will have thirteen cards. Then the auction begins, the dealer speaking first. This is the first phase, and there is more about this part of the game in the next chapter. For now, just know that you and your partner compete against the other two players, who are also partners. You will be vying for the right to name one of the suits as the wild suit ("trump" in bridge lingo) in the second phase of the game. You can also bid to play without a trump suit. In addition, you are competing in the auction by raising the number of tricks you and your partner will propose to win.

Suits

With fifty-two cards in the deck, you will need to understand the symbols for the cards. This book will also use diagrams and graphs to explain what is happening. Symbols will be used for each of the suits: Spades are represented by ♠, hearts by ♥, diamonds by ♦, and clubs by ♣. You will quickly understand the chart that represents the cards a particular player is holding in his or her hand.

Card Symbols Chart

Representation	Actual cards
♠ AKJ84	ACE, KING, JACK, EIGHT, FOUR
♥ Q1085	QUEEN, TEN, EIGHT, FIVE
♦ 83	EIGHT, THREE
♣ K10	KING, TEN

The suits will always be represented in the order of spades on top, hearts next, then diamonds, and then clubs. They are in this order because spades is the highest-ranking suit and clubs is the lowest. In the auction, the order of the bids from lowest to highest is clubs, diamonds, hearts, spades, and no-trump (NT).

In the auction, you and your partner will try to name a suit as the trump suit when, collectively, you have at least eight cards in that suit. You and your partner may also want to play the contract without a trump suit. Then you are playing no-trump.

Important Bridge Terminology

Some of the bridge terms you will come across may seem strange, even inexplicable. Don't worry. They will become second nature to you much more quickly than you might imagine. What follows are some terms you should add to your bridge knowledge. Most of them are in the Glossary at the end of this book, but some additional explanation can help you get started.

- **Trick.** Four cards played in clockwise succession by each of the four players, starting at trick one with a card from the player to the left of the declarer (the player who first named the denomination of the final contract) and later starting with the player who won the previous trick. There are 13 tricks in the play of each deal.
- **Auction.** The process by which the final contract is achieved. The dealer starts the auction with a bid or a pass. A deal is passed out if there are four successive passes at the start, but in most cases the auction continues until there are three consecutive passes.
- **Contract.** The number and denomination (suit or no-trump) representing the number of tricks your side must win. If you and your partner bid to 3 ♣, for example, you have contracted to take nine tricks with clubs as trumps. If you fulfill your contract, you can earn a bonus. If you fail, you incur a penalty. Contracts go all the way from 1 ♣ (seven tricks) to 7NT (13 tricks).
- **Game.** Whenever your side fulfills a contract that produces a score of 100 or more (see the next chapter for scoring basics), you have earned a game bonus. You can earn a game bonus by bidding and making 3NT, 4 ♥, 4 ♠, 5 ♣, or 5 ♦.

- **Call.** Any bid, pass, double, or redouble. A bid is always a call, but a call is not necessarily a bid. A bid requires a number and a suit (or no-trump). Pass, double, and redouble are calls, not bids.

- **Hand.** Thirteen cards. This is different from a deal, which is all fifty-two cards dealt and played by the four competitors. Players refer so often to a full deal as a "hand" that the terms have become interchangeable.

- **Duplicate.** The form of the game played at bridge clubs and tournaments. Cards are not mixed up and reshuffled when a deal is over. The same deals are played over and over by different players, and the scoring comes from comparisons after all the rounds have been played in a session.

- **Proprieties.** These are the rules governing behavior at the bridge table. These principles apply to your relations with your partner and the opponents. Strive to be cordial and respectful to all. The proprieties also provide a guide for fair and ethical conduct in competition. It is considered a violation of the proprieties, for example, to frown or gesture as a way of communicating with your partner or to play a card or make a bid with undue emphasis.

- **Director.** The director at a duplicate bridge game is the "umpire" or "referee." The director gets the game going, records the scores, and makes rulings when players make mistakes in procedure. It would be unusual to see a director in a social game.

- **Irregularity.** New players, especially at duplicate, will encounter this aspect of bridge—a mistake in procedure—more often than others. An irregularity can be a lead out of turn, an exposed card, an insufficient bid—the list goes on and on. In social bridge, these errors are usually overlooked. In a club game or tournament, the director must make a ruling by consulting the Laws of Duplicate Contract Bridge.

Becoming familiar with these terms will help you feel more at ease in a bridge setting, especially if it is a tournament or a club game. As part of your effort to study the game, make the *Laws of Contract Bridge* part of your library of bridge books.

Bridge Etiquette

Bridge is a partnership game and participants are expected to conduct themselves in an honorable fashion at all times. It is interesting to note that the Laws of Contract Bridge and the Laws of Duplicate Contract Bridge do not address the matter of cheating. It is assumed that, absent evidence to the contrary, contestants are honest and that achievement has been fairly earned.

FACT

The proprieties of bridge demand that spoken communication with your partner is limited to the numbers one through seven, the names of the four suits, *no-trump*, *double*, and *redouble*. All other words are strictly forbidden, as are gestures and other means of conveying pleasure or displeasure with your partner's bids or plays.

The laws do, however, address the subject of what is known as proprieties—and there are rules about how bridge players communicate with each other. It is highly inappropriate, for example, to indicate displeasure by gesture, comment, or facial expression with a partner's bid or play. You are free to deceive the opponents through the bids you make or the cards you play, but *not* in the *manner* in which you make your bids or plays.

Partnership Skills

Perhaps the most important skill you can cultivate is that of being a good partner. If you are known as a calm, supportive partner, you will be in demand at the bridge table, even if you never become an expert.

No one wants to sit across the table from an enemy. You already have two of them at the table. If your partner is also an antagonist, you are in deep trouble. Your chances of enjoying the most enjoyable of games will dwindle sharply.

You will find as you become more keenly interested in bridge and its many nuances that you will thirst for improvement and knowledge. You must remember, however, that players progress at different paces. You might well learn more rapidly than your partner. Be patient and supportive.

ALERT!

It is important for your development as a player to learn the correct way to play the game. You don't want to be branded as a *coffeehouser*— a player with dubious ethics. The term comes from the bridge play at European coffeehouses, where conversation was often designed to give information or guide partners in ways that are frowned upon.

Upgrade Your Game

If you have had some casual experience with bridge, you will learn the modern style of play that has developed over the last few decades. Bridge has become far more interesting with the advent of modern bidding styles. Soon you will learn how to compete with the contemporary tools of bidding and easily modify your bridge game.

Relearn the Game

You may have experience with bridge. If so, you should prepare to learn the game anew. Modern bridge is based on decades of development, and current styles may run contrary to your experience from years ago. Do your best to learn the modern style and adapt what you already know about the game.

Your success in bridge will depend on two things. First, your willingness to learn, and secondly, your willingness to unlearn any preconceptions you may have about bridge. If you have played before, you may have to make significant changes in your approach as you drop some bad habits. If you started playing bridge without a knowledgeable mentor to help you out, you may have some serious "unlearning" to do. This may cause you some anxiety, but this book is designed to help you move away from your old ways to the modern style of communication.

It can be very helpful if you find a partner whose experience level is similar to your own. You can learn together and practice the new principles. The two of you can share ideas and new information as you practice bidding together.

Online Play and Resources

The convenience of playing online has converted many players from regular club habitués to chronic computer contestants. There are dozens of games every week on the three main websites (see Appendix A), and it's fair to say you can play any time of the day or night online. The primary websites also offer dozens of games that award ACBL masterpoints (see Chapter 18) in games as short as twelve deals.

You don't have to play in a structured game, however. You and your partner can simply invite two other players to join you at a table, and you play until you need to stop—half a dozen deals or 100. It's up to you.

The Internet is also a resource for learning from the best players in the world. Most of the major matches—certainly the world championships— can be viewed live on Bridge Base Online (see Appendix A). There is also a complete record of the bidding and play for review later if you can't or don't want to stay up to watch a bridge match in China.

You also can take bridge classes online, consult with experts about your problem hands and bidding systems, and there are numerous websites with an incredible amount of information and instruction. See Appendix A for more information.

How to Use This Book

For starters, beware of information overload. Don't try to absorb everything all at once. It will be easier, of course, if you have experience at card games, possibly even bridge. For example, if you ever played Spades, you already know about tricks.

It's the bidding that will take some study and concentration. Keep in mind that most experts consider bidding to be, by far, the most important aspect of the game. No matter how well you play, if you consistently fail to get to the right contract, your results will suffer.

Many of the principles of bidding are not intuitive, and there are many rules of bidding that will be covered in later chapters. If that sounds intimidating, don't be concerned. Once you absorb the basics, it will all seem logical. The key is to take each section slowly, making sure you understand the principles.

CHAPTER 2

The Rules

Grab three other people and get ready to play bridge.
A card table would be nice, four comfortable chairs,
a deck of cards (two would be better) a pad of paper,
and you're just about set. Sit down and look across the
table. That person is your partner. Your opponents,
who are also partners, are to your left and right.

A Quick Review

First, review what you know. In each suit, the highest-ranking card is the ace. The lowest is the two. In the bidding phase of the game, the suits rank from the lowest, clubs, to diamonds, hearts, and spades, the highest. The cards are dealt in clockwise rotation, one to each player until all the cards are dealt. Each player will hold thirteen cards.

The player who dealt the cards begins the auction, which proceeds in clockwise rotation. Each player in turn must bid, pass, double (only after an opponent's bid), or redouble (only after an opponent's double). Some of these terms may seem mysterious at this point, but don't worry. They will be clarified.

Each bid is an offer by the bidding side to win a certain number of the thirteen available tricks. A player can propose a contract in a suit, in which case that suit becomes trump and can be used to control the other suits. It is also possible to play without a trump suit. Contracts of this kind are called "no-trump" contracts. In the hierarchy of the auction, no-trump outranks even spades.

Starters

The auction begins when the dealer makes a call, which as you remember from Chapter 1 can include a pass. A deal is considered passed out when there are four consecutive passes at the beginning of the auction. The cards should be dealt again, the deal passing to the next player in the rotation—e.g., from North to East.

When you have two decks, one can be shuffled while the dealer is distributing the cards. Then the second deck is ready to go at the completion of the first deal.

Scoring Basics

In all forms of the game, players receive rewards for achieving their contracts. Players receive scores based on how many "odd" tricks they take. An odd trick is any trick in excess of the "book" or first six tricks. In other words, if you bid 2 ♠, you are contracting to take two odd tricks. If you do so on the nose, you receive 60 points.

If your contract is in a minor suit (clubs or diamonds), you receive 20 points for each odd trick you take. If it's a major suit (spades or hearts), you receive 30 points per odd trick. If you play in no-trump, the first odd trick is worth 40 points, subsequent odd tricks 30 each.

Both sides are striving to achieve 100 points to make "game," and most party or rubber bridge games are played to win two out of three games. Party bridge games have scoring "above the line" and "below the line." To achieve a game score, you must have 100 points below the line.

Points below the line are achieved only through successful contracts—and only for the number of tricks contracted for. That is, if you contract for 2 ♠ and take nine tricks, you get 60 points below the line (the two odd tricks you contracted for) and 30 above (the overtrick). If you win the auction on the next deal and play 2 ♠ again, making your contract, you score another 60 points below the line. The total exceeds 100, so you have achieved game. If you do that again, you have won the rubber.

E-QUESTION

Are there other ways besides overtricks to get points above the line in rubber bridge?
If you double the opponents and defeat them in their contract, the premium for defeating the contract goes above the line. It does not count toward your game bonus. Nor does the bonus for making slam (taking 12 tricks in the case of a small slam and all 13 tricks in the case of a grand slam). That also goes above the line.

Of course, you can get your game bonus in one fell swoop by simply bidding "game" in a major (4 ♥ or 4 ♠), a minor (5 ♣ or 5 ♦), or 3NT. You also get credit for game if you bid a slam. Your slam bonus goes above the line, however.

When you have a score of less than 100 below the line, you are considered to have a "leg" toward your game bonus.

Double Your Fun

You now know a bit about the mechanics of the auction—bids, passes, and other calls—if not the actual meanings of the bids, but what is doubling and redoubling?

You will learn more about doubling in later chapters. For now, it's important to know that when one player doubles an opponent, it's because the doubler thinks the opponent has bid too much, and she wants to increase the penalty for failing to make the contract.

If the opponent who is doubled has confidence in his bidding, he can redouble, increasing the bonus for making the contract. When there is doubling and redoubling going on, someone has made a big mistake. Finding out who made the blunder is part of the excitement of the game.

E-QUESTION

When someone doubles, is it always for penalty (they think I'm going down)?
There are many meanings of *double* in the parlance of bridge, especially in the world of tournaments. The most common non-penalty double is the so-called "takeout" double. That's when one player opens in suit and the player in the next seat says, "Double." The doubler is asking his partner to "take out" the double by bidding his best suit.

After a double or redouble, if another player makes a bid of any denomination, the double or redouble is canceled.

Doubles and redoubles notwithstanding, you will find that the scoring in duplicate is quite a bit different from the scoring in social games.

In duplicate, each score you achieve is separate from all the other scores. You do not add up trick scores to make your game. If you don't bid to the game level, you don't get credit for it. If you do bid and make game, however, you get a bonus right away—an extra 300 if you are not vulnerable and an extra 500 if you are. You also get credit for the overtricks. So if you bid 4 ♠ and make 11 tricks (you needed only 10), you get plus 150 for the five odd tricks and another 300 if you are not vulnerable for a total of

450. As you will learn later in this book, those overtricks can be very big in calculating your final score in a duplicate game.

Let's Play

You have a partner in bridge who sits opposite you at the table. The people to your left and right are also partners, but they are your opponents. Your opponents might be lovely people away from the table, but when you play bridge, they are the opposition and your goal is to score more points than them. That doesn't mean you should be rude or hostile. They are your friends, after all, and bridge is just a game. It's important to always maintain that perspective.

First you must shuffle and deal the cards. The dealer, sometimes determined by a cut of the cards, distributes the cards in clockwise rotation, starting with the player on his left, and continues until all fifty-two cards have been distributed.

It's important to shuffle the cards thoroughly to achieve a truly random deal. Believe it or not, this topic has been the subject of a scientific study in Great Britain, where it was determined that seven is the "perfect" number of times to shuffle the cards before dealing them.

Once you have received your cards from the dealer, sort them so you can clearly see them. Most people alternate the black and red suits to keep them straight. There's nothing more embarrassing than having to admit that your "ace of diamonds" was actually a heart.

Bid 'Em Up

Once all players have their cards sorted, start the bidding. The auction, of course, is essential. Without the bidding there is no contract. Without the contract, there is no play. We will take the phases one at a time, starting with the bidding.

Each player will have at least one chance to bid, and in many deals there will be a spirited competition for the final contract.

To illustrate an auction, here is a representation. After the cards have been dealt, the dealer starts, or "opens," the bidding. The auction has begun.

West	North	East	South

The compass points are used to identify players at the table. You could be any of the positions. North and South are always partners and sit opposite each other at the table, as do East and West, who are always partners.

Each auction starts with a call by the dealer. Remember, that a call can be a pass. If any person bids before there are four passes at the outset of the auction, the bidding continues until there are three consecutive passes.

How the Bidding Works

In the auction, each bid must represent a number or suit higher than the previous one. For example, a bid of 1 ♠ cannot be followed by the bid of one of any of the other suits. If someone bids 1 ♠ and you want to mention hearts, you must bid at least 2 ♥. You can, of course, bid a higher-ranking suit at the one level, as when 1 ♣ is followed by a bid of 1 ♦, 1 ♥, or 1 ♠.

If someone bids 1 ♣ and the next person bids 1 ♠, then the bid will be won by the person who bid 1 ♠ because spades are ranked higher than clubs. If the next person bids 2 ♣, that is sufficient to be a legal bid because a bid of a larger number of tricks always beats a bid of a smaller number.

Rank Rules

If the number of tricks is equal, the higher suit beats the lower. Once the auction starts, it continues until there are three straight passes. The last bid becomes the contract.

If you won the auction at 3 ♥, you and your partner must collectively make the "contract," that is, win nine tricks (three plus book).

ALERT!

The side that "wins" the auction has an advantage because they usually have decided on the trump suit that best fits their hands, giving them a good chance for a positive score. When a trump suit has been named, those cards can keep the opponents' high cards from winning precious tricks. The other side of the equation, of course, is that there is a penalty when you do not take the number of tricks required by your contract.

Sometimes a "victory" in the auction can be a loss for your side. Bidding can be a delicate process, and some guesswork is often needed. You will notice as you get into the game that the more experienced players make accurate guesses more often than their less-skilled counterparts. In bridge, as in other aspects of life, experience is the best teacher.

Listen Closely

Every opening bid has a meaning that is conveyed to everyone at the table. Because it is important for partners to communicate well, players tend to bid as accurately as possible. You can take advantage of that information as you formulate your own plans. For example, say an opponent opens 1 ♠ and her partner raises her to 2 ♠.

Most people play five-card major openings, so the opener has five. Players rarely raise their partners with fewer than three trumps, so now you know the opponents have at least eight spades between them. If you are looking at four low spades in your hand, you can just about count on your partner to have one spade at most, possibly none. You can use this information in deciding whether to compete—and all you had to do was listen to the bidding.

FACT

The final bid of the auction becomes the contract for the number of tricks to be won by the winning pair after three consecutive passes end the bidding. The first player of the winning pair to have named the suit or no-trump in the contract becomes "declarer" and takes the starring role in the next phase of the game—the play.

You and your partner will use information from the auction to decide which suit to bid and how high to compete if the high-card strength is evenly distributed between your side and theirs.

The bids in the auction also convey the message about the ability to win tricks and points in the second phase of the game. In most social bridge games, the bidding is oral—players speak their bids.

In clubs and at tournaments, players use bidding boxes. Each box contains cards with all potential calls—all bids from 1 ♣ to 7NT, Pass, Double, and Redouble. As the auction progresses, players take the cards from the box and place them on the table. The players do not speak.

Box It Up

Bidding boxes are in favor, even in some home games, because they are placed on the table during the auction and not taken up until the bidding is over. All players can see the auction at all times, eliminating the need for reviews of the bidding.

In a tournament or a club setting, silent bidding via bidding boxes also makes for a quieter room. That is good for concentration and helps keep other tables from inadvertently finding out what they aren't supposed to know because of a loud penalty double or triumphantly bid grand slam.

To help you remember the rank of the suits, place them in alphabetical order: Clubs, Diamonds, Hearts, and Spades. The lowest bid is 1 ♣, the highest is 7NT.

There are fifteen words used in the auction phase:

- The numbers one through seven
- The names of the four suits
- *No-trump, pass, double,* and *redouble*

These are the only words you are permitted to use, and you should speak them, if your bidding is oral, in an even tone without undue emphasis.

The Bidding Ladder

Take a look at the following bidding ladder. You can see that the lowest bid is 1 ♣. The first person to bid can start the auction with a bid of 1 ♣ or any higher bid. Each following bidder must make a bid that is higher on the bidding ladder; otherwise, the player must pass.

Bid Values Increase as You Move Up and to the Right

7 ♣	7 ♦	7 ♥	7 ♠	7NT
6 ♣	6 ♦	6 ♥	6 ♠	6NT
5 ♣	5 ♦	5 ♥	5 ♠	5NT
4 ♣	4 ♦	4 ♥	4 ♠	4NT
3 ♣	3 ♦	3 ♥	3 ♠	3NT
2 ♣	2 ♦	2 ♥	2 ♠	2NT
1 ♣	1 ♦	1 ♥	1 ♠	1NT

At the end of the auction the final bid will be the contract. The contract will state what suit, if any, will be trump, and what goal you will try to achieve in the second phase of the game when you will play the hand.

How You Play a Contract

The specific goal in the second phase is to take tricks. The contract will state how many tricks you will attempt to make and what suit, if any, will be trump. If you succeed in the second phase of the game, the play of the hand, and make your contract, you will win points. If you do not succeed, the opponents will win points.

Sometimes, you deliberately overbid with the goal of losing fewer points than you would have if you didn't outbid the opponents. This is known as a "sacrifice" bid, which is a better strategy in duplicate bridge than it is in other forms of the game.

Making the Contract

Once the final contract is determined, the second stage of bridge begins: the play of the cards. Each partnership will try to win as many tricks as possible. To begin, the person to the left of the declarer will play any card, usually face down—in case that person is confused about whose lead it is. Once she is assured it is her lead, the opening leader faces her card on the table.

At that point, declarer's partner puts his hand down on the table for all to see. This is called the "dummy." This is not a disparaging term, just bridge lingo. Declarer's partner arranges the cards in suits, usually alternating black and red cards. If declarer is playing a trump contract, the trump suit goes on declarer's far left, dummy's far right.

Touch and Go

Play proceeds in a clockwise rotation. In rubber or party bridge, declarer selects a card from dummy and waits for the next player—often referred to as "third hand"—to make his play. If everyone follows suit to the opening lead, the highest card played wins the trick. Whoever wins the trick takes those four cards and puts them together in front of him.

In a duplicate game, declarer calls for a card from dummy, and dummy plays that card. Declarer does not touch dummy's cards or the cards of the opponents. When a trick has been "quitted"—everyone has played to it—the side that won the trick places it, face down, vertically on the table in front of her. The side that lost the trick puts it down horizontally.

The lead comes from the hand that won the trick. If dummy won the trick, declarer chooses a card from dummy to lead to the next trick. Play continues in clockwise rotation until all thirteen tricks have been played.

Declarer and the defenders count their tricks at the end to see whether declarer made his contract.

Each player will try to win tricks for her side. If your partner is winning the trick, it would be wasteful to try to win it yourself, as when partner has led the king of a suit and you have the ace. You know the king is going to win. You would play the ace only in the most extreme and unusual circumstance. Of course, if the ace is the only card in the suit that you hold, you must play it, wasteful or not.

If declarer is playing a trump contract and leads a suit you are out of, you can win that trick with your lowest trump.

You and your partner do not have to win a trick. Your side can purposefully choose to lose a trick, which is a key strategy in certain situations.

Winning Points

If you make your contract, you win points. When you don't make your contract you "go down" or "go set" and you suffer a penalty, which is awarded to your opponents. The penalties are accrued through tricks. The shorter you fall in your attempt to fulfill your contract, the higher the penalty for failing. That's why it's sometimes attractive for your opponents to double you. If they assume you won't make a contract of 2 ♠, for example, they may double it to ensure you are penalized even more than you would be for simply not reaching your goal of winning eight tricks (book plus two).

Your First Bridge Hand

You and your partner are sitting across from each other at the table and your opponents are to your left and right. You have sorted your hand and you hold these cards.

Dlr:South
Vul:None

```
        N
    W       E
        S
```

♠ K Q 10 3 2
♥ 4 3 2
♦ A Q 2
♣ A 10

West	North	East	South
			?

In the diagram, the suits are ranked highest to lowest. You have five cards in the spade suit. The "Vul: None" notation at the top of the diagram refers to vulnerability. This will be discussed in detail in later chapters.

Right under the card symbols are the compass points, which refer to the positions at the table. You could potentially be sitting at any of the positions, but for the purposes of this book you will be South unless otherwise noted. As a result, your partner will usually be North (sitting opposite you), and your opponents would then be East and West.

Now, you ask, "Why is there a question mark under South?" Because, in this example, you (South), as the dealer, will have to decide whether or not to bid.

Your First Bid

As the dealer, you will have the opportunity to open the bidding or pass. Simply decide what you want to bid and say the words, in this case "one spade." As the dealer, or the first person with an opportunity to open the auction, there is no restriction. If you choose not to bid, you will say the word "pass." After someone bids rather than passing, ensuing bids must be higher in denomination or level.

E-QUESTION

Do you have to bid?
No, you may pass if you choose as long as the auction remains open (there have not been three consecutive passes). If you pass, this conveys information to partner that you do not have a hand that is appropriate for bidding at this time.

Let's say you bid 1 ♠. If anyone else wanted to bid, he would have to make a bid that appears higher on the chart, perhaps 1NT or 3 ♣ or 4 ♦. He cannot bid anything that appears lower on the chart, such as 1 ♥ or 1 ♦. As the auction progresses this is still true. You may not make a bid that is lower than the current bid.

One of the irregularities discussed previously is an "insufficient bid." For example, your right-hand opponent opens 1 ♠ and you bid 1 ♦. That is an insufficient bid—it is not higher in rank or in level. If you are playing in a tournament, it's time to call the director. In a home game, the other players will probably just let you bid 2 ♦ and get on with the game.

So, how long does the auction last? The auction begins with the dealer. The dealer can pass or bid. Then the next person to the left has an opportunity to bid or pass (or double—more on that later). The opportunity to bid continues around the table until each person has a turn. If all four players pass, the cards are shuffled again and a new deal starts. But if any of the four players makes a bid at his or her first turn, the auction is open. The auction then stays open until three players in a row pass.

Each time it is your turn, you may bid, pass, double, or redouble (if an opponent has doubled). If you pass on your turn, it does not prohibit you from bidding at your next turn or any later turn.

Follow Your Instincts

Always follow your instincts when playing bridge. Your instinct is to make a bid with the hand on page 21. Okay, say the words "one spade." What you have essentially said is "if the next three players pass, I have proposed a contract for me and my partner to win seven of the thirteen possible tricks with spades as trumps."

Remember the list of the fifteen words of bridge; you have used two of those words to offer a contract of "one spade." The biggest factor in a bridge auction is determining how much your hand is worth in the auction.

The integrity of the game requires that you make all your bids with the same cadence and inflection. The proper expression of a bid of 1 ♣ would simply be "one club." If you were to hesitate or express reluctance and say something like, "Oh, well, I think I will bid one club," then improper information might be conveyed to your partner. This is a big no-no.

Playing the Dummy

Here is your hand from the previous discussion, this time accompanied by the dummy.

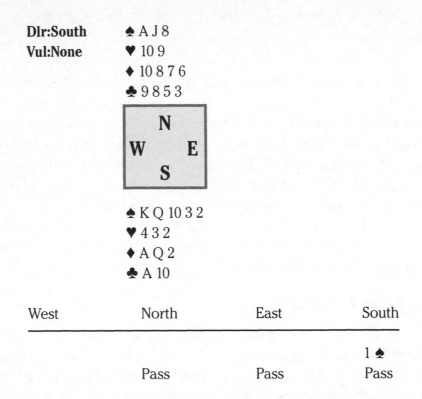

Dlr:South	♠ A J 8
Vul:None	♥ 10 9
	♦ 10 8 7 6
	♣ 9 8 5 3

♠ K Q 10 3 2
♥ 4 3 2
♦ A Q 2
♣ A 10

West	North	East	South
			1 ♠
Pass	Pass	Pass	

The auction is over because you opened the bidding, followed by three passes. West makes the opening lead of a low club. Now the spotlight turns to you.

Everyone has a minute or so to look at the dummy. The play of the cards continues clockwise around the table. The next card will be played from dummy, and you, as declarer, will decide what card to play from dummy. When you decide, you pick a card or tell dummy what card to play. Your right-hand opponent will play a card to the trick and then you will follow.

A club was led and you do have a club in dummy, so you must play a club. You will play the ♣ 3 from dummy and your right-hand opponent will play a club, almost certainly a face card. You, as declarer, will play last to this trick. You will play the ♣ A. You have won the trick from your hand, so you are required to lead the first card to the next trick from your hand. If you had won the trick with a card you played from the dummy's hand, you would play the first card from dummy in the next trick.

Before you lead, think for just a moment. Look at just the spades in the two hands combined. This is the trump suit, and because of that, you will want to take control of the suit. The reason is simple. You have five spades in your hand and three in the dummy. That is a total of eight of the thirteen spades in the suit.

Make a Plan

Let's imagine your opponents have only five spades between them. Now look at your spade suit from your perspective as declarer and count the number of tricks you can win in that suit. When you pull all the trumps out of the opponents' hands, you alone will have trumps remaining.

ALERT!

Whenever you are playing a hand, either as declarer or as one of the defenders, take some time before you play a card to the first trick. Look at your hand and dummy and give some thought to the auction. It is important to make a plan. Remember, even a plan that fails is better than no plan at all.

On your first bridge hand, you can absolutely make seven tricks and succeed at your contract. You will win five spade tricks, the ace of clubs, and the ace of diamonds for a total of seven tricks. You will make your contract.

CHAPTER 3

The Language of Bidding

Bridge is a game of tricks, and accurate card play is paramount to success, but if you consistently find yourself in a poor contract, it won't matter if you can play the spots off the cards. It is well known that two average players in tune with each other in the bidding often have an advantage over two experts with sketchy communication. If you want to succeed, learn to bid.

Counting Points

You can thank Milton Work for his pioneering efforts to help with the language of bidding and for helping to give the bridge world one of its most basic tools—the point count. Work, a Philadelphia lawyer and expert whist player, eventually left the practice of law and took up bridge as his profession in the early part of the previous century (he died in 1934). Work was instrumental in publicizing the point-count method of hand evaluation that is still in use today.

The method was developed by an obscure player named Bryant Campbell, but it is known as the Work point count method because it was through Work's writings that the system gained almost universal acceptance.

It is a very simple system. You evaluate your hand on a points system, with the following parameters.

Card	Point Value
Ace	4
King	3
Queen	2
Jack	1

Using this scheme, each suit has 10 high-card points, so a deck has 40 altogether. The average bridge hand has about 10 points.

Many bridge authorities consider the Work point-count method to be flawed. For example, in the context of a 4-3-2-1 method of high card evaluation, most experts consider the ace to be worth more than four points, a jack less than one. Nevertheless, the Work system is the one used by just about everyone in bridge today, either exclusively or as the cornerstone of more esoteric evaluation methods.

One of the first things you will learn about bridge bidding is how to count points, and it's a great way to get started in the game. You will learn some other methods of hand evaluation later in this chapter, but you will be on solid ground—and certainly in tune with other bridge players—if you count your points the way Work did.

So, how does this apply to the language of bidding? Well, while you were sitting there counting your points, your partner was doing the same, and it is through the bidding that the two of you will exchange information about the relative strengths of your two hands. Your objective is to reach the best contract, be it a part score, game, or slam. A part score is a bid for less than enough points for game—for example, 2 ♠ (you must bid 4 ♠ for game).

Bare Minimums

If you are the dealer, you will have the first chance to speak. When you pick up your hand and sort it into suits, you then count your high-card points. You are trying to decide whether you should open the bidding. If you do, what does it mean? A simple opening bid conveys a lot about the thirteen cards you are holding in your hand. Make sure you know what you are saying when you take that first step.

FACT

The bidding presented in this book is the system known as Standard American. There are other systems used by some tournament players and a variety of systems played primarily in other countries. Learning Standard American will put you in a great position to play with anyone in North America.

Opening bids come in a variety of flavors, so to speak, and it's logical to start with the one level. Here are all five bids you can make at the one level and what they tell your partner about your hand (that HCP abbreviation means high-card points).

- 1NT: 15–17 HCP, balanced.
- 1 ♠: 12–21 HCP, five or more spades, may be balanced or unbalanced.

- 1 ♥: 12–21 HCP, five or more hearts, may be balanced or unbalanced.
- 1 ♦: 12–21 HCP, probably more or better diamonds than clubs, may be balanced or unbalanced. In any case, a minimum of three diamonds.
- 1 ♣: 12–21 HCP, three or more clubs, may be balanced or unbalanced.

You noted, no doubt, the reference to "balanced" in each of the descriptions of one-level opening bids. A hand is considered balanced if it has one of three shapes: 4-3-3-3, 4-4-3-2, or 5-3-3-2. Here are some examples:

♠ KQ103
♥ 1092
♦ A92
♣ A65

♠ K732
♥ QJ92
♦ A92
♣ A10

♠ KQ1093
♥ QJ2
♦ A92
♣ A4

The first has four cards in spades and three cards in each of the other suits. The second has four spades, four hearts, three diamonds, and two clubs. The last has five spades, three hearts, three diamonds, and two clubs.

Note that none of the hands has more than one doubleton. These are considered balanced hands. Any other pattern is described as unbalanced, although some players consider any hand without a singleton to be at least a little bit balanced. As you progress in your experience and learn more about the game, you will form your own opinions on this subject. At this point, stick to the rules as written here.

Just for practice, count the high-card points in each of the example hands. Did you get 13, 14, and 16 points, respectively, for the three hands? Excellent! For the record, each is a fine opening bid.

In bridge language, a *doubleton* is a holding of just two cards in a suit. A *singleton*, naturally, is one card in a suit, sometimes identified as a *stiff* because it's more or less "dead"—it must be played the first time the suit is led. When you have no cards in a particular suit, you are said to be void.

Twelve Is Enough

You will note that the one-bids of a suit in the list of openers gave a minimum high-card point count of 12 for opening bids of one of a suit. If you and your partner are more comfortable with setting your minimum at 13 HCP, you will do just fine, but most players today open with 12, even fewer when a hand is very "shapely," that is with two long suits. Experience teaches that shapely hands play very well when partner has support for one or both of them.

The reason for discussing the issue of what constitutes a minimum opening bid, at least in terms of high-card points, is that when you open, your partner will have to decide what message to send you about her hand.

FACT

In figuring whether to go for a part score, game, or slam, keep these general guidelines in mind. To make game in 3NT—you must take nine tricks without trump cards to help you out—usually requires about 25 high-card points between the two hands. The same goes for game in a major, which requires 10 tricks but with the assistance of your trumps. Game in a minor, on the other hand, requires 11 tricks, so you need 27 or 28 HCP or some extra distribution.

Remember, the reason for the exchange of information between partners is to determine how high the bidding should go. For example, if you have an opening hand yourself and partner opens the bidding, you will get to game in some denomination almost all of the time—and expect to make it with normal breaks in the key suits.

Hand Evaluation

The point-count method of assessing the strength of a hand is a good starting point, but there are many factors to consider in determining how "valuable" a hand is. The "value" of a hand, of course, is what it represents in trick-taking potential.

Take the following hand, for example.

♠ AK765
♥ 4
♦ Q542
♣ A54

If your partner opens the bidding with 1 ♠, showing at least five by agreement, your hand has enormous trick-taking potential. Your partner can draw the opponents' trumps (there are at most three) and still have trumps left to deal with any losers she might have in hearts. This is a very powerful hand to put down as dummy.

It is a common error among new players to count "points" for so-called "distribution" (doubletons, singletons, and voids) in deciding whether to open the bidding. That is a mistake. Shortness has value only when you and your partner determine that you have at least an eight-card fit in some suit. Never count points for shortness as the opening bidder.

Now look at the hand from a different perspective. Suppose you are the dealer. You will open 1 ♠. If the auction develops in such a way that you determine partner is short in your long suit, your hand doesn't look so good, at least not for play in spades. Now, if you find out that partner has a good holding in diamonds, your hand comes back to life—that singleton heart has returned as an asset, and the long spade suit might end up being another source of tricks.

As you can see, the "value" of your hand depends in large measure on what you learn from the bidding. That's why accurate communication between partners is so important.

Length Rules

It is a mistake to assign value to a short suit as the opening bidder, but there is a distributional feature of your hand that can be positive—one or more long suits. Many experts assign extra "points" to a hand for every card in a suit in excess of four.

♠ AQJ1098
♥ A4
♦ 542
♣ K10

This hand above is a good example of this principle at work. If you stick strictly to high-card points, it's a 14-point hand. You would open the bidding with 1 ♠ and, assuming partner responded, you would rebid 2 ♠, showing your extra length.

Most experts, however, would look at this hand in a different way. Yes, there are only 14 HCP, but the length and strength of the spade suit argue for a more aggressive assessment. Most would rebid 3 ♠, which normally promises 16–18 HCP. In this case, the upward evaluation of the hand is justified because the spade suit is so good and the side cards are an ace and a king, known in the jargon of bridge as "quick tricks" because you can use them immediately if you need to.

So, take your 14 HCP and add two points for the extra two spades. Now you have 16, enough to justify a jump rebid.

Suit Quality

Not all suits are created equal, and it's the spot cards that often make the difference.

Here's an example.

♠ QJ109876
♠ QJ65432

Suppose you are in a spade contract. Which suit would you like to be playing with? Of course, that's a silly question. With the first suit, you will take five tricks even if partner is void in spades. You simply knock out the ♠ A and ♠ K and you have five tricks. With the second suit, you would be in dire straits if you had to play it opposite a void. You might end up taking only three tricks, two if you are really unlucky. Both suits have the same number of high-card points, but the spot cards in the second hand argue for caution, especially in competitive bidding, which will be covered in Chapter 5.

Suit quality is less of a consideration when opening the bidding, largely because in many cases you have no choice, as in the following hand.

♠ J5432
♥ A
♦ QJ109
♣ AJ5

Yes, the spade suit is anemic, but you must open the bidding with 13 HCP, and you must open 1 ♠. The quality of the suit might be a consideration later in the auction, but for now you must soldier on and bid what you have. There's no law that says partner can't help fill in some of the gaps, perhaps holding ♠ Q1098.

The point of discussing suit quality is to reinforce the principle that high-card points are not the only tool you can use in the bidding process.

The Importance of Shape

Many expert players devalue hands that are "flat," and the worst shape possible is the dreaded 4-3-3-3. Unless such a hand is blessed with an abundance of high-card points, the trick-taking potential is seriously reduced. Think about it: no long suit to develop for extra tricks, no shortness that could allow for ruffs. Dull shape such as this should set off warning signals in your head.

Then there are the freaks—hands with extreme distribution, such as seven cards in one suit, six in another and two voids! If you hold such a hand and find that partner has support for one of your suits, you can take lots of tricks.

Most "shapely" hands fall somewhere in between completely flat and the 7-6 freaks. A hand with five cards in each of two suits can be a big trick taker, and you will learn later in this book how to describe such hands when the opponents get the first shot in the bidding. Such hands are more common than you might think.

The bottom line is that you can be more aggressive in the bidding when you have a shapely hand, which brings up the so-called Rule of Twenty, a notion that has gained a lot of support in recent years. Warning: The "rule" also has detractors, for reasons that will become clear.

Basically, the Rule of Twenty is a formula for helping you determine whether to open the bidding on hands that fall short of the 12 or 13 HCP most bidding systems advocate.

Here's how it works: Take the number of cards in your two longest suits, then add the number of high-card points. If the sum is 20 or higher, open the bidding.

Players who use this rule as a substitute for thinking or judgment are doing themselves and their partners a disservice. The Rule of Twenty is a useful guideline, but it should not be followed blindly. Here are a couple of examples to bring home the point.

♠ AJ1076
♥ AJ987
♦ 9
♣ 54

Using the Rule of Twenty, you count the HCP (10) and add the number of cards in hearts and spades, the two long suits, and you come up with 20. This is a perfectly respectable opener, and if your partner has good support for one of your suits, you have the chance to take a lot of tricks.

Now look at the other extreme.

♠ 95432

♥ 107543

♦ AQ

♣ A

This is a poor hand for opening the bidding. The negatives are that the two long suits are very weak, and the high-card strength is in short suits. Yet this hand qualifies for the Rule of Twenty: There are 10 HCP and 10 cards in hearts and spades. You are begging for trouble if you open this hand, however. Put the ♣ A in the spade suit and the ♦ AQ in the heart suit, and you're back in business—open 1 ♠.

Augmentation

Instead of blindly following the Rule of Twenty, some players adjust it to what they call the Rule of Twenty-Two. The parameters for the rule of 20 are still in place, but with an additional requirement: two quick tricks. The new rule, then, is that high-card points and cards in the two long suits must add up to 20, and you can open as long as you have two quick tricks.

For reference, here is your guide to quick tricks:

Tricks	Requisite holding
2 Quick Tricks	A–K of the same suit
1½	A–Q of the same suit
1	A or K–Q of the same suit
½	K and any card

The reason you want to include quick tricks in your calculation is that, in today's atmosphere of competitive bidding, if you open on a shapely hand with little or no defense (aces and kings) and your partner doubles the opponents, you will regret having opened when their contracts come rolling home. Two long suits without quick tricks will not help you on defense.

The other part of the equation is that partner will begin to doubt your openers, so even when the opponents step out of line and your side should be doubling, partner won't cooperate because he has seen too many bad opening bids from your side of the table. He is now gun-shy.

It won't hurt your bidding at all if you forget about the Rule of Twenty.

Major Suits

The foundation of the bidding system in this book is what is known as five-card majors. That is, when you open the bidding with 1 ♥ or 1 ♠, you promise a suit of at least five cards. One of the advantages of making this agreement is that it makes it much easier for you and your partner to find an eight-card fit in a major suit. Knowing that partner has at least five cards in the suits he opens makes competitive bidding easier as well.

New Style

This is not how bridge started out—nor is this the universal rule for opening in a major suit. In many European countries, notably Great Britain, four-card major openings are standard. Perhaps the most famous American bridge player of all time, Charles Goren, taught and played a four-card major system. One of the all-time great players in bridge history, Bob Hamman, is an adherent of four-card majors.

Dissidents notwithstanding, nearly every bidding system associated with Standard American teaches five-card majors. The popular bidding system known as two-over-one game force (usually written as 2/1) is based on five-card major-suit openings. It is what virtually everyone you are going to play against will be using.

Following the point-count rules and common sense, an opening bid of one of a major strongly suggests at least 12 high-card points but as many as 20 or 21, at least five in the suit and some defensive (quick) tricks. The bid is not forcing, which means that if the partner of the opening bidder is very weak, she can simply pass. The next chapter will describe responder's choices after an opening bid.

FACT

> The 2/1 game force system is self-descriptive. If you open the bidding in one of a suit and your partner bids at the two level, you are forced to game. In the vast majority of cases, neither partner can pass until some game has been reached, the exception being when the partnership discovers that the hands are serious misfits.

Safety in Numbers

Why do so many players employ five-card major openings? It's partly because of the measure of safety that the system offers.

Most players, and certainly most new players, abhor the thought of playing in the dreaded 4–3 trump fit (declarer's hand has four cards in the trump suit, while dummy has only three). What that means is that the opponents have almost as many trumps as you do, and if both suits are less than robust, it can be a dicey affair (not to mention when the opposing trumps split badly). If you routinely open four-card majors, you will find yourself playing 4–3 fits much more often than your five-card-major counterparts. That makes many players nervous. They prefer the comfort of knowing partner has at least five when he opens a major.

When you are blessed with two major suits and enough to open the bidding, start with the longer suit. If they are of equal length, open 1 ♠. Do not violate this principle because you like one suit better than the other.

♠ J5432
♥ AKJ107
♦ A7
♣ 5

In the hand above, do not open 1 ♥ just because your spade suit is weak and your heart suit robust. Don't think there's a problem? Well, how about this scenario: Partner bids 1NT in response to your 1 ♥ opener. Now what? If you bid your spade suit now, it shows a much stronger hand than you have. Why? Because if partner has to prefer your first suit, he will have to do so at the three level. If you choose to rebid 2 ♥, you have told a lie about your heart length. Rebidding the suit shows six of them. You can see that you are getting into a mess.

If you open 1 ♠, as you should, and partner bids 1NT, you have an easy second bid of 2 ♥. You may even get a chance to bid your hearts again to show the extra length.

Minor Suits

If you use the five-card major system, you will find that the level of comfort you enjoy when you open a major suit is not there with your minor-suit openings. You will find that you often have to open 1 ♣ or 1 ♦ on a three-card suit, even something as bad as ♣ 432. That might make you nervous, but it is the price you pay for the system you play. At least when you play in a duplicate game, you will know that just about every other player holding your cards will have to make the same bid as you.

When do you open 1 ♣ or 1 ♦ on a three-card suit? Here are some hands that qualify:

♠ AK98
♥ AQ76
♦ J6
♣ 432

You have to open the bidding with your 14 high-card points, but if you open 1 ♥ or 1 ♠, you promise a five-card suit. What choice do you have?

♠ AK98
♥ AQ76
♦ J106
♣ 43

Again, you must open the bidding, and when your hand looks like the one above, you must start with 1 ♦. Fortunately, that particular distribution—four hearts, four spades, three diamonds, and two clubs—is the only time you are forced to open on a three-card diamond suit. With any other shape, a 1 ♦ opener will deliver at least four diamonds.

Remember, too, that most of your opening bids of one of a minor will not look so pitiful. In fact, most of the time you will have a reasonable holding in your minor. It's only when you have four cards in each of the majors—not a bad thing, when you think about it—that you are forced to open the bidding on a weak minor-suit holding.

When you have three cards in each minor and no five-card major, open 1 ♣ unless the disparity between the suits is too great, as with ♦AKQ compared to ♣ 754. If the opponents outbid you and your partner is on lead, which suit do you want her to start with?

Because of the need to open one of a minor on a three-card suit now and then, players tend to want to show a "real" club or diamond suit when they have only five. They can't wait to rebid in their five-card minor to show that it wasn't three low cards. Do not get into this habit.

When you rebid a suit, in almost all cases it should show at least six of that suit. This is important because when the auction heats up, with the opponents bidding their heads off, the difference between five and six in partner's long suit could be critical to your decision to bid on, pass, or even double the opponents.

What do you do when you have four cards in each minor? Some players prefer to start with 1 ♣, allowing them to raise diamonds if partner bids that suit. Others prefer to start with 1 ♦, giving them the flexibility to show the second suit if partner bids a major.

This is something you should discuss with your partner, and you should agree on a style. There is some merit to the argument that a bidding sequence such as 1 ♦—Pass—1 ♠ —Pass; 2 ♣ should show an unbalanced hand—that is, a hand with shortness somewhere, or perhaps with two cards in each major and nine cards in the minors. This is another topic for discussion with your partner.

There is one hand type with which you should ignore the rule about opening your longer suit first when you hold a five-card suit and a four-card suit.

> ♠ 7
> ♥ AQ7
> ♦ QJ108
> ♣ A8754

If you open 1 ♣ and partner bids 1 ♠, you are not well placed. You do not have enough high-card strength to rebid 2 ♦, which would show 17 or more HCP. If you rebid 1NT, you show a balanced hand, which you do not have. If you rebid 2 ♣, you show a six-card suit, another distortion of your hand, albeit not a terrible one.

It is simpler to open 1 ♦ and, if partner bids 1 ♠, rebid 2 ♣. You won't be ecstatic if partner gives preference to 2 ♦ holding three of each minor, but that's better than strongly implying what you don't have.

Note that if partner's response is 1 ♥, you will happily raise to 2 ♥. There will be more about that in the next chapter.

Openers at the Two Level and Higher

Each bid should tell a story, and many of the bids at the two level are highly descriptive. Most of them are meant primarily to annoy the opponents. Here is the menu:

- 2 ♣: Your big bid, describing a powerful hand with 22 or more high-card points if balanced. If unbalanced, it is a hand with lots of tricks, usually from a long, powerful suit.
- 2 ♦, 2 ♥, 2 ♠ : What is known as a weak two-bid, usually describing a six-card suit and 5–10 high-card points (the range can be different if you and partner prefer).

- 2NT: A balanced hand with 20–21 high-card points (you can have a different range if you prefer).
- 3 ♣, 3 ♦, 3 ♥, 3 ♠: Weak hand (circumstances can dictate extreme weakness) with a long suit, usually at least seven cards.
- 3NT: A balanced hand even stronger than a 2NT opener (perhaps 24–25). Some players agree that it shows a long minor suit of at least seven cards headed by the AKQ.
- 4 ♣, 4 ♦, 4 ♥, 4 ♠: In the minors, bids at the four level usually show eight-card suits. The majors are similar, but for tactical reasons 4 ♥ or 4 ♠ can sometimes be bid on a seven-card suit.
- 5 ♣, 5 ♦: More pre-emption (the removal of bidding space). These are usually based on eight- or nine-card suits.
- 5 ♥, 5 ♠: Bids carrying a specific message: Bid six of my suit if you have one of the top three honors, bid seven if you have two. This is not a weak bid.

Most pre-emptive bids are weak, and there is some risk in starting the bidding at a high level with a weak hand, but the rewards can more than compensate. Robbed of bidding space by your pre-emption, the opponents will often have to guess what to do. In such cases, they will guess wrong a certain percentage of the time.

As pointed out earlier, experienced players guess correctly more often than newcomers, but even top players are not impervious to the havoc that can be wreaked by an opening bid of, say, 5 ♦.

Bridge is a bidder's game, and if you give the opponents an unimpeded shot at finding their best contract, they will do so most of the time. That's bad news for you.

CHAPTER 4

Communicating with Your Partner

You and your partner have a distinct advantage when one of you makes the first bid of an auction. You have immediately started your exchange of information about your respective hands, and you have put the opponents at a disadvantage because there is risk involved for them if they intervene. Maintain that edge by honing your skill at communicating with partner.

Partner's First Response

Once your partner opens the bidding, if the next player passes, it's up to you to begin describing your hand.

You will hold a variety of hand types, each of which will require different treatment. Your hands will vary in strength as well, another facet about which you must tell partner. Bear in mind that once partner has revealed something about his hand—most descriptively by opening one of a major—your assessment of your hand will be expressed in "support points," a combination of your high-card points and, if you have support for the suit partner has opened, any distributional values you might have, such as doubletons, singletons, or voids.

When partner opens one of a suit and you have at least three-card support for a major or four-card support for a minor, you can count points for short suits. Traditionally, with four-card trump support for partner's major, you can count one point for a doubleton in a side suit, three support points for a singleton, and five for a void. With three-card support for a major, count no extra for a doubleton, one for a singleton, and two for a void.

Assuming partner has opened at the one level, there are four kinds of hands you will have to describe:

- **Bad hand:** usually less than 6 HCP. Pass tells your story.
- **Minimum strength:** usually 6–9 high-card points, perhaps a "bad" 10.
- **Medium strength:** usually a "good" 10 to a "bad" 12 points.
- **Game-forcing strength:** a hand with which you would probably would have opened the bidding yourself, possibly even more.

The matter of "good" and "bad" points is worth addressing. Good points are aces and kings, four-card support (or better) for partner's major-suit opener, and suits with good intermediate cards (9s and 10s). "Bad" points are in hands with dull shape, three-card support, and high-card points in queens and jacks, especially doubleton queens and tripleton jacks. Some experts go so far as to add value to a hand that has no jacks.

FACT

In the parlance of bridge, a two-card holding of a queen and a jack is a "quack," an especially dubious value considering that it represents 3 high-card points that might not take a trick. Beware of quacks in evaluating your hand.

Your response when partner opens the bidding at the one level depends in large measure on what the opening bid was. The most descriptive one-level opening bid is 1NT, which requires a completely different set of responses, all of which are covered in Chapter 17.

That leaves the openings of 1 ♣, 1 ♦, 1 ♥ and 1 ♠, which, as has been noted, have a very wide range, from as little as 12 HCP to as many as 20 or 21.

Major or Minor Opening?

Responder's choices differ greatly depending on whether opener started with a major or a minor.

If the opening was 1 ♣ or 1 ♦, responder's first priority is to attempt to locate a major-suit fit with opener. Most bidding systems are designed for that purpose.

If responder has a major suit of four cards or longer, she will simply bid that suit at the one level. A bid of 1 ♥ in response to an opening of 1 ♣ has a very wide range, from as little as 6 HCP to a true monster. All opener knows after responder bids 1 ♥ is that responder has four or more hearts. At that point, responder has said nothing about the strength of her hand.

ESSENTIAL

Many new players make the mistake of thinking they have to make some kind of strength-showing jump bid when partner opens one of a minor and they have an opening bid as well. They somehow get the idea that a bid of 1 ♥ with 17 HCP does not do the hand justice. They forget that when partner opens 1 ♣ and they respond as an unpassed hand, their bid is 100 percent forcing. Opener is not allowed to pass a response from a hand that has not yet passed.

When partner opens one of a minor, in formulating your response you will focus on your major suits.

- With one four-card major, bid it.
- With two four-card majors, bid 1 ♥. That does not deny four spades, and it allows opener, should he have four spades but not four hearts, to continue describing his hand by bidding 1 ♠. You can raise to the appropriate level at your next turn.
- With five of one major and four in the other, bid the longer suit.
- With five cards in each major, start with 1 ♠. You may have a chance to bid hearts later to show your second suit.
- With six cards in a major, bid it. You plan to rebid your suit later (the stronger your hand, the more you will bid at your second turn).
- With a balanced hand, no four-card or longer major, and 6–9 HCP, bid 1NT. If partner's opening was 1 ♣ and you have four or more diamonds, you might select 1 ♦ as your response instead of 1NT.
- With a balanced hand, no four-card major, and 11–12 HCP, bid 2NT.
- With a balanced hand, no four-card major and 13–15 HCP, bid 3NT.
- With an unbalanced hand, 6–9 HCP, no four-card major, and four-card or better support for partner's minor, bid two of opener's suit.
- With an unbalanced hand, 10–12 HCP, no four-card major, and four-card or better support for partner's minor, bid three of opener's suit.
- With an unbalanced hand, 13 or more HCP, no four-card major, and four-card or better support for partner's minor, make some forcing bid, perhaps 1 ♦ in response to 1 ♣ or 2 ♣ in response to 1 ♦. If your hand just isn't right for a bid of 2 ♣ over 1 ♦, you might have to bid a three-card major. Some game-forcing hands you will hold after partner opens one of a minor can be awkward to bid. Fortunately, they don't come along that often.

Some examples will help explain how to decide on the best bid. Partner has opened 1 ♣. What is your bid with the following hands?

♠ 987
♥ K765
♦ 8
♣ AQJ76

Bid 1 ♥. You have good support for partner's 1 ♣ opener and 10 HCP, but if you raise clubs first, you deny a four-card major. If partner raises your heart suit, your hand increases in value, and it would not be outrageous to simply jump to 4 ♥. It would not be out of line, however, to simply make an invitation to game.

♠ A987
♥ K765
♦ 8
♣ AJ107

You will still bid 1 ♥. If partner raises, you will go straight to game. If partner bids 1 ♠, you will bid game in his suit. If partner bids 1NT, denying four-card heart support and four spades, you will bid 3NT. Yes, the singleton diamond makes you nervous for play in no-trump, but if partner can't raise hearts or bid spades, he probably has a stopper or stoppers in diamonds.

♠ 987
♥ K76
♦ 87
♣ AQJ76

Bid 3 ♣. This is a so-called "limit raise," which shows 10–12 HCP, and no four-card major, but at least four clubs. If there is a game in the offing, it will most likely be in 3NT, so do not count distributional points when making a limit raise in a minor. Short suits will not help partner take tricks in no-trump.

♠ AJ10
♥ AKJ765
♦ K8
♣ Q4

Bid 1 ♥. You know you are going to at least game—perhaps slam—but the right place to play is not known at this point. For example, if partner rebids in clubs, showing at least six of them, you will give serious thought to investigating a slam in clubs. Don't worry, partner will not pass 1 ♥.

♠ QJ8
♥ KQ9
♦ 986
♣ QJ76

Bid 2NT, showing your balanced distribution and enough high-card points to invite game. You also deny a four-card major.

♠ 987
♥ 765
♦ 86
♣ AQJ76

Bid 2 ♣, the most descriptive bid you have. There are many losers, but you have too much to consider passing and 1NT is not a good choice with such weakness in three suits. If you have so much strength in the club suit, partner should be able to cover some of your losers in the other suits.

Major Suits

When partner's opening bid was in a major, your options are limited by the strength of your hand. Rather than making your life harder, however, that limitation makes things easier in the sense that you don't have to choose from a wide variety of bids, which can be perplexing at times.

Your first priority when partner opens one of a major is to raise partner's suit. That requires at least three cards in the suit that was opened. When the opening is 1 ♥ or 1 ♠ and you have support for the suit:

- With 6–9 support points (perhaps a "bad" 10), bid two of the opener's suit.
- With 10–12 support points but only three card-support, bid a side suit at the two level, planning to support partner's major suit at your next turn to bid.

- With 10–12 support points and at least four-card support for opener's major, bid directly to the three level in the major—a limit raise.
- With 13 or more high-card points and support for opener's major, bid a new suit at the two level. You will judge your next bid by opener's response. If he indicates a minimum opener, you will probably sign off in game.

There are more sophisticated ways of raising opener's major when you have a game-going hand with support. These will be covered in Chapter 7.

Handy Tool

You will find yourself using 1NT as a response to one of a major more often than you might expect, in large measure because a bid of a new suit at the two level in response to a major-suit opening requires at least 10 high-card points. Suppose partner opens 1 ♠ and you are holding this hand:

♠ 3
♥ QJ10987
♦ K1062
♣ J7

You sense that if your side is going to play the contract, it should be played in hearts. Your partner might have a hand such as:

♠ AJ765
♥ K
♦ Q75
♣ K1083

No matter what suit your partner plays in, your hand, with that nice long heart suit, will be of almost no use to her. By contrast, if you can manage to play a heart contract, you can do pretty well. With dummy's ♥ K to help fill out your suit, you have at least five trump tricks in your hand. Partner's ♠ A makes six, and you can take at least one trick in diamonds by driving out the ace of that suit. You are up to seven tricks now, with at least a couple of chances for an eighth trick.

So, how do you get to 2 ♥? Partner is never going to bid the suit, and you don't have enough high-card strength to bid 2 ♥ in response to partner's opening bid.

The solution is to bid 1NT. With the hand shown for your partner, she will bid 2 ♣, and now you can give partner the news by bidding 2 ♥. That bid says to your partner that you have a long heart suit (usually at least six cards), no support for her major suit, not enough strength to bid 2 ♥ directly over 1 ♠. A disciplined partner will pass, happy that she has an honor in your suit, even if it is a singleton.

Sometimes, partner will pass 1NT, usually when she has only a five-card major and no second suit to show—in other words, 5-3-3-2 shape—and a minimum opening bid.

From partner's perspective, when she holds such a hand, 1NT is as good a place to play as any.

Keeping It Low

When partner's opening bid is 1 ♥ and you do not have the three-card support needed to raise opener's suit, at least you have one more option available to you at the one level. If you have four or more spades, you can bid 1 ♠. If partner raises you to 2 ♠, which he will do when he has four spades, you have found a playable spot. If partner rebids 1NT, that is likely to be your place to play when your response is in the minimum range (6–9 HCP).

Bidding 1NT in response to an opener of 1 ♥ sends this message: "Partner, I don't have support for your major suit, I don't have four or more spades, and I don't have enough high-card strength to bid at the two level." That's a lot of information in one bid, which is the essence of bidding accuracy.

Opener's First Rebid

When you open the bidding and partner responds, you have started a dialogue. At your second turn in the auction, your job is to continue the conversation by making the most descriptive bid possible.

Opening bids come in different ranges:

- **Minimum:** 12 to 15 high-card points.
- **Intermediate:** 16 to 18 high-card points.
- **Maximum:** 19–21 high-card points.

Of course, there are other features of your hand that you will want to make known—extra cards in the suit you opened, perhaps a second suit.

The main message you want to send, however, relates to the strength of your hand—and it is possible to send two messages with one bid.

♠ AJ10765
♥ KQ6
♦ 107
♣ K10

You open 1 ♠, to which partner responds 1NT. You have a six-card spade suit, and you are definitely in the minimum range for your opener. You can tell your story in one bid: 2 ♠. Your partner now knows that you have an extra spade but no extra strength. Suppose, however, that your hand looks more like the following:

♠ AKJ765
♥ A8
♦ AJ10
♣ 93

Now you have 17 high-card points along with your extra spade. Your proper rebid is 3 ♠, sending the message that you have at least six spades plus 16–18 HCP.

These two examples show the principle at work, but the rank of the suit you opened can make a big difference in how you rebid.

Minor or Major?

When you open 1 ♣ or 1 ♦, partner's response will center on the major suits. If she has one, she will bid it. Most of the time, if partner does not bid 1 ♥ or 1 ♠ when you open a minor, she doesn't have a four-card major. The exception is when responder to 1 ♣ bids 1 ♦, which does not deny a four-card major.

> When your partner has opened 1 ♣, you usually bid your suits "up the line." That is, bid the lowest-ranking suit (diamonds) first if you have four of them. Be careful, however, when you have a minimum responding hand with four diamonds and four hearts. In that case, it is better to bid 1 ♥. The reason is that if the next player bids 1 ♠ before your partner can make her rebid, you could "lose" the heart suit because neither you nor partner will be strong enough to mention the suit at the two level.

As opener after you have started with one of a minor, if partner bids one of a major, your responsibility is to describe your hand as accurately as possible. If partner has responded 1 ♥ to your opening and you have four-card support, raise to the appropriate level. Bid 2 ♥ if you have 12–15 support points, 3 ♥ with 16–18 support points, and 4 ♥ with 19 or more support points. The same applies to a response of 1 ♠ when you have four-card support.

Here are your priorities after opening one of a minor:

- Raise partner's major to the appropriate level. Any other bid denies four-card support.
- Rebid one of a major when partner has responded 1 ♦ to your opening bid of 1 ♣.
- Rebid 1 ♠ over the response of 1 ♥ if you do not have four-card heart support.
- Rebid a six-card or longer minor suit at the two level with 12–15 high-card points, at the three-level with 16–18 HCP.
- Rebid a lower-ranking suit (clubs after opening 1 ♦) at the two level with a minimum to intermediate hand. Note: You can rebid 2 ♣ after opening 1 ♦ with as much as 17 HCP, just short of a jump shift rebid.
- Rebid a lower-ranking suit at the three level (3 ♣ after opening 1 ♦) with 18–19 HCP.

- Rebid 1NT with a balanced hand of 12–14 HCP. If partner has responded 1 ♥, this denies four-card heart support. It also denies four spades.
- Rebid 2NT with a balanced hand of 18–19 HCP. This denies four-card support if partner responded 1 ♥, but it does not deny four spades. The priority in this case is to show the strength of the hand. If partner has four spades, she can bid the suit over 2NT.
- Rebid 3NT with a very strong six-card or longer minor suit, 17–19 high-card points, and no support for partner's major.

The one rebid not covered in this list deserves a special mention. It is a bid called a "reverse." It occurs most often after an opening of one of a minor and the response of 1 ♠. If you rebid 2 ♦ (after having opened 1 ♣) or 2 ♥ (after having opened either minor), you are showing a strong hand, usually at least 16 high-card points. The reason you must have extra strength is that if your partner has to go back to your first suit, he must do so at the three level. You don't want to be that high if you have a minimum opener and partner has a minimum response. For more on this topic, see Chapter 7.

Major Issues

If you have opened one of a major, you will have plenty of choices for rebids, always striving to make the most descriptive rebid possible.

Here are your priorities after you have opened 1 ♥ or 1 ♠ and partner has responded:

- After opening 1 ♥, raise a response of 1 ♠ to the appropriate level with four-card support, 2 ♠ with 12–15 support points, 3 ♠ with 16–18 support points, and 4 ♠ with 19 or more support points.
- Pass with a minimum opener when partner makes a minimum or "limit" raise of your major.
- Consider making a game try with an intermediate hand when partner makes a minimum raise. Bid game if partner makes a limit raise.
- Pass partner's response of 1NT with a minimum opener and a balanced hand (no side four-card suit).

- Rebid a six-card or longer suit at the two level with a minimum opener, at the three level with intermediate values.
- Raise partner's response of 1NT to 2NT with intermediate values (18 to a poor 19 HCP) and a balanced hand.
- Raise partner's response of 1NT to 3NT with maximum (good 19 to 20) and a balanced hand.
- Bid a lower-ranking side four-card suit at the cheapest level with a minimum to intermediate opener. As noted with minor-suit openers, you can have up to 17 HCP for a rebid at the two level.
- Bid a lower-ranking suit at the three level with 18–19 HCP.

With a six-card or longer major suit and a hand that should make game when partner responds to your opener, you can just charge into 4 ♥ or 4 ♠, but that can make it difficult to reach slam when your partner has some potentially useful cards but no bidding space to show them.

Many experienced players take this into account and use a bit of creativity in the bidding, perhaps making a jump shift rebid on a three-card suit. That can provide some extra bidding room that would be lost if you simply jumped to four of your major.

This is somewhat esoteric and might be tricky for newer players, but it's something to keep in mind for adding to your repertoire as you gain experience.

The Captaincy Principle

Of all the concepts you will study in learning the game of bridge, there are few more important than the captaincy principle.

It is as simple as it is elegant: In the bidding, when one member of a partnership limits her hand, that player's partner becomes the "captain" of the auction. The captain makes the decision about how high the bidding should go.

The easiest way to illustrate the principle is to consider the auction that begins with 1NT. That is the ultimate in a limiting bid. Most players open 1NT with 15–17 high-card points. That narrow range allows the partner of the 1NT opener to make an accurate assessment of where the two hands should go. The partner of the opener is the captain and cannot be over-ruled in any decision he makes.

For example, if responder to 1NT bids 2 ♥, she is indicating that she has at least five in her suit but not enough high-card points to consider going any higher than the two level. It is a signoff bid and, no matter how good opener thinks his hand is, his only option is to pass. Responder, after all, knows about his partner's hand. The 1NT opener, however, knows nothing about his partner's hand except that he wants to play 2 ♥.

Consider the following auctions and see if you can identify the bids that limit one hand or the other.

West	North	East	South
1 ♣	Pass	1 ♥	Pass
1NT			

Answer: 1 ♣ is somewhat limited, but 1 ♥ can be as little as 6 HCP or very strong. 1NT limits the opener to 14 HCP (if he had, say, 15, he would have opened 1NT, not 1 ♣). The 1 ♥ bidder is now the captain.

West	North	East	South
1 ♠	Pass	1NT	Pass
2 ♣			

1 ♠ is limited in a sense (as was 1 ♣ in the first example), but still offers a wide range of possibilities. 1NT strongly implies that the bidder does not have 10 high-card points, but that is the only limiting factor. Opener's 2 ♣ bid is limited by the failure to rebid 3 ♣, showing 18–20 HCP, but the range for opener's hand is still pretty wide at 12–17.

West	North	East	South
1 ♦	Pass	1 ♥	Pass
2 ♥			

1 ♦ is limited in the same way as the other opening bids in this exercise, 1 ♥ is not limited, but the raise to 2 ♥ is definitely limited. Opener is showing roughly 12–15 points in support of hearts. If any further action is to be taken, it will have to be by responder.

Here's an example of an auction where the captaincy principle is violated.

Suppose East holds this hand:

♠ QJ9
♥ J1054
♦ K763
♣ 32

Now consider this auction:

West	North	East	South
1 ♠	Pass	2 ♠	Pass
Pass	3 ♣	3 ♠	

East's bid of 3 ♠ is a big no-no because it violates the captaincy principle. East limited his hand by bidding 2 ♠, and there is nothing about his hand that has changed. By limiting his hand, East made West the captain of the auction. In the given auction, it's West's decision about what to do over the 3 ♣ bid (known as "balancing" because North does not want to let the opponents play a comfortable 2 ♠). What if West's hand is something like the following?

♠ K8763
♥ A4
♦ 109
♣ KQJ9

After West hears North bid 3 ♣, she will be licking her chops in anticipation of the chance to double in the expectation of a juicy penalty. West will not be pleased to have that chance pre-empted by her partner.

Write this down and study it with your partner. Once you have described your hand, all further decisions in the auction are left to your partner.

After the First Round of Bidding

On most occasions, opener will limit her hand with her rebid. In that case, responder is the captain and will make a decision about the strain (suit or no-trump) and the level. It's pretty easy when responder is minimum and opener has described minimum values. If a fit in a suit has been found, responder will usually pass. When there is some doubt about where to play, more bidding will ensue. For example:

West	North	East	South
1 ♣	Pass	1 ♦	Pass
1 ♥	Pass	?	

East might have a hand such as:

♠ A954
♥ J10
♦ K7632
♣ Q8

West has not denied four spades, so East will bid the suit to provide more information to West.

When responder is confident the partnership has found the best denomination to play in, she will pass with minimum values, make an invitation to game with intermediate strength, and simply bid game in the appropriate suit (or no-trump) unless she has enough extra strength to consider probing for slam.

If a fit has not been found and responder has a minimum hand for the bidding, she will usually take a preference for opener's first suit. In most cases, responder will not introduce a new suit, which is forcing (opener cannot pass) in most systems. With no fit for either of opener's suits, assuming two have been bid, responder will bid 1NT if possible. 2NT is not an option without at least 11 HCP because 2NT is an invitational bid.

FACT

Modern bidding is designed to help partners discover when two hands have at least eight cards in the same suit (usually a major) between them. This is known in the vernacular as a "golden fit." It is highly advantageous in many cases to have four cards of the suit in each hand, providing opportunities for using the trumps separately and generating extra tricks.

When responder has a strong hand and wants to play game, she can simply bid it if a fit has been found, bid 3NT with a balanced hand and no established fit, or she can jump in a suit of six cards or longer.

West	North	East	South
1 ♣	Pass	1 ♥	Pass
1 ♠	Pass	?	

East would bid 3 ♥ with this hand:

♠ AQ
♥ KQ10654
♦ J103
♣ J9

Bidding 3 ♥ would show a six-card suit and enough to play game. Opener, with a doubleton heart, would probably bid 4 ♥. With a singleton heart, opener likely would choose 3NT.

Responding hands with invitational values are more difficult to bid without certain sophisticated bidding tools that are beyond the scope of this book.

What you want to take from this chapter is an understanding of and appreciation for good communication between partners. If you and your partner are on the same wavelength, you will probably get by just fine in most cases without fancy conventions. In any case, no system, no matter how fancy or highly developed, can cater to all possibilities.

Important Bidding Principles

A good bridge player has many positive attributes. Among the most important of them is discipline. Not only does he know the right bids, he knows when to make them—and when not to.

Suppose you have the following hand:

♠ Q5
♥ K43
♦ K32
♣ AJ1096

You open 1 ♣, as anyone would, and partner bids 1 ♠. Now your right-hand opponent comes in with 2 ♥. You have a good opening hand, but it's not strong enough to bid at the three level (don't admit it if you were considering raising spades with only two), not to mention the fact that you have only five clubs.

Because of the interference, your only choice is to pass. Remember, you have a partner over there, and she heard you open the bidding. If her hand justifies it, she will take some action, but from your pass she will know you are probably minimum, you don't have as many as three spades (you would have raised her in that case), and you don't have enough strength in hearts to double for penalty. Did you think you could convey so much information simply by passing?

Discipline enters the picture in other ways, such as when you have described your hand and partner makes a bid that does not look good from your side of the table. Perhaps partner has bid your singleton. A disciplined player, understanding that he has shown his hand and partner is in charge, does not try to "improve" the contract by bidding again. He trusts his partner and passes.

Bidding in Third and Fourth Seats

When your partner passes as dealer and the next hand passes as well, things change. Whereas you would not consider bidding with a hand as weak as 10 high-card points in normal circumstances, you will often do so in third seat (that is, when your partner is the dealer).

The reason is that if you play a disciplined style with sound opening bids, partner will pass on occasion when she has a 12-point hand, and she will certainly pass with 10 or 11. If you hold a hand of 11 points yourself, you must consider that the majority of the high-card points could be with your side. That means you should be able to make something.

In essence, you are opening light in third seat as a way of "protecting" your plus score. This is more important in duplicate bridge than in party or rubber bridge, but it is a principle with which you should become familiar. Here are the basics:

- Open light in third seat only with hands with which you will be comfortable passing whatever bid your partner might make. If you have a relatively balanced hand with 10 HCP and at least three-card support for all other suits, it's okay to open the bidding. Unless you are forced to bid, however, plan on keeping your mouth shut for the duration of the auction. If you have as few as two in some suit partner might bid, just pass. It will be bad for partnership harmony if you pass partner's bid and put down a dummy with only two trumps.

- If you open the bidding in third seat and voluntarily bid again, it shows a full opening hand.

- Bid the suit you want your partner to lead—and that means you can break the cardinal rule about opening a major suit with only four of them. Take this hand, for example:

♠ AKJ10
♥ Q107
♦ 874
♣ J109

This is a reasonable third-seat opener. You have only four spades, but do you really want your partner to lead one of the minors if the opponents compete and buy the contract? Bid your best suit. No matter what partner bids, you can pass.

Final Shot

When there are three passes to you, the situation changes yet again. If you pass, you will get no score. That's not great, but at least it's not a minus. Again, this is more important at duplicate, but the principle is good to know.

There is a time-tested way to determine whether to bid in fourth seat. It's called the Rule of Fifteen, and it's pretty easy. Simply count up your high-card points, then add that to the number of spades in your hand. If the sum is 15, open the bidding with whatever bid your system calls for. If the sum is 14 or less, pass it out.

A famous woman player from Great Britain had a somewhat different view of the Rule of Fifteen. Her view was that if the player in fourth-seat held a singleton or void in spades, that meant there was a fair chance partner had some spades, so she bid even when her hand didn't meet all the parameters of the Rule of Fifteen.

The reason spades figure into the equation is that it is the "boss" suit. The opponents may be light in values, but if they have the spade suit they can outbid you. If you hold extra strength or some length in spades, that lowers the chances that the opponents can get in there with the highest-ranking suit.

The Rule of Fifteen is a bit of an oversimplification, but in the main it is valid.

CHAPTER 5

Competitive Bidding, Part 1

In many ways, bridge is like war except with friendly opponents (it is a social game, after all). This is especially true when neither side holds a significant advantage. Both sides scratch and claw, with whatever weapons they might have at their disposal, as they try to gain an advantage. In the arena of competitive bidding, the bold often hold the edge.

5

The Opponents Open the Bidding

The side that takes the first shot usually has the advantage, but when the opposition is well armed, it often doesn't matter who gets in the first blow.

When one of your opponents opens the bidding, you have some choices. You can:

- **Pass.** This tells your partner you have nothing to say at the present time.
- **Overcall in a suit**—as in bidding 1 ♠ after your right-hand opponent starts with 1 ♥. Your 1 ♠ bid is an overcall. Making this call generally shows a suit of five or more cards of decent quality. The overall strength of the hand should be appropriate to the level of the bid and the vulnerability.
- **Overcall in no-trump,** usually either 1NT (showing a balanced hand, a stopper in the suit that was opened, plus 15–18 high-card points) or 2NT (a conventional bid showing at least five cards in each of the two lowest unbid suits).
- **Make a cuebid of opener's suit** (as in 1 ♣ —2 ♣). This is another conventional way to show two-suited hands.
- **Make a takeout double.** A direct double of an opening bid tells partner that you have the rough equivalent of an opening hand and at least three-card support for the unbid suits. Partner is not allowed to pass unless he has a long, strong holding in opener's suit.

As you can see, there are many options available for competing. Experience will teach you the right one for each different situation.

Roads Not Taken

Astute players use information about options their partners could have taken to draw inferences as the bidding and play progress. You can make deductions about your partner's hand from her failure to take some action that was available to her.

Listening to the bidding is more than just hearing the calls. Really listening means interpreting the messages and using them to your advantage.

It is usually safer to take action in the direct seat—that is, next to bid after an opponent opens—than when both opponents have bid and exchanged information. The more they know about each other's hands, the better they will handle your interference.

Principles of Overcalling

There is danger in overcalling, but there is also danger in not overcalling (you may miss a big reward).

Fasten your seatbelt because once the opponents take the first shot, the auction is now competitive and you are in for a battle. Overcalls are your weapons in this competitive auction. You will serve a specific purpose when you make an overcall.

Why Overcall?

Here are some reasons why you might want to be involved in the opponents' auction:

- To try to interfere with the opponents' communication
- To tell partner about a good suit
- To tell partner what suit to lead if you end up as defenders

When the opponents have opened the bidding and you have an opportunity to get in there, the direct seat may be your only chance. You will feel pretty silly if you have a legitimate one-level overcall, decide to pass, and find that the bidding is at the four level when it comes back to you. The following auction is not uncommon.

West	North	East	South
		1 ♥	Pass
4 ♥	Pass	Pass	?

Perhaps your hand was worth a 1 ♠ bid, something like:

♠ QJ987
♥ 98
♦ KJ63
♣ Q10

How do you feel about entering the auction now? It could be an utter disaster. Your partner might have good spade support for you, maybe even enough to make 4 ♠ or at least push the opponents one level higher, but you left your partner out of the loop with your failure to overcall.

Overcall Parameters

Your first goal is to tell your partner that you have a suit with lots of cards in it. For overcalls, that's usually five or more at the one level, often six or more at the two level or higher. You know that the opponents have some strength because they opened the bidding, and you also know what suit is strong for them, because you heard their bid. When you overcall, you are offering to play the hand with your strong suit as trump.

You do not need as many points to overcall as you do to open the bidding. The hurdle for opening the bidding is 12 HCP with adequate quick tricks or any hand with 13 HCP or more. All you need to overcall on the one level is a good suit and 8 or more HCP.

Your second objective in overcalling is to tell your partner what suit to lead later if the opponents win the auction. You want your partner to lead your suit.

And finally, you want to take up bidding space to try to limit the opponents' opportunity to communicate. Remember those obnoxious, preemptive three-level bids? Well, some overcalls can have the same effect. If you make an overcall, they can only use the available bids that are higher on the bidding ladder.

When the opponents open at 1 ♣ or 1 ♦, you have lots of space left on the one level and all of the higher bids. When the opponent opens a higher-ranking suit, like 1 ♥ or 1 ♠ or 1NT, you will have to be a bit more careful, but it's a bidder's game and no one promised you a rose garden. Get in there and bid when you think it's right.

Let's look at some hands that you would love to overcall when the opponents open the auction—and the reason you will make the overcall.

    ♠ AKJ75
    ♥ 87
    ♦ 9753
    ♣ 75

Your right-hand opponent opens 1 ♣. Are you game?

You can certainly get into this auction. You do not need to have as many points as the opener. The 13-point hurdle the opener has to jump over does not count for you. All you have to do is fit one or more of the criteria for joining this auction:

- 8–17 HCP and most of the points concentrated in your suit if you are at the lower end of the HCP range.
- A five-card suit.
- You have jammed the auction by bidding 1 ♠. The opponents will have to bid at least 1NT to stay in this auction. You certainly would not mind playing this hand, but even if you don't end up as declarer, you will be pleased to have partner lead this suit if you end up as a defender.

There is, of course, a downside to overcalling. One of your opponents could have a stack in your suit, meaning you would probably be doubled. That will happen from time to time, but, as the famous quote goes, "Faint heart ne'er won fair lady."

Overcalling just to make noise is a bad policy. You should have a purpose when you get into the bidding. Ask yourself (1) whether your hand provides a reasonable shot at a plus score, (2) whether it will be helpful to partner if you enter the auction, and (3) if it will interfere with the opponents' communication. Remember, you have told your opponents the same information you have told your partner. They will use this information against you just as you try to use the information about their bids against them.

Higher Plane

Overcalling at the one level is relatively safe because it's tough to exact a meaningful penalty against you when you need only seven tricks for your contract. The two level is vastly different territory, and you must exercise extreme caution in overcalling at the two level when you are vulnerable.

This following hand, for example, would be a reasonable overcall in diamonds if the opening bid is 1 ♣.

♠ Q64
♥ 109
♦ AKJ54
♣ 743

If the opening bid on your right is 1 ♥ or 1 ♠, however, it would be suicide to bid that five-card suit at the two level. That is not even close to a two-level overcall at any vulnerability and it would be madness if you are vulnerable. A vulnerable two-level overcall would look more like this:

♠ 764
♥ K9
♦ AKJ1098
♣ K10

That's a bare minimum two-level vulnerable overcall.

Takeout Doubles

There are many ways to compete when an opponent opens the bidding, and a must for your bidding toolbox is the takeout double.

As described earlier in this chapter, when you double an opponent's opening bid—and that includes bids higher than one—it sends a message to your partner that you are short in opener's suit and have at least three cards in the other suits. Your partner is directed to pick her best suit—sometimes "best" means longest—and bid it an appropriate level. The parameters for responding to a takeout double are covered in the next chapter.

Suppose your right-hand opponent opens 1 ♥. Which of the following hands is appropriate for a takeout double?

♠ Q1098
♥ 6
♦ AJ43
♣ KQ72

This hand has perfect shape, the requisite high-card count, and excellent support for any suit partner might bid. This is a textbook takeout double:

♠ Q109
♥ 643
♦ AJ43
♣ KQ7

Pass is best after your right-hand opponent bids 1 ♥. The shape is the worst possible. You have what is known as the "death holding" in opener's suit and you have only three spades. When you double one major, partner will strain to bid the other major. This is not great support. Again, right-hand opponent has opened 1 ♥.

♠ J1098
♥ 6
♦ QJ43
♣ K872

This one has perfect shape but is short of high cards. Pass.

♠ Q109
♥ A543
♦ AQJ4
♣ 82

One of the most common errors among beginners is making a takeout double with a hand of this kind. Yes, there are 13 HCP, but where are the clubs? What will you do if you make a takeout double with this hand and partner bids clubs? Pass and let him languish in a 4–2 trump fit? He won't enjoy that. Bid 2NT? That shows a hand stronger than a 1NT overcall—roughly 19 HCP. It may be counterintuitive to pass with an opening hand, but you have to do that sometimes.

Occasionally you have the wrong shape initially but get a second chance in the bidding.

Try this one on for size.

♠ QJ109
♥ 64
♦ AQ432
♣ A2

Your right-hand opponent opens 1 ♥, and unless you feel like overcalling 1 ♠ on that four-card suit, you must pass. You can't double with this hand for the same reason you couldn't double with the previous example hand. But wait! What if the auction proceeds as follows:

West	North	East	South
		1 ♥	Pass
1NT	Pass	2 ♣	?

Now you are well placed to enter the bidding with a double. There are now only two unbid suits, and you have support for both. Now is the time to double. Your partner should understand that this is for takeout, showing spades and diamonds, and she will understand from the auction why you didn't double at your first opportunity.

Other Competitive Doubles

The double has many uses in bridge besides penalty and takeout. In today's modern game, one of the most common uses for the double occurs after your side opens the bidding.

In days past, when partner opened one of a minor and the next player bid 1 ♠, the following hand type presented a serious problem.

♠ 87
♥ QJ62
♦ KJ94
♣ J62

If your right-hand opponent had passed, you would have happily bid 1 ♥. You have more than enough to respond, and you could tell your story in one quick bid. When your right-hand opponent overcalls 1 ♠, however, you are no longer so happy. You have no spade stopper, so 1NT won't work, and raising partner to 2 ♣ with that anemic holding has little appeal. Well, what about hearts or diamonds? To bid either of those suits, you will have to go to the two level, which requires a minimum of five cards.

Furthermore, you have only 8 HCP, and bidding at the two level shows at least 10 HCP.

This kind of hand is the reason that Alvin Roth, one of the all-time great players, invented a tool that has become a staple of just about every bidding system worldwide.

It's called the negative double, the negative stuck in there to, you might say, "negate" the penalty aspect because it's not meant to punish the opponent for a bad bidding decision. It's for takeout.

FACT

The negative double was originally known as the *Sputnik* double because when Roth and his partner, Tobias Stone, introduced the new bidding device in 1957, the Russian space satellite was getting a lot of publicity. The *Sputnik* name is still used with the convention in some countries.

In the formative years of bridge, a double after an opponent's overcall was for penalty, but you don't get many chances for a significant penalty of a one bid. Roth, one of the great bidding theorists of all time, reasoned that the double in the given situation was more useful as a way to show the other two suits.

Here's how it works. When your partner opens one of a suit—usually a minor—and the next player overcalls, a double indicates that you have enough to respond and usually four-card support for the unbid suits.

With negative doubles, the emphasis is always on the majors. This is the formula:

- When an opening of 1 ♣ or 1 ♦ is overcalled by 1 ♠, double shows a four-card heart suit and probably—but not necessarily—four or more cards in the other minor.
- When an opening of 1 ♣ or 1 ♦ is overcalled by 1 ♥, a bid of 1 ♠ shows at least five spades. With only four spades and enough to respond, employ the negative double.
- If 1 ♦ is overcalled by 2 ♣, double indicates possession of at least one four-card major.
- The negative double can be used when you hold a suit longer than four cards but without the 10 high-card points needed to bid at the two level. You can double, and if partner bids your suit, decide whether to raise or just pass. If partner bids some other suit, you can bid your long suit to reveal the nature of your hand and the reason for the negative double.
- There is no upper limit in terms of high-card points for a negative double, although most of the time you will have a relatively modest hand. You could, however, have a very strong hand but choose to use the negative double to find a fit in a major suit.

The negative double is one of the handiest of the conventions you will learn as you progress. It has almost universal acceptance.

How High

When opener's rebid in response to a negative double will be at the one or two level, assuming the next player passes, you can make a negative double on minimum values, roughly 6–9 HCP. If opener will have to bid higher than the two level, the HCP requirements for a negative double will increase.

Discuss with partner how high the opponents can bid before negative doubles become penalty doubles. Most experienced partnerships agree that negative doubles are in effect through the three level. That is, if partner opens one of a minor and the next player bids 3 ♠, double is still for take-out. Of course, when you are forcing partner to bid at the four level, you must have a relatively strong hand.

Information, Please

One of the best uses of the double is to help your partner out with his opening lead. Suppose your left-hand opponent opens 1NT and, after partner passes, your right-hand opponent (RHO) bids 2 ♣, a conventional bid called Stayman. It is completely artificial and is used to inquire of the opener whether he has one or more four-card majors.

FACT

Bridge writers frequently use terminology and jargon that may be unfamiliar to newer players. The notation *RHO* signifies your right-hand opponent and *LHO* your left-hand opponent.

Now, suppose your holding in clubs is something along the lines of KQ1098. It certainly appears likely that the opponents are going to end up playing the contract, and if the 1NT opener bids a major suit that is raised by his partner, that means your partner will be on lead. So, what suit do you think will be the best lead for your side? That's right! You want partner to lead a club.

So, how do you get partner to cooperate? You double, that's what. When you double an artificial bid, it shows that you have length and strength in the suit. So if your partner finds himself on opening lead, he should start with a club unless he has a great excuse, such as being void in the suit.

If you play in tournaments, you will encounter many artificial—not to say esoteric—bids that give you the opportunity to help partner with his opening lead, or even find a suit that you and your partner can bid as a way of competing.

Be careful about doubling artificial bids if it is likely you are going to be on lead against the final contract—as when it is clear your right-hand opponent is going to play a spade contract and she has bid some suit you can double. Doubling gives the opponents a chance to exchange more information, and you could be providing declarer with potentially useful information.

Some examples of artificial bids you might encounter:

- **Jacoby Transfers over 1NT and 2NT.** In the simplest form, bidding diamonds asks the opener to bid hearts; bidding hearts asks partner to bid spades. Transfers are useful because they keep the stronger hand concealed, which is an advantage in most cases.
- **Stayman.** Already mentioned.
- **Gerber.** An ace-asking convention of 4 ♣.
- **Responses to the 4NT (Blackwood) convention,** also asking for aces.

There are many other artificial bids. The key is to be aware of the opportunity to indicate length and strength when the opponents bid some suit you know they don't intend to play.

Avoid doubling an artificial bid without true strength in the suit. For example, you would not be too keen for partner to lead a suit in which you held six to the jack. You double mainly with the idea that leading that suit for your side will develop tricks.

Responding to Partner's Overcall

Overcalls come in a variety of types, anchored by the simple overcall—they open the bidding, you bid something at a minimum level, as in 1 ♥—1 ♠. Or, they open the bidding, your partner passes, the next hand responds in some way, and you bid, as in 1 ♥—Pass—2 ♥—2 ♠. This, too, is a simple overcall.

Requirements for simple overcalls were covered earlier in this chapter. What was not discussed was your responsibilities as the partner of the overcaller, the "advancer" in bridge lingo. What should you do when your partner overcalls?

ALERT!

When your partner overcalls, the more of her trumps you hold, the more aggressive you can be in the bidding, especially if you have shortness in some other suit. If you can bid to a high level immediately in response to your partner's overcall, you rob the opponents of precious bidding space, and you have the protection of lots of trumps between the two hands.

Your action as advancer depends on your hand, and your choices are as follows:

- With no trump fit for your partner's suit, fewer than 10 high-card points and no good suit of your own to bid, pass.
- If you would have raised your partner's suit if he had opened the bidding instead of overcalling, do so directly unless third hand has bid and you will have to go to the three level to raise. Your raise to the two level does not promise much.
- If you have trump support and your hand evaluates to 10 or more support points, make a cuebid in opener's suit. That is, if opener started with 1 ♣ and partner overcalled 1 ♠, a bid of 2 ♣ by you tells your partner that you have trump support and at least 10 support points.
- With at least four-card trump support and some shape—a singleton or void—and a weak hand, make a jump raise in partner's suit (for

example, bid 3 ♠ if partner overcalled 1 ♠). You have a cuebid available to show a forward-going hand, so partner will not misunderstand your jump raise.

- With no fit for partner but with at least 10 HCP and a stopper in opener's suit, bid 1NT. On rare occasions, you will have enough to bid 2NT (12—14).

If your partner knows he can rely on you to raise with support after he overcalls, he won't bid his suit again after you pass unless he really has the goods.

Balancing

In bridge, especially in duplicate, the auction frequently turns into a skirmish between the two sides as they fight to win the contract. It is losing strategy to go quietly, and it will behoove you to become familiar with a practice called balancing. In some countries, it's called "protection." No matter what it's called, the objective is the same: getting the opponents out of their comfort zone.

Suppose the bidding goes this way:

West	North	East	South
		1 ♠	Pass
2 ♠	Pass	Pass	?

You are South and it's your turn to call. If you pass, the opponents get to play in 2 ♠. Is that okay with you? Your answer should be in the negative.

So, what can you do about it? First, consider what the relatively quiet auction has told you. Neither of your opponents seems to be loaded. West's 2 ♠ could be based on a mere 6 high-card points. If East had more than a minimum opener, she might have made some move toward game. It's logical to conclude that the high-card points are pretty evenly distributed between your side and theirs. You should make some move to get the opponents to a higher level. How you do that will depend on the makeup of your hand.

Suppose you hold:

♠ 32
♥ Q987
♦ KJ65
♣ K109

You didn't have enough strength to enter the fray directly over 1 ♠, but you should make a takeout double at this point. You may be thinking, "Wait! I have only nine high-card points!" That's true, but the auction strongly suggests that your partner has some of the missing strength. Think about it—the opponents are stopping in 2 ♠. If opener has 12 or 13 HCP and responder has 6 or 7 HCP, that's about 20 total. You have 9 HCP, so partner probably has 10 or 11 points.

That's what balancing is all about—inferring that your partner has a modicum of strength. By taking action, you are—in a very real sense—bidding your partner's cards as well as your own.

Here's another hand, same auction:

♠ 63
♥ 72
♦ KJ652
♣ KQ106

If you chose to balance at this point, what do you think is your best call? It might seem strange, but your proper bid is 2NT. You don't want to double because your hand will not be a good dummy if partner bids 3 ♥. You could bid 3 ♦, but that will work out badly if your partner is short in that suit.

You can bid 1NT in the passout seat as an offer to play the contract, but any no-trump bid by a passed hand at the two level or higher will almost always show the minor suits with a lack of support for the other suits. Make sure you and your partner are in accord on this principle.

Involve your partner in the final decision by bidding 2NT, which can mean only that you have length in the minors. 2NT cannot be an offer to play in no-trump at the two level. If you had that kind of hand, you would have overcalled 1NT at your first turn.

Discretion Rules

You don't always balance when the opponent stops at a low level. For example, you would pass if you held this hand in the passout seat (same auction):

♠ QJ109
♥ A3
♦K652
♣ 843

The opponents have landed in your best suit. Why disturb them? Further, your holding in spades makes it clear your partner is short in spades, yet he took no action.

Another major factor in deciding whether to balance will be the vulnerability. If your side is vulnerable, you should be very leery of balancing when whatever you do (doubling or bidding) will require going to the three level (or making partner do so). The opponents already know a lot about each other's hands and they will be quick to double you at the three level—and that can work out very badly, especially in duplicate. Balancing when vulnerable might be trading minus 110 (leaving the opponents to play in 2 ♠) for minus 200, 500, or worse.

You Open and They Compete

A vitally important principle of competitive bidding when your side has opened can and probably should be written in stone: Support with support.

That is, when you have support for partner's suit and enough strength to bid, let her know it as soon as possible. There's nothing worse than making an ambiguous bid, planning to support partner's suit later, then finding that the bidding is in the stratosphere by the time it gets back to you.

By failing to show support, in many cases you will have deprived your partner of valuable information. You will be forced to guess what to do, which is never a good thing. It's a time-tested principle of competitive bidding that you always want to make the other person make the last guess.

When partner opens the bidding, here are some basics for an accurate exchange of information. If partner has opened one of a major and the next player bids a suit at the one level or two level:

- With 6–9 (or a "bad" 10) support points and at least three cards in partner's major, make a minimum raise, as in 1 ♥—1 ♠—2 ♥.
- With a "good" 10 or more support points, bid the overcaller's suit. This is known as a cuebid. It does not say you have the overcaller's suit. It says that you have trump support for your partner but that your hand is too good to make a simple raise. You could even have an opening hand yourself, so even if your partner tries to sign off below game, you will bid it yourself.
- Without support for partner but with 8–10 HCP and at least one stopper in the opponent's suit bid at the one level, bid 1NT.
- Without support for partner and 11–12 HCP and at least one stopper in the opponent's suit bid at the one level, bid 2NT.
- Without support for partner and 13–15 HCP and at least one stopper in the opponent's suit, bid 3NT.
- Without enough strength to bid at the two level, or without long suit to bid and no stopper in overcaller's suit, double for takeout (this is the "negative" double discussed earlier in this chapter).
- Without support for your partner but with a good suit of your own and at least 10 HCP, bid your suit at a minimum level. Partner is not allowed to pass, so you should get more information about her hand when she takes another call.

The key in this situation is to act when you have some high-card values. Don't pass and hope to catch up later. That rarely works out well for your side.

Biting Your Tongue

There will be times when your partner opens the bidding and the next player bids a suit in which you are loaded. You will have visions of a four-digit number for your side after you double. If you and your partner have agreed to play negative doubles—and you should—you will have to pass. Double by you would be for takeout, not penalty.

That sounds terribly frustrating, right? It would be if you haven't discussed all the nuances of playing negative doubles. When your partner opens the bidding and the next player bids, if you pass and the bidding comes back to your partner, she will look at her hand and, if short in the overcaller's suit, she will double as a way of "protecting" that big plus score you were hoping for.

You will, of course, happily pass your partner's "reopening" double, which ostensibly is for takeout. By passing, you will be converting it to the penalty double you wanted to make directly.

Some hands will not be appropriate for a reopening double. If, for example, your partner opened a seven-card suit, she will be worried about how many tricks she will take in her long suit. If she has a second long suit, it might be better to bid that suit than to make a double. In such cases, if you were hoping to be able to penalize the opponents for a risky overcall, you can bid game in no-trump or partner's second suit if your hand is appropriate.

In the long run, you will benefit more from playing negative doubles than you will lose on occasion by not being able to exact heavy penalties.

CHAPTER 6

Competitive Bidding, Part 2

In the competitive bidding arena, communication and judgment are key elements of a successful game plan. You will not do well if you are timid in the bidding, but you must temper your aggression. Knowing when to pass is as important as knowing when to strike a blow.

Responding to a Takeout Double

There are two ways to get into the bidding when one of your opponents beats you to the punch with an opening bid—the overcall and the takeout double.

The parameters for takeout doubles were covered in the previous chapter, but it bears repeating that, with rare exceptions, the proper takeout double is roughly an opening hand with at least three-card support for any unbid suits.

The takeout double is not exclusively used in the direct seat after an opening bid. Third hand can also make a takeout double if opener's suit is raised or if responder bids a new suit. For example, if opener started with 1 ♣ and responder bids 1 ♥, a double by third hand shows support for diamonds and spades and roughly the equivalent of an opening hand.

There are two exceptions to the rule requiring support for unbid suits when a takeout double is made.

One is when you have a powerful hand (usually at least 17 high-card points) and a long, strong suit, something such as ♠ AKJ10976 or ♥ KQJ987.

The other is when you have a balanced hand with a stopper in the suit that was opened and more high-card points than it would show if you simply overcalled 1NT—19 or more when a 1NT overcall would be 15–18.

When you make a takeout double and subsequently bid your own suit or no-trump, you are showing extra values. This is not a forcing bid—responder can still pass with a truly bad hand but should strain to bid again, especially with support for the suit partner has bid after doubling.

It is easy for the responder to the takeout double—sometimes known in bridge parlance as the "advancer"—to overlook this maneuver, and it might take a missed game or two for you and your partner to get used to this nuance. Just remember, making a takeout double and changing suits on your partner (or bidding no-trump) shows extra values—*not* simply that you doubled without support for unbid suits.

Tell Your Story

When your partner makes a takeout double of an opening bid and the next player passes, the spotlight is on you. You have one responsibility—to tell your partner what you've got. You should assume that partner has a normal takeout double and respond accordingly.

Here are the guidelines for successful communication with your partner after he makes a takeout double:

- **With 0–8 high-card points,** bid your best suit at a minimum level.
- **With 9–11 high-card points,** make a jump bid in your best suit.
- **With a good 12 or more high-card points,** start by cuebidding the opponent's suit. This tells your partner that your side belongs in game. The focus from that point usually will be to find a major-suit fit of at least eight cards. If you do not uncover a fit in a major, attention will turn to no-trump.
- **With no good suit to bid but at least one stopper in the suit that was opened,** bid no-trump at the appropriate level: 1NT with 8–10 high-card points, 2NT with 11–12 HCP, and 3NT with a good 13 or more.

Suppose partner doubles 1 ♣ for takeout and the next player passes. What is your action with the following hands?

♠ KQ3
♥ 62
♦ 10965
♣ 7632

Bid 1 ♦. True, you have no high-card points in that suit, but it would be poor strategy to bid a three-card spade suit in this case. Remember, your partner could have as few as three spades and still have a hand that qualifies for a takeout double.

♠ KQJ3
♥ 62
♦ 1096
♣ 7632

Bid 1 ♠. You have a good suit, but you are short of high-card points. Change the hand just a little, however, and you have a rosier view.

♠ KQJ3
♥ 62
♦ QJ65
♣ 763

Now your hand is too good for a simple 1 ♠ response. Think about it: You would bid 1 ♠ with zero high-card points and four spades to the 5. Your hand is much better than that. You must let partner know when your hand is well above the minimum. Bid 2 ♠.

When you make a takeout double and partner responds at a minimum level, it is prudent to assume her hand is at the bottom of the range for her bid. If the auction becomes competitive and partner has another chance to speak, she can always take another bid if she is close to the maximum. Trust partner to take action when appropriate.

There is one occasion when you will make a cuebid without sufficient values to force to game. It's when your partner doubles a minor-suit opening and you have both majors. Here is an example:

♠ KQJ3
♥ QJ62
♦ Q9
♣ 763

This hand is good enough to make a jump bid to show invitational values, but which major should you choose? You could end up in a 4–3 fit if you guess wrong, but you don't have to guess. If partner has doubled a 1 ♣ opener, simply bid 2 ♣. If partner has only one major suit of at least four cards, he will bid it. If he has both, he will start with 2 ♥. You can then raise to 3 ♥ to show that your cuebid was based on an invitational hand. In considering whether to go on to game, he will use the information you have provided to help make that decision.

Be careful about cuebidding without invitational values. If your hand falls short of the strength to invite game, simply bid the higher-ranking suit first, even if they are the same length.

When you are considering your bid in response to partner's takeout double of a suit, you should envision your hand as providing support for one of partner's suits. For example, when you hold six cards in a suit for which your partner has implied support, count two extra "support points" for the fifth and sixth cards. With that principle in mind, a hand with 8 high-card points and a six-card suit would count as 10. Make a jump bid to show your strength.

There are many considerations beyond just high-card points in evaluating your hand after partner has made a takeout double. For example, except for aces, honors you hold in the opener's suit should be discounted or at least devalued. Remember, partner will tend to be short in opener's suit when he makes a takeout double. If you think four to the queen in opener's suit is worth anything, consider how many tricks you are likely to take in that suit if partner puts a singleton 2 down in dummy.

Improved Holdings

On the other hand, honors in suits that partner has promised can be increased in value because they should be complementary. For example, you would not ordinarily assign much value to a doubleton queen. If partner has promised that suit by way of a takeout double, you can look at that queen in a different light. It might still be worthless if partner has only low cards in the suit, but it has potential at least.

The one card in opener's suit that is good is the ace, especially facing shortness in your partner's hand. Having three or four to the ace opposite a singleton in dummy will give you the option of ruffing those low cards.

No Passing Fancy

When partner makes a takeout double and you have a really dreadful hand, your natural inclination is to pass. Players are taught not to bid without values, right? Unfortunately, the worse your hand is, the more important it is to bid. If you have a poor hand and partner has a minimum takeout double, you probably won't defeat their contract. That will annoy your partner and erode the trust between you. Just make the smallest "noise" you can and hope for the best.

FACT

When you are faced with having to bid on a bad hand opposite a takeout double, don't let the opponents know of your discomfort. Make your bid cheerfully and—outwardly, at least—without a care in the world. If the opponents sense you are in trouble, they are more likely to double when they have the balance of power. Bid with confidence.

There is one occasion on which you can pass your partner's takeout double—when you are loaded in opener's suit. In that sense, you are selecting opener's suit as trumps and converting the takeout double to a penalty double. In most cases, partner will lead a trump if she has one, so your suit should be strong—something like QJ10964. Partner leads a trump because, just as when you are declarer, one of your first duties is to rake in the opponents' trumps so they can't be used for ruffing. You want to do the same to declarer.

The Doubler's Second Call

When you have made a takeout double and partner has responded, you will use the information you have gained from the response to decide what, if any, action to take next.

There are two separate scenarios to consider after you have doubled and your partner has responded.

- Opener passes partner's response to your double.
- Opener bids again.

If opener passes, any move you make will be inviting game. Why else would you take action? Consider this auction, with you as South:

West	North	East	South
		1 ♣	Dbl
Pass	1 ♠	Pass	?

What does it mean if you now bid 2 ♠? First, consider that partner's 1 ♠ bid shows 0–8 support points. If you bid 2 ♠, it should be an invitation to game in spades, asking partner to bid 4 ♠ if she is close to the maximum for her bidding, typically 7 or 8 support points.

So, what should you have to bid 2 ♠? Well, if partner is supposed to go to game with 7 support points, you need something along the lines of about 18 support points yourself. This is what a 2 ♠ bid in the given auction should look like:

♠ KQJ3
♥ AQJ6
♦ K1095
♣ 7

You have 16 good high-card points and a singleton. This is about a minimum for a free raise to 2 ♠.

E-QUESTION

What is a "free" bid or raise?
A bid or raise is said to be "free" when it is made at a time when passing is an option. For example, if your partner opens 1 ♥ and the next player bids 1 ♠, you are under no obligation to bid—partner will have another chance to call. If you bid another suit or raise partner to 2 ♥, it is said to be free. Similarly, if your partner makes a takeout double and the next player bids or redoubles, you are off the hook. You do not have to respond, so any bid you make is said to be a "free" bid.

It's a different situation when there is competition. Going back to the auction in question:

West	North	East	South
		1 ♣	Dbl
Pass	1 ♠	Pass	?

If you have four-card support for spades and a normal takeout double, it is important for you to bid 2 ♠ at this point. Why? If you don't, your partner will assume you don't have four spades and, holding only four herself, will probably sell out to the opponents even if she has a decent hand in the context of the bidding. She will not be that keen to play a 4–3 fit. If you suppress that four-card support, you will lose the part-score battle that is so important in bridge.

When the opponents have the boss suit—spades—the rules change slightly. If opener rebids his suit after you make a takeout double and partner has bid at a minimum level, you should have extra values to raise to the three level, even with four-card support. Partner will keep that in mind if the bidding gets back to her. She will compete with an appropriate hand.

Heavy Lumber

The parameters for doubling and bidding a suit of your own have been discussed, but a couple of examples are in order—along with an important principle.

Here are two hands good enough to double and then bid your own suit.

West	North	East	South
		1 ♥	Dbl
Pass	2 ♦	Pass	?

♠ AKQJ76
♥ Q7
♦ AQJ
♣ 75

Bid 2 ♠, showing your strong hand and very good suit.

♠ AK4
♥ 75
♦ KJ
♣ AK10976

Bid 3 ♣. If your partner has a heart stopper and a smattering of points, he will probably bid 3NT. Remember, your bid of 3 ♣ is not forcing, and if your partner can't make a move over your strong bid, you probably don't want to be any higher.

Greater Efficiency

The reason you double with extra strength, planning to bid your own suit after partner's response, is that the simple overcall has a very wide range, which hampers the bidding process to a degree.

When your hand is so strong that you need very little from your partner to make a game, partner will frequently have what you need but be unable to move over a simple overcall. For example, suppose you hold:

♠ Q4
♥ 75
♦ K7653
♣ J1087

Your left-hand opponent opens 1 ♣. Your partner overcalls 1 ♠ and right-hand opponent passes. There's not much you can do. It's bad policy to raise your partner's simple overcall with a doubleton, and you certainly don't have enough to bid 1NT even though you do have a club stopper of sorts (a 1NT bid in this position shows a minimum of 9–10 high-card points and a stopper).

So you pass, as does opener. Now suppose this is your partner's hand:

♠ AKJ1087
♥ 82
♦ AQ5
♣ A9

You have just missed a game that should have been bid. Clearly, your partner should have doubled first, then bid spades over your response of 2 ♦. You would happily raise to 3 ♠ —you don't mind raising with a doubleton honor because partner will have six spades more often than not—and you would soon be in 4 ♠.

Gotta Get to Game

Making a takeout double and later bidding your own suit shows strength, but it is not forcing when responder to the double has bid at a minimum level. Any minimum bid could have been forced and advancer might have zero high-card points.

When advancer makes a bigger "noise" with his response—that is, jumps in a suit or bids no-trump—any new suit by the doubler is 100 percent forcing to game. Advancer must keep the bidding open, even if he cannot raise opener's suit.

Discussing this with your partner will save a lot of headaches and teeth-grinding over missed games. There are few things as frustrating as taking 11 or 12 tricks in a contract of 2 ♠.

Competing Against Pre-empts

In today's bridge world, the opponents are much more aggressive than in the early days of the game. That means you will occasionally find yourself faced with the problem of starting the bidding at the three level or higher.

Pre-emptive bidding is a two-edged sword, of course. Jumping around at high levels can cause your side more problems than you cause for the opponents, particularly when you open at a high level and find your partner with a good hand but no support for your suit. You will see when the dummy hits—partner will pass most of the time—that your bid has kept the opponents out of trouble and landed you in a minus position.

Nevertheless, the pitfalls of aggressive pre-empting do not appreciably slow down some players, so you will have to learn ways of coping.

Fire versus Fire

An obvious tool is the takeout double, but some cautions are in order. The higher the pre-empt, the more you should have for a takeout double. What would qualify as a reasonable double of a 1 ♣ opener would fall woefully short of the requirements for a takeout double of 3 ♣, for example.

When the opponents possess the spade suit, even the three level is gone after an opener of 3 ♠ unless you or your partner can bid 3NT.

When an opponent starts the bidding at the two level or higher, especially in first seat, you risk going for a number if you bid or double. Why does the first-seat pre-empt make a difference? Mainly because nothing is known about the other two hands. The next player could be loaded and ready to double you. On the other hand, if you pass, it could be your partner with the goods, so going quietly could result in your missing game.

With that in mind, it is best to be consistent in your approach. If you generally have a conservative style—you don't bid on marginal hands—your partner will take that into account if the opening pre-emptive bid comes to him after two passes. Similarly, if you normally take an aggressive stance, partner will know you probably don't have much if you pass. This will help partner make more accurate guesses in close situations.

Minimum Standards

Do not let emotion dictate your action. Yes, it is annoying to have an opponent start with 2 ♠ against you. If you let that get under your skin and you bid just to show them they can't push you around, your results will suffer in the long run. Your partner should have confidence in your bidding.

It's difficult to outline specific guidelines because pre-emptive bidding takes many forms, and the methods available will vary from pair to pair. In general, it will probably pay to be slightly aggressive in combating pre-emptive bids, especially when the vulnerability is favorable (they are, you aren't). Vulnerable overcalls should be sound and based on good suits, and you should be very sound when the vulnerability is unfavorable (you are, they aren't).

The level at which you have to bid also makes a difference. You can be a bit more frisky if you can get in there at the two level, as when the opponents open with a weak 2 ♦ or when partner might be able to bid at the two level over your takeout double.

The Rule of Eight

A handy tool for helping you get into the bidding over weak two-bids is known as the Rule of Eight.

Here's how it works. When your RHO opens with a weak two-bid, figure that your partner will have, on average, about 8 high-card points scattered through his hand. If you think that partner's 8 HCP will be enough for you to have a shot at whatever you are considering bidding, go ahead and take the plunge. If you need substantially more help than the average hand partner will provide for you, look again at your thirteen cards and reconsider your decision to get involved.

If you and your partner are in accord about the use of the Rule of Eight, be sure to apply it when it is your turn to bid after partner overcalls. When your partner bids over a two-level opener, be aware that he is counting on you for about 8 HCP. If that's all you have, it's best not to raise partner's bid, even with trump support. If you have good trumps and 9 or 10 support points, you can raise.

The Rule of Eight has other applications. Say dealer opens a weak 2 ♥. If you now bid 3 ♠, that is a strong bid, not a weak one. You don't pre-empt over pre-empts. Just as with a two-level bid, the overcaller is counting on her partner for about 8 support points. The difference is that when the overcaller bids 3 ♠ instead of 2 ♠, she is saying to partner, "I'm counting on you for 8 support points. If you have them, put me in game if we have a fit in spades—or do something else intelligent. If you don't have the points or we don't have a good spade fit, pass."

The Rule of Eight loses its effectiveness when the opponents are opening the bidding at the three level and higher, so be a bit more careful when you have to start at higher levels.

Suit Quality

When you overcall at the two level or higher, it generally shows at least a good suit. You are not always blessed with extra length or good intermediate cards in a hand that cries out for some action. For example, say an opponent opens 2 ♥ in front of you and you hold this hand:

♠ K7654
♥ 82
♦ A3
♣ AK109

You have a ratty spade suit, but you have a good hand with prime cards (aces and kings). You can't overcall in no-trump because you don't have hearts stopped and you don't have the high-card strength anyway. A takeout double is out because you can't support diamonds and if you bid 3 ♠ over 3 ♦, it shows a much stronger hand than you have (not to mention a much stronger suit). Passing is a very wimpy action. Yes, you could get nailed if opener's partner has a big spade stack behind you and some high-card points, but partner could also have those spades and HCP, so passing might let the opponents steal your game from you.

You might be a bit uncomfortable bidding 2 ♠ with this hand, but you have to do it.

Compensation

Be sure, however, that if your suit is not of the best quality or length that you have compensating values. Translation: It's okay to overcall a somewhat ratty suit if your hand is pretty good and passing doesn't feel like a reasonable option.

The bottom line is that when the opponents are taking up your bidding space, you will have to make some compromises.

Cuebids

The cuebid takes many forms in bridge. To many players, the various cue-bids are essential to survival in the competitive bidding arena.

One of the most popular and easiest to use is the Michaels cuebid, named for its inventor, Mike Michaels.

In the old days, if someone opened one of a suit and the next player bid two of the same suit—as in 1 ♣—2 ♣—that showed a very strong hand and directed partner to pick his best suit. It was more or less a takeout double on steroids.

Hands that qualified for the super-strong takeout were few and far between, however, so Michaels devised a better use for the direct cuebid. Here they are:

- **Over one of a minor,** the bid of the same minor shows at least five cards in each major in a hand that is either somewhat weak or very strong. When the hand is very strong, the Michaels bidder is just waiting to see which major his partner likes better so that he can make a strong game invitation or a raise to game in that suit.
- **Over one of a major,** a bid of the same major shows at least five cards in the other major and at least five cards in either minor. When advancer doesn't fit partner's major, he bids 3 ♣ to tell partner, "Pass if this is your minor suit—or correct to diamonds."

The Michaels cuebid is a handy convention that comes up more often than you might think, and it's great when you uncover that big trump fit. You can blow the opponents out of the water by jacking up the bidding in a hurry. It's not so great when you don't have a good fit in one of the Michaels bidder's two suits. Furthermore, if the other side ends up playing the contract, the information provided by the cuebid will help declarer play as though she can see all the cards.

Still, few duplicate players would consider playing without Michaels. For more discussion of this convention, see Chapter 15.

Info, Please

Another vital use for the cuebid in competition occurs when the other side opens the bidding and your side overcalls. You will always raise your partner's overcall when possible, but it's best, considering how light the overcaller might be, not to have to make a jump raise to show a raise with a bit extra.

That's where the cuebid comes in. Consider this auction (you are South):

West	North	East	South
1 ♥	1 ♠	Pass	?

Now suppose you hold this hand:

♠ KJ65
♥ 82
♦ AQ3
♣ 7654

You will certainly raise partner's overcall, but if you bid just 2 ♠, partner will pass with this hand:

♠ AQ1098
♥ KQ3
♦ J1087
♣ 2

As you can see, game is almost certain, but North will never make a move toward game over a simple raise, which could be based on as little as 6 HCP.

Of course, if you have to jump to 3 ♠ to show your good support—akin to a limit raise of an opening bid—you might catch your partner with this hand:

♠ AQ1098
♥ K3
♦ 654
♣ 983

A 1 ♠ overcall is perfectly reasonable with that hand, but the partnership is now too high.

You can avoid this kind of problem when you have a limit-raise type of hand (or better) by cuebidding to show it. If your partner thinks game might be in the offing over a limit raise, she can make a game try in one of her suits. If she signs off to show no game interest opposite a limit raise, you have succeeded in staying at a safe level.

Getting to No-trump

You have seen the cuebid in use when partner makes a takeout double and you have a good hand. You show it by bidding the opener's suit.

When you and your partner have found a big fit in a minor and figure you have enough for game, you usually prefer to play in 3NT, which scores better in a duplicate game and also requires two fewer tricks than 5 ♣ or 5 ♦.

One way to get there is to use the cuebid to ask partner for a stopper in opener's suit.

Here is a typical auction (you are South):

West	North	East	South
1 ♥	2 ♣	Pass	2 ♥
Pass	3 ♥	Pass	3NT
All Pass			

The first cuebid (yours) says you have a fine hand in support of clubs. Partner makes a second cuebid to say, "If you can stop hearts, we can probably take nine tricks in 3NT."

Your hand might be:

♠ AJ10
♥ K103
♦ QJ10
♣ Q873

Partner could have something like:

♠ K54
♥ 6
♦ K65
♣ AK10965

You will make 3NT with ease on the combined hands.

In the Balancing Seat

Balancing—taking some action when passing will end the auction—was covered in an earlier chapter, but only in routine auctions, such as when an opening bid of one of a suit is followed by two passes or when the opponents bid and raise a suit and opt to bid no higher. It is established that it can be beneficial to try to push them one level higher with some kind of action.

When the opening bid was at the two level or higher and the next two players pass, the person in the passout seat will have objectives that differ vastly from the typical balancing decision.

The fact that the opening bidder has started the auction so much higher means that if you bid, you may have to do so at a level that is not justified by the cards you hold. Yes, as in other balancing situations, you will be bidding partner's cards as well as your own, but even if partner has more than you have a right to expect, it might not be enough.

Also, when balancing over a pre-empt, you are not trying to push the opponents to a higher level. You are trying to claim what is yours. In many of these cases, it's your hand. You just have to figure out where to play it.

No Bid, No Fit

In these days of aggressive bidding, it is normal for the partner of the pre-emptive bidder to increase the pre-emption when he has support for opener's suit. There is a measure of safety when your side has an abundance of trumps, and most astute players take advantage of that, especially when not vulnerable, even more so when the opponents are.

What that means for you in the balancing seat is that if the bidding goes 2 ♥—Pass—Pass, there is a fair likelihood that your RHO does not have a fit for the opening bidder. That might or might not be a danger sign. Just because opener's partner lacks a fit does not mean he is loaded and just waiting for you to take some action so that he can pounce on you with a penalty double. He could simply have a weak hand. If that is the case, however, why didn't your partner do something?

Here are possible explanations for partner's failure to act over the pre-empt:

- Partner has a poor hand that does not justify taking action.
- Partner has a good hand but does not have a long suit to bid and does not have a stopper in opener's suit and cannot make a takeout double because he cannot stand for you to bid a particular suit.
- Partner has a good hand and a hefty holding in the opener's suit and is hoping you will balance with a double so that he can convert it to penalty by passing and thereby collect a big number.

You must consider all of these possibilities when you find yourself in the balancing seat after an opening pre-empt has been followed by two passes.

If you find a partner who is disciplined enough to pass a good hand over a pre-empt when she has no good action, sign her to a long-term contract if you can. She is a winning player, in contrast to those who have been heard to say after a bidding disaster, "But I had to bid . . . I had 14 points."

Being short in opener's suit is the first hint that a double might work out best for your side. Be careful, however, about doubling just because you have only one or two cards in opener's suit. If your hand is weak, your partner's trump tricks may be the only tricks for your side. To double in the balancing seat when partner might pass for penalty, you should have a minimum of two quick tricks.

Dummy Quality

Second, consider whether you will be happy about putting your hand down as dummy should your partner bid in response to your double. Sometimes partner will have length in opener's suit without good spots and will decide to bid even when she has a few of opener's trumps. Sometimes partner has no semblance of a trump trick and simply has to bid. She won't be happy to find a doubleton in the suit she selects.

Of course, there will be many occasions when your course of action in the passout seat will be clear-cut. Perhaps you will have a long, strong suit to bid. You might have the equivalent of a 1NT opener (with a stopper in opener's suit). You can show that by bidding 2NT in the balancing seat. You might have a classic takeout double with a bit extra to compensate for the higher level of the bidding.

The bottom line, however, is that those nasty pre-empts will make your life miserable when you don't have any easy decision in fourth seat. As with other competitive decisions, you will be well served to try to be consistent in your courses of action, and disciplined enough to pass when you know it's right. You will not win every battle with a pre-empt—that's why players throw them at you—but you will profit in the long run with a sound, disciplined approach.

CHAPTER 7

Bidding Accuracy

Worthy opponents will often interfere even when you
open the bidding and your side has the balance of
power. Sometimes, however, they don't just have the
assets to get involved, leaving you with a clear path
to the correct contract. Be sure you have the tools to
take advantage of that rare quiet time.

New Minor Forcing

You have a sound foundation based on opening bids of five-card majors. You know that you respond with 6 high-card points, and when partner opens one of a minor and you have four cards in each major, you bid 1 ♥. When partner opens one of a major, you raise when you have support.

You have most of the bidding rules down pat, and it's easy when your hand falls on either end of the strength spectrum after partner opens the bidding. With just enough to respond to partner's opener, you plan to make one bid and pass unless opener shows extra strength with his next bid. When you and partner both have opening hands, you will get to game.

It's the responding hands that fall in the middle range that can cause problems without what some players refer to as "gadgets."

One of the most useful of those bidding tools is called New Minor Forcing. That sounds fancy and complicated, but it is really very simple.

Before you learn about how it works, it's important to know why it's needed.

Say you have the following hand:

♠ AK765
♥ A654
♦ 732
♣ 2

Your partner opens 1 ♦. You bid 1 ♠. So far, so good. Now partner rebids 1NT, showing 12–14 high-card points and a balanced hand. You have 11 HCP, so you know you should be in game if partner has 14, so clearly an invitational bid is in order. So, what is your next move?

First, consider the meanings of the bids you might make, discounting a bid of either of your minors: 2 ♠ shows a six-card or longer suit and a weak hand. 2 ♥ correctly describes your distribution in the majors but does not come close to describing the invitational strength of your hand. 2NT is correct from the standpoint of high-card points, but that singleton club is worrisome.

Furthermore, partner will pass holding:

♠ Q3
♥ K983
♦ AQJ6
♣ 954

If that is partner's hand, the opponents could take the first five or six club tricks, and if even they take only five club tricks, unless spades divide 3–3 (against the odds), partner will have to depend on the diamond finesse. He could easily go down in 2NT, but do you see the possibilities in hearts? 4 ♥ requires only a normal split in hearts for game to make. The losers are one club, one heart and one diamond (if the finesse doesn't work). With a working diamond finesse, you could take 11 tricks in a heart contract.

So, why can't you bid 3 ♠ to invite game in that suit? Well, that shows a six-card suit, which you don't have. What about 3 ♥? That would show at least 5–5 in the majors with enough strength for game.

So what is the answer?

It's called New Minor Forcing (often written as *NMF*), and this is how it works in basic form:

When opener starts with one of a minor and rebids 1NT over responder's bid of one of a major, responder's bid of the *other* minor is artificial and almost always indicates that responder has five of his major and enough high-card strength to invite game.

Some sample auctions:

West	North	East	South
1 ♣	Pass	1 ♠	Pass
1NT	Pass	2 ♦	

West	North	East	South
1 ♦	Pass	1 ♠	Pass
1NT	Pass	2 ♣	

In both cases, responder has chosen the unbid or "new" minor for his second call. This bid indicates at least 11 high-card points, although you also use the convention with enough strength for game (responder is simply trying to find the best denomination for the final contract).

So, what are opener's responsibilities when his partner employs NMF? There are two separate scenarios, depending on which major responder bid (the minor that was opened is of less importance). Here is the bidding:

West	North	East	South
1 ♦	Pass	1 ♥	Pass
1NT	Pass	2 ♣	

Opener's responses:

- 2 ♦ denies three hearts or four spades (see note below) and usually shows extra length in diamonds.
- 2 ♥ shows three-card heart support but a minimum opener—12 to a poor 13.
- 2 ♠ a minimum with four spades and fewer than three hearts. Note that because 1NT in the given auction normally denies four spades, this is a matter for partnership agreement.
- 2NT shows a minimum with a doubleton heart and fewer than four spades.
- 3 ♣ shows a hand with clubs and diamonds, without three hearts.
- 3 ♥ shows a maximum opener with three-card heart support.
- 3NT shows a maximum without three hearts or four spades.

Opener's rebids are slightly different when responder started with 1 ♠.

West	North	East	South
1 ♦	Pass	1 ♠	Pass
1NT	Pass	2 ♣	

Reminder: NMF also applies when opener started with 1 ♣ and responder bids 2 ♦ over 1NT. Here are opener's responses in the given auction:

- 2 ♥ shows a minimum with four hearts, usually without three spades.
- 2 ♠ shows a minimum with three spades. This bid does not deny four hearts.
- 2NT shows a minimum without three spades or four hearts.
- 3 ♣ shows a hand with diamonds and clubs, without three spades.
- 3 ♦ shows a maximum with extra length in diamonds without three spades.
- 3 ♥ shows a maximum with four hearts but without three spades.
- 3 ♠ shows a maximum with three spades.
- 3NT shows a maximum without three spades or four hearts.

There are many different variations on the use of NMF. For example, some partnerships agree that in the given auction, a 2 ♦ response to the NMF bid of 2 ♣ shows three-card heart support *and* four spades.

Inferences

One of the benefits of using NMF comes from what opener knows about responder's hand when the convention is *not* used. For example, opener may have three-card support for responder's major, but if responder invites game by bidding 2NT, opener knows that responder almost certainly has no more than four of his major, so opener will not show three-card support even if he has it. After all, if responder held five of the major, he would have started the invitational process with NMF.

Also, when you employ NMF, you show at least invitational values, but you could have more. With enough to force game, you can agree with partner that if you use NMF and rebid your major suit, that shows at least six of them with enough strength to force game and with at least mild slam interest. Otherwise, you would simply blast into game over the 1NT rebid, right?

Here's another benefit to using NMF. Supposed you hold this hand:

♠ QJ93
♥ 8
♦ Q6
♣ J109854

Partner opens 1 ♦. You respond 1 ♠ (you are nowhere near strong enough to consider bidding your six-card club suit). If partner raises your 1 ♠ bid, you are perfectly happy. But what if opener rebids 1NT? You know your best contract almost surely is in clubs (partner has at least two of them for his 1NT rebid) and your hand definitely does not look like a good dummy for a no-trump contract.

So what can you do? Well, because you play 2 ♣ as a forcing, artificial bid with invitational values, that option is not available. You can, however, bid 3 ♣ as a signoff. This shows exactly what you have: four spades, at least six clubs, and no interest in game. Yes, it sounds strong, so partnership discussion ahead of time is necessary—and you might screw it up the first time or two that you use it. This device is very valuable in turning a poor 1NT contract into a making suit contract.

It works the same when partner opens 1 ♣ and you have four of a major, at least six diamonds, and a hand with no game interest opposite a 1NT rebid.

Fourth Suit Forcing

Another important bidding weapon is called Fourth-Suit Forcing (FSF). Just as with New Minor Forcing, the focus is often on finding a fit in a major suit, but there are significant differences between FSF and NMF.

For starters NMF is used only over a 1NT rebid by opener. FSF is just what it says it is: a call in the last unbid suit. Here are a couple of examples:

West	North	East	South
1 ♦	Pass	1 ♥	Pass
1 ♠	Pass	2 ♣	

West	North	East	South
1 ♥	Pass	1 ♠	Pass
2 ♣	Pass	2 ♦	

In each auction, East's second bid is ostensibly artificial—although the bidder may indeed have a substantial holding in the suit—and *100 percent forcing to game*. It's a rather simple concept. After one player employs FSF, the duty of that player's partner is to describe her hand to the best of her ability. Often, that involves bidding no-trump with stoppers in the fourth suit. It is not uncommon for the FSF bidder to have a poor holding in the fourth suit. FSF is also commonly used to try to uncover an eight-card fit in a major.

The advantage of using FSF is that the partnership can keep the bidding low while exchanging information with each other for possible slam exploration. Take the first auction cited:

West	North	East	South
1 ♦	Pass	1 ♥	Pass
1 ♠	Pass	2 ♣	

East might have a hand such as:

♠ AQJ9
♥ AKJ10
♦ A9
♣ 764

East's plan is to force to game by bidding the fourth suit. After West further describes his hand, East will show his spade support. This can mean only one thing—East is interested in slam in spades. If not, why didn't he just jump to 4 ♠? All East needs to hear is a cuebid in clubs and he will be off to the races.

ALERT!

Many useful bids come in unassuming packages, and a good example is Fourth-Suit Forcing. It is counterintuitive to assign a strong meaning to a low-level bid, so partnership discussion is vital to avoid bidding mishaps.

Sometimes, FSF is just a "mark time" bid, used when the direction of the auction is not clear. In those cases, what is missing is usually a stopper. Consider this hand:

♠ AK7
♥ A1098
♦ Q1095
♣ 76

Partner opens 1 ♦ and rebids 1 ♠ over your response of 1 ♥. You know you belong in game, but you don't have a stopper in clubs. You could bid 3 ♦, but that is an invitational bid and you have enough to force to game.

Your only choice is to bid 2 ♣, game forcing. If partner bids 2NT, you will raise to 3NT. If partner bids 2 ♥, indicating three-card support, you will try 2 ♠, clearly indicating further concern about the club suit for no-trump play. If you end up playing in a 4–3 major fit, it is best to play in spades rather than hearts.

When considering a game in a 4–3 fit, do your best to play in the suit that will allow you to take ruffs in the hand with three trumps—the short side. If you will have to ruff from the four-card holding, a bad trump split could doom your contract.

If your partner does not fancy playing in spades, at least you have good diamond support. You won't be keen to play game in five of a minor, but that may be your best chance.

There are no complicated rules with FSF, and it is simple to execute. In response to FSF, you simply make the most natural bid suggested by your hand, comfortable in the knowledge that you don't have to jump to show strength.

What Is a Reverse?

For many new players, the reverse is an enigmatic bidding tool that is frequently overlooked or "missed" in the bidding. It is important, however, to recognize a reverse when your partner employs the device.

The term probably arises from the fact that you bid two suits in reverse order of their rank (normally you bid a higher-ranking suit first).

In its simplest form, a reverse is a second bid, usually by the opener, at the two level or higher in a higher-ranking suit than the original bid. Here's an example:

West	North	East	South
1 ♦	Pass	1 ♠	Pass
2 ♥			

Another:

West	North	East	South
1 ♣	Pass	1 ♥	Pass
2 ♦			

One more:

West	North	East	South
1 ♥	Pass	1NT	Pass
2 ♠			

These bids always show strength. Why? Because if responder prefers opener's first suit, he has to take the preference at the three level. You don't go around forcing the bidding to that level with a 12- or 13-point hand. Here is a typical hand for a reverse:

♠ AJ3
♥ AQ109
♦ AQ1095
♣ 7

You open this nice hand with a bid of 1 ♦. If partner responds 1 ♥, you will bid game in her suit. But what if partner responds 1 ♠? Your rebid should be 2 ♥. This shows your strength—at least a good 16 high-card points, often 17 or 18.

When your partner makes a reverse bid, the weakest response you can make is to go back to her first suit. That bid can be passed. Any other bid is forward going and usually will end with the two hands playing game.

If partner bids 3 ♦, a preference for your first suit, you will bid 3 ♠ to show your exact hand pattern.

You may be thinking, "How does this show my hand pattern?"

Bidding in reverse fashion *always* shows more cards in the first suit bid than in the second. You do not reverse with equal length in your two suits.

Therefore, when you open 1 ♦ and rebid 2 ♥ over partner's 1 ♠, you must have at least five diamonds and four hearts. When you later support spades, you are showing at least three of them. With five diamonds, four hearts, and three spades, your hand cannot contain more than one club.

Stay Alert

Because the reverse is not a jump bid, it doesn't "sound" strong, so new players frequently miss the implications of the bidding and have been known to pass. A reverse can be based on a good 16 HCP, so it is not forcing to game. After all, responder might have only 6 HCP himself, not enough for game opposite 16 or even 17 HCP. Nevertheless, a reverse is pretty close to a forcing bid. Responder should come up with some response, even if it is just going back to opener's first suit.

When opener reverses, responder's second bid of 2NT is not showing weakness. It is forward going, although not forcing, so with 9 or more high-card points and no other clear action, just bid 3NT. After all, you know your side has at least 25 HCP.

Take care not to confuse the sequence 1 ♣ —Pass—1 ♥ —Pass—1 ♠ with the reverse principle. A rebid of a higher-ranking suit at the one level is not a reverse because responder can take a preference at the two level.

Powerhouse Hands

When you have been dealt a true "rock"—a very strong hand with a lot of tricks—it is important to have the right machinery in place to take advantage of your good fortune.

It is not within the scope of this book to outline an entire structure for responding to strong openings such as 2 ♣—strong, artificial, and forcing—but there are some principles worth covering regarding very strong hands.

One of the most useful principles involves your constructive auctions after a strong 2 ♣ opening. Most partnerships employ the 2 ♦ bid over the strong 2 ♣ as "waiting." This does not say your hand is bad, although it might be. 2 ♦ says only that you do not have the requisite holding to make a positive response of 2 ♥, 2 ♠, 3 ♣, or 3 ♦—at least a five-card suit with two of the top three honors.

When your partner opens 2 ♣ and rebids in a suit over your 2 ♦ bid, there will be times when you have support for partner's suit. You will, of course, show that support, but the level of your raise, especially of a major, will say a lot about your hand.

Suppose you hold:

♠ Q103
♥ 7632
♦ K8765
♣ 7

Partner opens 2 ♣ and you respond 2 ♦. Partner bids 2 ♠, which improves your hand immensely. Your natural inclination is to jump to 4 ♠ to show how happy you are to hear partner's news.

That would be the wrong bid.

If you jump to game in partner's major suit, it should send a clear message: "Partner, I have support for your suit but I have no aces, kings, or singletons." Knowing that, your partner will not try for slam unless he has a truly unusual hand.

When you do have support and a control such as an ace, king, or singleton, slow it down. Bid 3 ♠. This tells partner you have trump support and some other good feature of your hand. He will take it from there, usually cuebidding one of his controls to start the slam exploration. The key is that you let partner know your hand has some potential for more than just game. Partner could have something like:

♠ AKJ976
♥ 4
♦ AQJ
♣ AQ5

If you bid 3 ♠, partner will bid 4 ♣, and when you bid 4 ♦, he will know that his A–Q in that suit are "working." You will almost certainly land in a very good slam. If you had a different hand, one that dictated a jump to 4 ♠, your partner would not risk the five level with any kind of inquiry. That's just good communication between partners.

Long Suits

When you have an extremely powerful hand with a long suit, you can send a special message with your rebid. Take this hand, for example:

♠ A3
♥ AKQJ10976
♦ K8
♣ 7

You open 2 ♣ and partner responds 2 ♦. Do not rebid 2 ♥. Instead, rebid 3 ♥. This tells your partner that the trump suit has been chosen. You don't care if your partner is void in hearts. All you want her to do is to show controls, starting with aces. You will bid your aces "up the line"—starting with the lowest ranking, so that if you skip one of the suits, it denies an ace in that suit. With no aces or kings, partner will raise to game.

E-QUESTION

My partner opens 2 ♣ and jump rebids to show a solid suit and asking me to cuebid controls. What if I have a king or two but no aces? How do I show that feature?

When partner bids in that fashion and you have at least one king, bid the lowest level of no-trump. If partner wants to know which king(s) you have, she will bid clubs. You then start bidding kings up the line.

There is some dispute over whether you should open 2 ♣ with a limited number of high-card points but a lot of tricks in your hand, as with:

♠ AQJ109876
♥ A
♦ K65
♣ 8

No matter how spades divide, you are a lock for seven spade tricks and the ♥ A, plus you might get the ♦ K by leading up to it. That's eight and a half tricks. The problem is that there are only 14 high-card points, well short of what is considered the norm for a 2 ♣ opener. In some tournament settings, an opening of 2 ♣ with such a hand will get you in trouble. It's not the worst bid ever made, but the opponents will feel that you have taken advantage of them with a "strong" opener that is really based on trump tricks, not high-card points.

Forcing and Non-Forcing Bids

This might seem to be an innocuous subject, but there are few events in bridge as annoying as having one's partner pass a bid you believe to be forcing.

What does "forcing" mean? It means that the partner of the person who makes the "forcing" bid is not allowed to pass.

Here is a simple example of a forcing bid:

West	North	East	South
2 ♣	Pass	?	

East is not allowed to pass 2 ♣. It is a forcing bid. In theory, West could be void in clubs.

West	North	East	South
1 ♥	Pass	4NT	Pass
?			

4NT is also forcing. It is not an offer to play in no-trump. It is an inquiry about the number of aces held by West.

West	North	East	South
1 ♥	Pass	2 ♣	Pass
?			

2 ♣ is a natural bid, showing at least 10 high-card points but potentially a lot stronger than that. West is not allowed to pass 2 ♣.

West	North	East	South
1 ♣	Pass	1 ♥	Pass
?			

This is more subtle, but 1 ♥ is every bit as forcing as a 2 ♣ opener, a Blackwood 4NT bid, or a response of 2 ♣ to an opener of 1 ♥. East is just getting started in this auction. No limit has been placed on his hand. He could have 18 or 19 high-card points.

Double Trouble

This chapter is mostly about uncontested auctions, but it's worth noting that there is such a thing as a forcing pass in competitive bidding. Suppose the auction goes this way:

West	North	East	South
1 ♥	Pass	3 ♥	3 ♠
4 ♥	4 ♠	Pass	Pass
?			

East's 3 ♥ invites game, and West accepts. The opponents are clearly sacrificing in 4 ♠. When East passes North's 4 ♠, it does not mean she wants to go passively. East is saying her action in this case is not clear, and she is leaving the decision to West whether to double or bid on. The one thing West is not permitted to do is to pass. In that sense, East's pass is forcing. West must act in some way—by doubling 4 ♠ or by bidding on.

Responder's Reverse

Another example of a forcing bid is when responder to an opening bid reverses in his second chance to bid. For example:

West	North	East	South
1 ♦	Pass	1 ♥	Pass
1NT	Pass	2 ♠	Pass
?			

East is showing a strong hand and is forcing to game by bidding 2 ♠. West's 1NT rebid usually denies four spades, so opener may have a difficult decision in his third turn to bid, but he is not allowed to pass.

Here is a good rule of thumb for deciding whether to bid on over an action by partner that you don't completely understand: If it sounds forcing, it is. Your partner will be less annoyed with you if you bid on over a non-forcing bid than if you pass when he wants you to keep bidding.

Harmony in bidding is vital to success at bridge. Make sure you and your partner understand which bids are forcing and which are not.

What the Opponents' Bidding Tells You

Your auctions will not be the only ones that are uncontested, and while the opponents are exchanging information, you should be listening in. Here is a prime example of how you can gain by what the opponents are saying to each other. You are South.

West	North	East	South
		1 ♠	Pass
2 ♦	Pass	3 ♦	Pass
3 ♠	Pass	4NT	Pass
5 ♦	Pass	6 ♠	All Pass

This is your hand:

♠ A2
♥ QJ109
♦ 6543
♣ 854

What is your lead?

The ♥ Q looks like the textbook lead, but not if you have been listening to the bidding. Review the auction one more time. Remember the bidding and raising of diamonds by the opponents? How many diamonds are there between the East and West hands? That's right—at least eight. You have four yourself, so how many does your partner have? Now you're making progress—partner is very likely to have a singleton or void in diamonds. So get that low diamond on the track, planning to take your ♠ A the first time the suit is led so you can lead another diamond. Presto! Partner ruffs and the slam is down.

There are many other examples of how you can make inferences from calls that are made—and those that are not made. Suppose you are on lead against 3NT with a weak hand with no obvious lead. You know because your hand is so bad that your partner has a fair amount of high-card strength. Now suppose you are South and the bidding went this way:

West	North	East	South
		1NT	Pass
2 ♦	Pass	2 ♥	Pass
3NT	All Pass		

West's 2 ♦ was a transfer to hearts, and when West bid 3NT she was giving her partner a choice of games. With three or more hearts, East would bid 4 ♥ instead of passing 3NT. Now suppose your hand is:

♠ 1063
♥ Q543
♦ 987
♣ 654

What is your lead? A heart is out of the question. West is known to have a five-card suit. You can only be helping declarer if you lead a heart. So it will be one of the other suits.

What Didn't Happen?

Do you have anything to go on? Well, consider that your partner had a chance to double the artificial bid of 2 ♦ but chose not to. Can he have a substantial holding in that suit? It's rather unlikely, so choose between clubs and spades.

The best option is probably a club because the ♠ 10 could be a rather important card, say if dummy hits with ♠ J98 and declarer has ♠ AQ54. Your lead of a spade in that case would pick up the entire suit for declarer, giving him four tricks instead of the three to which he is entitled. Go with the club lead.

FACT

When someone opens the bidding at the three or four level and you become declarer, you can use the information about the long suit to get a more accurate count of the opponents' hands. If a player makes an opening that shows a seven-card suit, you really have to count only six more cards in her hand.

The truly difficult opponents are the ones who get to their final contracts with short auctions that tell very little about their hands. That's a lesson you can apply to your own auctions.

It's fun to conduct a lengthy, scientific auction to just the right spot, but beware of passing too much information to the people sitting at your left and right.

When to Double and When to Bid On

One of your toughest tasks as a bridge player will be to decide when to double the opponents and when to bid on in a highly competitive auction. When both sides have long trump suits, it will often be the side with the higher-ranking suit that wins out.

Those annoying opponents will do their best to make life difficult, especially when the vulnerability is in their favor (you are vulnerable, they are not).

The form of scoring can make a difference in your decision. Say this is your hand:

♠ AKQ106
♥ AJ105
♦ 65
♣ K5

This is the bidding with you as South. You are vulnerable, the opponents are not.

West	North	East	South
			1 ♠
2NT	4 ♠	5 ♦	?

You know you are going to defeat 5 ♦, but to compensate for your vulnerable game you will have to beat it four tricks for plus 800. That might be in the offing, but chances are you won't get 5 ♦ that much. It's probably best to bid on, hoping partner has the ♥ K and a singleton diamond and that the ♣ A is to your right. The fact is that plus 300 or 500 will be a poor score, and if you go down in 5 ♠ the difference between plus 300 and minus 100 won't be much.

In a team game, you can't afford to speculate. If you bid one more for the road and go down, you might lose a vulnerable game swing if your teammates don't find the save at the other table. At teams, you will profit in the long run by just taking the plus score. Double 5 ♦. If partner has an exceptional hand, she can always pull it. Your double is a suggestion, not a command.

CHAPTER 8

Developing Bidding Judgment

You know how to count points now, and you know all about quick tricks. You know some 12-point hands are better than others for opening the bidding. Experience will teach you that the auction will have a major influence on how you view your hand and its potential for helping your side. As you listen and learn, you are practicing the skills that will help you decide when to charge ahead and when to hold back.

What Are Wasted Values?

The process of hand evaluation is not intuitive, and many beginning players do not take into account the positional value of their honor cards. To illustrate the point, here's a simple example of a single suit distributed to all four hands:

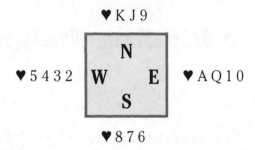

Look this over before deciding how many tricks the hand holding the KJ9 will take in the heart suit. If you said none, you are correct. No matter what card is played from the North hand (at the top of the diagram), the player sitting "over" the KJ9 has a winning card to cover it. The situation changes radically if the layout is this way:

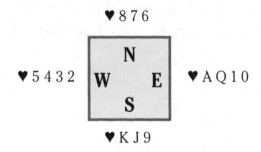

Now the hand holding the KJ9 will take two tricks. Only the ♥ A is a winner. Looking at the situation from the perspective of the hand holding the AQ10, three tricks are available if the king and jack are on the right, but only one if the king and jack are on the left. If either honor is to the right, two tricks can be taken with AQ10.

You might wonder what all this has to do with the evaluation of a complete hand? Well, as the bidding progresses, you will receive strong clues about the location of the honor cards in the other players' hands—and that includes your partner.

In bridge parlance, honor cards to your right are said to be "under" or "in front of" your honors. Similarly, your honor cards compared with the player on your right are said to be "over" or "behind" her honor cards.

The "information" provided in the auction will not be guaranteed. For example, a player who overcalls 1 ♠ can be presumed to have honors in his suit, but that won't always be the case. There are hands that are good enough to warrant overcalls with relatively poor suits. That said, players do tend to have their values in the suits they bid when they compete.

You should remember, of course, that an opening bid in one of a suit does not promise any particular quality. When you have enough strength to start the bidding and a five-card major, for example, you will open one of that major even if it is headed by only the 10.

Keeping those points in mind, most players who overcall do so because they like their suits, so it is safe to infer that when someone overcalls against you—especially at the two level—some or all of the missing honors in the suit will be in the overcaller's hand.

Listen and Learn

All these factors should be taken into account when considering how a hand goes up or down in value—expressed in terms of trick-taking ability—as the auction progresses.

Consider this hand:

♠ QJ6
♥ AKJ98
♦ KJ42
♣ 3

You open 1 ♥ and your left-hand opponent overcalls 2 ♦. Your partner raises you to 2 ♥. Now what?

If your left-hand opponent had passed instead of bidding and partner made the same raise to 2 ♥, you would certainly consider making a game try, perhaps bidding 3 ♦, which asks your partner to evaluate her hand based on her diamond holding. With low cards in the suit (or perhaps shortness), your partner would sign off in 3 ♥, but if she had something good like the queen or the ace, she would probably accept your game try and bid game or show some other feature of her hand.

ALERT!

When your partner makes a "game try" in a suit after you have given her a raise in her original suit, she is asking you to decide on going to game or signing off based on your holding in the game-try suit. If you have a good holding in that suit, you must go to game no matter how you view your hand as a whole. It's important to partnership harmony to do as your partner asks.

It's a completely different story when you open 1 ♥ and the next player bids 2 ♦. In light of that bidding, your hand is no longer worth a game try. You may end up taking no tricks in the diamond suit, and it's not farfetched to envision all of the important diamond cards sitting "over" your king and jack. It's true that your partner might be short in diamonds, giving you the chance to ruff your losers, but your right-hand opponent will also be short in the suit. If you try to ruff losing diamonds in the dummy, your right-hand opponent will overruff unless your partner's trumps are very strong.

After the 2 ♦ overcall, it is best to go quietly with this hand.

Good Turns Bad

Consider this same hand again, but without interference by the opponents.

♠ QJ6
♥ AKJ98
♦ KJ42
♣ 3

Again, you open 1 ♥. After your left-hand opponent passes, your partner bids 4 ♦, a special bid known as a "splinter." A bid of 4 ♦ in this case means that your partner has at least four-card support for your heart suit, the equivalent of at least an opening hand, and a singleton or void in diamonds. Your partner could show the same sort of hand with spade shortness by bidding 3 ♠ or club shortness with a bid of 4 ♣. This convention is introduced to make the point that once your partner shows shortness in the diamond suit, you will re-evaluate your hand downward. The bid itself puts you in game, but you should not consider any move toward slam.

Just think about the play. The opponents, who have listened to the bidding, will lead trumps at every opportunity, trying to deprive you of those precious diamond ruffs in dummy. Even if they can't lead trumps more than once or twice, you still have losing diamonds to dispose of. Opposite a singleton or void, your ♦KJ are not pulling their full weight and are considered "wasted" values. If you end up ruffing them in the dummy, they might as well have been four low diamonds.

It's altogether different if your diamonds are headed by the ace. An ace is never considered to be a "wasted" card opposite a singleton. When the shortness is a void, the ace might be superfluous, but at least you might be able to make an important discard from the dummy when the suit is played.

Information, Please

The auction will often tell you when there is shortness opposite your high cards, and it doesn't have to involve anything as dramatic as a splinter bid.

Consider this sequence:

West	North	East	South
	1 ♥	Pass	1 ♠
Pass	2 ♦	Pass	2NT
Pass	3 ♠		

You are South. What have you learned about North's hand? First, you know that North has at least five hearts for his opening bid of 1 ♥. North's second bid shows at least four diamonds. Over your invitational bid of 2NT, North bid 3 ♠. Considering that you have promised only four spades, your partner's 3 ♠ must show three-card support (you know he does not have four spades or he would have raised to 2 ♠ directly). So there you have it: five hearts, four diamonds, and three spades. That leaves room for only one club. This information should help you decide whether to play in a suit contract or in no-trump.

Aces and Spaces

If you have the ♣ A but no other honors in the suit, you will probably choose to play in spades, even if you have only four of them. After all, you will be able to ruff clubs in the short trump hand (partner's) to keep your trump holding from being subject to a forcing defense, in which the opponents make you ruff in the long trump hand, causing you to lose control.

If you play in no-trump and hold only the ace in the suit, the opponents will knock out your only club stopper right off the bat. On this bidding, you can be sure that you will receive a club lead if you play in no-trump.

E-QUESTION

What is a "forcing" defense in a suit contract, and when is the best time to go for that strategy?
The forcing defense is aimed at reducing declarer's trumps in her longer holding to fewer than those held by a defender. The defender holding four trumps—even low ones—leads a suit declarer is short in with the idea of making declarer ruff. This is especially effective if declarer is playing a 4–3 trump fit.

If you then have to let the opponents in, they will have lots of clubs to cash. With something like three or four clubs to the KJ, you will probably choose to play in no-trump, protecting your tenace in the suit.

A tenace is a holding of honors cards in a broken sequence, such as A–Q or K–J. It can also be a holding of Q–10 or 10–8. The A–Q holding is known as a "major" tenace.

If you do get a club lead, and someone plays the queen, you will probably win the king and try to keep your right-hand opponent off lead so that he cannot play a club through your jack, which would be trapped if your left-hand opponent had started with the A–10 in the suit.

The important thing is that you envisioned your partner's hand to help make your final decision.

Too Many Trumps?

The expression "trump poor" is not widely used in today's game, but the concept is an important part of hand evaluation.

Consider that your partner opens 1 ♠ and you hold ♠ AQ7653. Your partner is known to have at least five spades, so you have 11 between you. Chances are good that your partner has the ♠ K, so even if the outstanding trumps split 2–0, they can be pulled with ease. That means that your ♠ Q is essentially a wasted card. Having a queen in another suit might make the difference between making or going down in a game or a slam. When you have an overabundance of trumps but a paucity of high cards where you need them, you are said to be "trump poor."

Working Values

Now that you know about wasted values, it's time to discuss the other end of the spectrum—working values.

A good auction will tell you when your high cards match up well with your partner's. Most of the time, these will be aces, kings, and queens—the fillers that help suits run.

Sometimes, though, the auction will tell you that your low cards are in just the right place. Here's your hand, followed by the auction:

♠ A10843
♥ K4
♦ 642
♣ KJ5

West	North	East	South
	1 ♣	Pass	1 ♠
Pass	2 ♥	Pass	2 ♠
Pass	3 ♠	Pass	?

Given this bidding, your hand is worth its weight in gold. Your partner has described a very good hand with her "reverse" (see Chapter 7), and once she bids 3 ♠, she has completed the picture of her hand to show five clubs, four hearts, three spades, and a singleton diamond. Note that you can bid 2 ♠ on a five-card suit when your partner has reversed.

You worried about diamonds when the auction started, but knowing that your partner is short in the suit means the opponents can take at most one trick there. Further, your honors in partner's two main suits can only mean they will help fill out those suits for lots of tricks. Partner could easily have a hand such as this:

♠ KQ9
♥ AQ87
♦ 5
♣ AQ1064

In fact, that's a minimum for a reverse, but slam in spades will be trivial with normal breaks—and if the opponents don't lead diamonds, you will take thirteen tricks.

Once you found out about partner's shortness in diamonds, your outlook became much more optimistic because you knew that those three low diamonds in your hand were not such a liability—and more important, you knew that your partner had to have high cards in the other suits, meaning your honors in those suits were complementary, another way of saying "working."

Switch your diamond and club holdings, however, and you don't like your hand nearly as much. The ♦KJ5 opposite a singleton is cause for concern. You still want to play game when you have a hand that good opposite a reverse, but you would not make a move toward slam.

Over and Under

Even cards in the opponents' suits can be looked upon as working values, especially when the final contract is likely to be no-trump.

Here's an example. Suppose your partner opens 1 ♠ and the next player bids 2 ♣. Now suppose you have an opening hand yourself with ♣ KQ6. Given the bidding, you can be virtually certain that your holding is worth two tricks in a no-trump contract. Players almost always lead their partner's suits, especially those bid at the two level, and it would be very surprising if the overcaller did not have the ♣ A for his bid. In a suit contract, you might take no tricks with that fine club holding if your left-hand opponent has a singleton and his partner has a quick re-entry.

ALERT!

Your holdings in the suits the opponents bid go up and down in value depending on which of your foes does the bidding. When you are "behind" the bidder (meaning she is to your right), count those honors for full value, especially for no-trump play. When you are "in front" of the bidder (she is on your left), de-value those high cards in most cases.

What that means is that, even when you have a good suit of your own, you might decide to ignore it and simply bid 3NT when you have enough high-card strength. In that way, the interference by the opponent is helping you to the right spot—so long as you are listening and evaluating as the auction goes along.

A Preference or a Raise?

There are subtle elements to bidding that may not be easy to detect when you are just starting out.

Here are two auctions.

West	North	East	South
	1 ♠	Pass	1NT
Pass	2 ♥	Pass	3 ♠

West	North	East	South
	1 ♠	Pass	1NT
Pass	3 ♥	Pass	3 ♠

Both auctions conclude with South bidding 3 ♠. Can you tell the difference? In the first, South had a hand worth a jump (limit) raise to 3 ♠ but he did not have the requisite four trumps in the modern style. The only way to show that hand is to bid 1NT as a one-round force, then make the jump bid, describing a hand with three-card spade support and limit-raise (game invitational) values.

As for the second auction, South's bid of 3 ♠ says only that he had enough to keep the bidding open and that he likes spades better than hearts. South is showing a relatively weak hand with two-card spade support at best. With modest values and at least three spades, South would have made a simple raise in spades rather than bidding 1NT.

> When your partner opens the bidding and you have a hand just barely good enough to keep the bidding open, make your bid as descriptive as possible. It may be your only chance to bid. Always keep in mind the maxim: Support with support.

In the case of the second auction, 3 ♠ is not a raise, it is a preference. South makes no promises about his spade holding. All he is saying is, "Partner, I understand that you have a very strong hand with spades and hearts.

Based on that information, 3 ♠ is where I want to play this contract. If you bid on to game, you do so on your own."

There will be occasions when your partner enters the auction at a high level, forcing you to bid. The following occurs more often than you might think:

West	North	East	South
1 ♠	Pass	4 ♠	4NT
Pass	5 ♣		

South's 4NT describes a two-suited hand with the minors. The 5 ♣ bid does not say anything about North's hand except that she prefers clubs to diamonds. North could have:

♠ 6532
♥ J98764
♦ 4
♣ 32

5 ♣ is in no way a forward-going bid. North was forced to choose between the minors, and she did so. South should not infer anything from the bidding except that North likes clubs betters than diamonds.

It's a completely different matter when the bidding is done freely, for example:

West	North	East	South
		1 ♠	2NT
3 ♠	4 ♣	Pass	?

In this case, North is doing more than taking a preference when South shows the minors with his bid of 2NT. North believes she has the values to compete in addition to a good trump fit. If there is anything the least bit exceptional about the South hand—perhaps five diamonds, six clubs, and a void—it will behoove that player to bid on.

Your Bidding Style

The concept of bidding style may seem somewhat nebulous. Chances are you already have a style without knowing it.

Do you tend to be conservative in competition? Do you go for the plus score rather than taking a risk? Or are you aggressive, bidding game every time it seems even remotely possible? Do you make weak, pre-emptive bids on any excuse? Do you have a hair trigger when it comes to doubling the opponents? Perhaps you fall somewhere in between super-conservative and wild.

A lot goes into determining one's style, and it is good to have one, even if you don't consciously decide on it.

An important part of developing one's style is comfort. If you don't mind going for numbers occasionally—even frequently—an aggressive style will make you a feared opponent. You will have some very big games to offset the disastrous sessions that will come when most of your maneuvers result in zeros.

Steady as She Goes

If you prefer a somewhat reckless style, be sure you have a partner who can stomach the bad games and enjoys throwing some curveballs himself.

The key is being consistent in your approach, whatever that may be. For example, you will face situations in which the opponents have put pressure on you with pre-emptive bidding after your partner has opened. You will find that you must either pass or bid game—no invitational bid is available and double is a poor third choice. You will be well served in these cases to try to take the same course of action each time you are forced to decide.

The last thing you want to do is guess what to do each time. Just do the same thing in all similar cases. If you try to guess and guess wrong, you could go on a losing streak of epic proportions. At least with a consistent approach, you will be right some of the time, perhaps even most of the time.

Being more aggressive when the opponents put on the pressure is probably the best way to go in terms of style. There will be times when it's right to push on, and on some occasions when it's wrong, the opponents will rescue you by bidding more themselves, providing a juicy penalty. If you bid confidently, you have handed the guess to them.

The Case for Sound Openers

In the not-too-distant past, conservative bidders were sometimes called Roth-Stoners, the appellation coming from the bidding system advocated by Alvin Roth and Tobias Stone. The Roth-Stone methods were very conservative, especially where opening bids were concerned. In their day, however, they had a lot of adherents.

Roth and Stone made up one of the top partnerships in the Fifties, and their ideas were popular in their time. They had great credentials, including a number of wins in high-level competition. Roth, now deceased, was a brilliant bidding theorist. He developed negative doubles and weak two-bids, among many innovations. Many players today adhere to his conservative approach.

In the Roth-Stone system, many 13-point hands did not meet the requirements for opening the bidding. Quick tricks (aces and kings) were also essential components of acceptable opening bids. Today, players are opening 10-point hands, some even weaker, with alacrity.

There are sound arguments for each approach, most of them applying to tournament or duplicate-style play.

Pay the Piper

Two important advantages of a sound opening bid structure are greater bidding accuracy in certain situations and more comfort in doubling the opponents for penalty.

When your partner opens the bidding and you can be confident she has the goods, you won't worry about getting too high trying for slam when your hand is borderline. It is very frustrating to make a slam try only to find that you are too high at the five level. Even worse is holding back because you can't be sure the five level is safe, then finding that partner had a very good opener and you missed an easy slam.

When you don't have a good suit fit, you generally play in no-trump after partner has opened the bidding. For that, you need high-card points. Shapely hands without high-card strength don't do you much good in no-trump.

In a sound opening bid structure, when you have a 12-point hand to go with partner's sound opener, you can be confident in most cases that you will be able to bring home nine tricks in 3NT.

In today's highly competitive arena, you can reap handsome profits by doubling the opponents when they overbid, which they will do frequently. It's easier to make them pay for getting involved in your auctions when you know that your partner's opening bids are sound and that he has at least a certain number of quick tricks.

To be sure, there are downsides to a conservative, sound opening bid structure. To start with, when you routinely pass 12- and even 13-point hands that others are opening, you lose the initiative and advantage that go with taking the first shot in the bidding.

Further, the player in third seat will be under more pressure than usual to "protect" against the possibility that opener has passed a hand that others have opened.

E-QUESTION

Why does the player in third seat after two passes have to consider opening on very thin values at times?
If you employ a sound opening bid structure, your partner will pass many hands others are opening, so just because partner has passed does not mean the balance of power is on the other side. You can't afford to pass if your side could have up to 23 or 24 points, so you must strain to keep the bidding open in third seat after two passes.

Think about it. If partner has passed a 13-point hand as dealer and you have a 10-point hand yourself, your side has a major advantage in high-card points—23 to 17. If you pass that 10-point hand and partner has 12 or 13, there is a good chance the deal will be passed out and you will receive a very poor score.

This will make for some dicey opening bids after partner and your right-hand opponent have passed. If your partner has passed with a normal non-opener, your side could be in danger of getting much too high when you "protect." It's like walking on a tightrope. Sometimes you will fall off, and in bridge, there's no net.

Can Light Be Right?

Busy opponents—those who open the bidding on any excuse and overcall in the same fashion—are difficult to play against.

For example, if you are sitting at the table in second seat with an opening hand and your right-hand opponent opens in front of you, your whole opening bid structure is now gone. You have to decide whether to enter the auction at that point and, if so, how. The player in third seat now knows that his partner has some high-card strength, sketchy though it might be, and if a big trump fit has been located because of the opening bid, the opponents can blow you out of the water with pre-emptive strikes.

Ruling the Roost

Many players use the so-called Rule of Twenty (see Chapter 3) to decide whether to open the bidding with hands in the 11-point range. You will find yourself opening the bidding more often when you use the Rule of Twenty, but you will also find yourself in a difficult spot when you fail to find a major-suit fit and must turn to no-trump. As stated previously, shapely hands that are light in high-card strength become liabilities when you and your partner lurch into a no-trump game with no good source of tricks.

Now consider the problem for the player who has been dealt a 12-point hand and hears his partner open the bidding. Most 12-pointers are considered openers, and it's axiomatic—or it used to be—that when you have an opener and your partner opens, you should get to game somewhere.

When one player opens the bidding and his partner has an opener, bidding game in some denomination is considered routine. The notable exception is when the two hands turn out to be misfits—neither player can support any suit his partner introduces. When such a situation becomes clear, wise players call a halt to the proceedings before the opponents start doubling.

When your partner's opening bid might be based on a scrawny 11 high-card points, bidding game with only 12 high-card points yourself could be tantamount to suicide. The problem is that you don't know. If you assume partner is light and hold back in the auction, you could miss game or slam. If you give partner credit for a legitimate opener and bid game with 12 points, you could be headed for a minus score. So what's the answer?

You could increase the minimum strength needed to commit your side to game as responder, perhaps going as high as 14 high-card points. That means you will be inviting game with 12- and 13-point hands. If that is palatable to you, it will allow opener to be frisky without continually getting too high in the bidding. Of course, opener must remember that partner's invitational bids are much "heavier" than normal.

In the Middle

There is surely a happy medium between the restrictive Roth-Stone approach and the anything-goes philosophy of opening bids. Here are some suggested guidelines:

- With 13 high-card points, open the bidding. Exception: 4-3-3-3 distribution, no aces, and mostly queens and jacks.
- Pass with 4-3-3-3 shape and 12 high-card points unless you have two quick tricks.
- Upgrade 12-point hands with no jacks.
- Adjust the Rule of Twenty to the Rule of Twenty-Two, the additional two points coming from two quick tricks. Make sure the high-card points are in your long suits. If not, pass.
- Upgrade hands with good intermediates (10s and 9s).

Following these guidelines will allow you to continue with normal responses to partner's opening bids.

It is worth stressing again that partnership discussion of such principles—along with agreement on a bidding style—is vitally important to success. Bridge is, after all, a partnership game. It is well known that two experts who are not in tune in the bidding will often be at a disadvantage against two lesser players with a good knowledge of their system, its nuances, and each other's tendencies.

CHAPTER 9

The Play of the Hand

You have to win tricks when you play the hand. You will develop cunning, guile, and deception. Some situations require that you win tricks immediately. Other hands will require that you lose tricks when it serves your purpose. You command twenty-six warriors and play them in concert to defeat your opponents. Compared to bridge, any other card game is like playing tennis with the net down.

Card Play

In the following situations you are going to be declarer. The cards will be listed as being in your hand or in dummy. You have to figure out how many tricks you are going to win. In this beginning exercise, neither the suit nor the contract matter.

In each case, you will be determining how many tricks you can win. Since the rules of bridge require that you lead from the hand that won the last trick, the situation will be set, giving you the lead from hand or from dummy. There will be a progression of examples that will develop your ability to take tricks.

You will, of course, have thirteen cards in your hand when you start to play in an actual game, but for the next few exercises we'll concentrate on one suit.

Counting Winners

```
DUMMY
AK

DECLARER
(VOID)
```

Count the winners for this suit between you and your partner.

If you are leading from your hand, you have no cards in this suit to lead to your winning ace and king in the dummy. If you are leading from dummy, you will be able to play both high cards. You will have to discard two cards in your hand from another suit.

FACT

When a suit is led and you are void in that suit, you may discard any card you choose. In a trump contract, you may use a trump card to win the trick, or you may discard. Discards are valuable in trump contracts. They are not as valuable in no-trump contracts.

Spotting Entries

Add just one card to your hand and you have an entry to the ace and king in the dummy.

DUMMY
AK
DECLARER
2

That is, you can lead the 2 to gain entry to the dummy's ace and king. Now, no matter what, you will win two tricks. If you are leading from your hand, you lead the two and win that trick and the next with your two winners. You have used the 2 to "get to" the dummy. When you play the king from dummy, you must discard from your hand.

When you lead a losing card toward a winning card, you have gained entry to the hand containing the winning card. It is a means of securing the lead in the hand of your choice. *Transportation*, in bridge terminology, is the ability to get from one hand to the other.

DUMMY
AQ
DECLARER
KJ

Guess how many tricks this combination of cards will win? No matter what, you will win two tricks. If you are leading from your hand you have transportation. You have two entries to dummy if you so choose (win the first trick in dummy with the queen and the next one with the ace). You may also use the king in your hand to overtake the queen if you want to be in your hand. When you plan well, you can have an entry to either hand, and you can win the second trick in whichever hand you choose.

The idea of transportation in bridge is fascinating. Getting from hand to dummy and back is what transportation is all about. It is about deciding where to win a trick when you have a choice.

Using Entries—Transportation

These are the cards of the same suit (the type of suit doesn't matter) between you and your partner:

```
DUMMY
KQ3

DECLARER
AJ
```

In this example you have a choice. You have two entries to your hand or you can win three tricks ending in dummy. The only way you can win three tricks is to play the ace first and play the 3 from the dummy. Next you would lead the jack and win with the king or queen. The other high card would win the third trick. You will win three tricks, and you will have one discard.

```
DUMMY
KQ43

DECLARER
AJ
```

Now, try this situation. No matter how you play this situation, you will win only three tricks at the very most (assuming no cards in this suit have been discarded by the opponents before you start playing it). If you do not play carefully, you will win only two tricks. Because you have so many face cards in the suit, it could be easy to mess this up. If you play the jack from your hand first, it will win because there are no higher cards in the suit held by the opponents. Unfortunately for you, none of the cards in dummy would then be higher than the only card left in that suit in your hand—the ace. In bridge parlance, you have "blocked" the suit.

In the given example, if you led the ace on the first trick, you would then lead the jack from your hand and overtake for the second trick. The third high card, or honor, would then win the third trick. You would then have only a low card in the dummy remaining. That low card probably wouldn't take a trick. You will win three tricks, and you will have one discard in your hand.

Unblocking and Counting Cards

Get a deck of cards and sort out these cards and set them up exactly the way they are set in the box below.

```
DUMMY
♠ KQJ54

DECLARER
♠ A3
```

No matter which hand leads, you must win the first trick with the ace. This technique unblocks the suit and allows you to win the remaining tricks in dummy. Next you will lead the 3 and win the second trick in dummy with the king, the third trick with the queen, and so on. If both opponents follow suit to the first two leads of this suit, all the cards in that suit will be good.

Let's back up a bit. You will now start to count the cards played. It's easy.

- **Trick #1**—Play the ♠ A from your hand and the ♠ 4 from dummy. The opponents each play a spade to the trick. Four spades have been played.
- **Trick #2**—You lead the ♠ 3 from your hand and win with the king in dummy.

Each opponent plays a spade. So now eight of them have been played. You have three cards remaining in dummy. That totals eleven cards. The opponents have two cards remaining between them. You have the QJ5 remaining in the dummy to win the last three tricks.

That ♠ 5 becomes a winner because it is the only one left in the suit. You have established the ♠ 5 as a winning card. Between your hand and the dummy, you held seven of the thirteen cards in the suit. As long as one opponent held two cards in the suit, you win five tricks.

Unblocking and Using an Entry

This example will have two suits.

DUMMY		DECLARER	
♠	♥	♠	♥
K	A	A	9
Q	A		8
J			7
10			6
9			5
8			4
7			3

The example is set up vertically to get you used to viewing the cards from the correct perspective. When you are declaring, you see the cards in vertical columns.

Declarer has eight cards, as does dummy. You are going to play these cards to win all eight tricks. How will you do that? If you play any heart card from your hand first, you will only win two tricks. The first trick you win will be the ♥ A in dummy. You will then have to lead a spade from the dummy and win with the ♠ A in your hand. You will have to lead a heart, and the opponents will win the next six tricks.

> The point is to win with high cards in the short hand. If a six-card suit is divided with four cards in your hand and two in dummy, then the dummy is the short hand. Short suits in dummy are valuable when you are playing in a trump contract.

Now, look at what happens if you unblock the spades first by playing the ♠ A. It wins the trick, and you are still in your hand. Next you lead a low heart and win it in dummy with the ace. Now you can lead all those good spades from the top down, winning each and every trick and discarding a heart on each of those tricks. You win eight tricks.

In review, you won the ♠ A and then led a heart to the dummy, winning with the ♥ A and then you led the spades, winning six more tricks.

Creating an Entry with Trump

DUMMY
♠ KQJ109872
♥ 6
♦ 432
♣ 4

DECLARER
♠ A
♥ A108764
♦ AK76
♣ AK

Look at the following set of cards. You will play the same cards in two different contracts. The first contract will be 7NT, the second 7 ♠.

You are playing this hand in 7NT and you are not happy. Look at what happens. Your left-hand opponent leads the ♣ Q. You win with the ace. You can win the ♣ K, the ♦ A and ♦ K, the ♥ A, and the ♠ A for a grand total of six tricks. Alas, you have no way to get to dummy. All those luscious spades are going to waste.

Let's try again. This time you will be playing in 7 ♠. The opponent leads the ♣ Q again, and you win with the ♣ A. You win the second trick with the ♠ A. Playing the high card from the short side in spades unblocks the suit. Next you play the ♥ A, winning the trick. Next you play a low heart from your hand. You have no hearts in dummy, so you can ruff with the ♠ 7. The term *ruff* means using your trump cards to win tricks. You have used the trump suit as transportation to the dummy.

Now you will win eight tricks in spades, one heart, two diamonds, and two clubs for a total of 13. Much more satisfying, no? This time it's the opponents with the keen sense of frustration.

Trump Suit Distribution

> **DUMMY**
> ♠ AKQJ10987
>
> **DECLARER**
> ♠ 6

Spades are the trump suit:

When the spade suit is led you will win with the ♠ A and then play them from the top, winning eight tricks. You have a nine-card fit. Since you hold nine cards in the trump suit, your opponents have four. How many times would you have to lead this suit to pull the opponents' fangs? That is, how many times do you have to lead the suit to get all their trumps away from them—and that is something you want to do because the opponents' trumps are potential winners for them. If you leave them outstanding and start playing your plain suits (non-trump suits), the opponents will be ruffing your winners.

How many rounds it takes to pull the opponents' trumps depends on how they divide. If the four trumps in the opponents' hands are divided 2–2, it will take two rounds to reel them all in. If they split 3–1 (more likely, according to the odds), you'll have to play three rounds.

ALERT!

The "distribution" of a suit is the number of cards of the specific suit in each of the four hands. First establish the number of outstanding cards. Do that by adding the number of cards you can see and subtracting that number from thirteen. For example, when you can see nine cards, the outstanding number is four.

If you lead the suit once and one opponent does not follow suit, then the four outstanding cards are distributed with zero cards in one hand and four in the other. You now know there are three outstanding trumps and they are all in one hand. If you lead the suit and both opponents follow, then you know there are two outstanding trumps left (split evenly or in one opponent's hand).

If you lead the suit twice and both opponents follow suit, then you know the suit has been cleared and you alone hold the remaining trump. You have pulled trump and cleared the suit.

FACT

When you have played a suit enough times to know that there are no more cards in the suit remaining in the opponents' hands, then the suit is cleared and you have all the remaining cards in the suit. A major goal when playing in trump is to pull trump until you clear the suit. In no-trump, a major goal is to clear your long suit so as to make your low cards winners.

In the next hand you also have the top nine spades, but the distribution of the suit is different.

DUMMY
♠ AKQJ

DECLARER
♠ 109876

How many tricks can you win in this suit? If you do not have an entry to your hand in another suit, you will win only four tricks. The last spade will be in your hand, but the lead will be in dummy. You will have no transportation in this suit. Every time a spade is led, it will be won in dummy. You have four entries to dummy, but if spades are trump, then you will win at least five tricks.

DUMMY
♥ AKQJ

DECLARER
♥ 109

You will win six tricks, and look—you actually have an entry to your hand. If you play the ♥ 7 or the ♥ 8 first, you can win with the ♥ 9 in your hand and then lead back to dummy to take the remaining tricks. You have one entry to your hand and two entries to dummy. You will win six tricks in this suit. How many trumps are outstanding? You have eight; the opponents have five. Again, they can be distributed only three ways. Let's list the distributions the way you should start to think about them: 5–0, 4–1, or 3–2. That means trumps can be five in one hand, none in the other, and so forth. If you get your mind around these numbers, they will become second nature to you and will help you with one of the most important chores you must master to become a good player—the ability to count.

Delayed Winners and Counting Losers

At times you cannot win a trick immediately. This is true whenever the opponents hold the ace of the suit. You need to find a way to get rid of your losers. First, learn to identify a loser in bridge.

DUMMY
KQ

DECLARER
J10

You have one loser. After the opponents play the ace, you have one winner. How many tricks can you win with this holding? Only one. You will win a trick with this suit if an opponent declines to play the ace on the trick, but in most cases you will win a trick *after* the ace has been played. At that point, you have one winner. The winner is not a quick trick, but it is a delayed winner. This holding has one loser, one eventual winner, one entry to your hand, and no discards. Add just one card, and see what happens:

DUMMY
KQ4

DECLARER
J10

This holding contains one loser, two eventual winners, one entry to dummy, and one discard in your hand. That little 4 is mighty. Its presence gives you another eventual winner, and a discard in your hand.

DUMMY
K

DECLARER
9643

The story on this holding is ugly. You have four losers, no eventual winners, no entries, and no discards. Even worse, the king is sitting there by itself in dummy. Both opponents can see it, so there's no way you could sneak past the ace, as you might do if the singleton king was in your hand.

DUMMY
QJ3

DECLARER
1094

No matter what, you will win one trick with this holding. When the opponents play the ace and king, you will have the queen remaining to win a trick. If you lead the suit, or if the opponents lead the suit; you will always win one trick. You have the QJ109 split between the two hands. All these cards are equal.

"Touching cards" are any number of cards that are next to each other in rank. The ace and king are touching cards, as are the 7 and 6. So, if you have the AKQJ10 in one hand, they are equal in value.

DUMMY
Q85

DECLARER
J2

If you lead this suit, you can be sure of winning a trick only if the ace and king are on your left. If the opponents lead the suit, you will always get a trick. If a low card is led from either side of the table, simply play low. Your right-hand opponent wins with the king and returns another card in this suit. You must play the jack from your hand. Lefty wins with the ace and plays another card in this suit; your queen will win on the board (another name for dummy). If you lead the suit, you won't win a trick unless your left-hand opponent has both high honors. If the honors (high cards) are split, you cannot win a trick if you lead this suit yourself.

When you play a card higher than one that has been played, you have "covered." You cover when you play a card just high enough to beat the prevailing high card. When you do not play a card higher, you have "ducked"; that is, you have played a low card.

You have learned the basic principles for counting and winning tricks. These principles will serve you well at no-trump contracts or trump contracts. There is a basic difference between the two types of contracts. In a trump contract you can use trumps to win tricks and provide entries when you become void in a suit. In no-trump contracts, you do not have the safety net of trumps, so your goal will be to develop tricks in suits that hold promise for promotion.

To this point, this chapter has only covered playing cards that are touching, or in sequence. In actual play, though, you will find that you have combinations of honor cards that are broken up with one or two intervening cards missing. The play that you are about to learn is called a "finesse." Here is how it works.

```
DUMMY
AQ

DECLARER
32
```

If you are playing from your hand, you lead a card toward dummy. You see that you do not have the king in this suit. You can certainly win one trick by playing the ace first. The queen will then lose to the king unless the king falls under the ace (very unlikely when you have only four cards in the suit). There's a better plan for winning two cards in this suit.

Lead the 2 from your hand, and if your left-hand opponent does not play the king, you will play the queen from dummy and see what happens. It may win the trick. In fact, it will win the trick if your left-hand opponent has the king and did not play it. In that case, you have finessed against the king and won two tricks.

If your left-hand opponent did have the king and played it on the first trick (a silly thing to do, usually), you will cover the king with the ace, winning the trick. The queen is then the highest-ranking card remaining and she will win a trick whenever she is played.

Also notice that if the king is on your right, you won't win two tricks unless your right-hand opponent is asleep or trying very hard to win your favor. The queen will always lose to the king but you have given yourself an extra chance to win a trick. A finesse is about trying to give yourself the best chance.

CHAPTER 10

Card Play Techniques

When you have a trump suit, you play differently than when you don't. In general, when your contract involves trumps, you want to get the opponents' cards in your trump suit "off the street," to use bridge parlance. There will be occasions when you delay that process, but it takes experience to know when to draw trumps and when not to. One thing is certain, if you attempt to run a long suit while the opponents hold trump cards, they will use them.

No-trump versus Trump—Different Techniques

In no-trump, you do not like short suits. In a trump contract, you love them. It is then that you use your trumps. Run out of cards in a suit? Good, start winning tricks with those trumps. In no-trump, if the opponents run out of cards in your long suit, they are helpless. In a trump contract, if they have trump left and a void in another suit, they are powerful. Similarly, if you run out of a suit in no-trump, the opponents can run wild playing that suit since you have no trumps to take control.

When you are playing in a no-trump contract, you count winners—immediate tricks such as aces, and tricks you have to develop, sometimes called "slow" tricks. In a trump contract you will count losers from the perspective of the hand with the longer trump holding—usually the declarer.

Counting Losers

```
DUMMY
AK8

DECLARER
Q3
```

Look at each of these hands and calculate how many tricks you are going to lose:

From the perspective of declarer, you have no losers in this suit. The queen will win a trick, after which you can lead the 3 to dummy to take the next two tricks with the ace and king.

```
DUMMY
Q3

DECLARER
AK8
```

Now the position is switched and you have a card, the 8, that won't win a trick. The good news is that you can see that the queen in dummy will take care of the 8, so you have no losers in this suit because the queen will help.

```
DUMMY
Q109

DECLARER
J87
```

There are two losers in this suit. The opponents' ace and king will each win a trick. You have to lead this suit twice, losing twice, before you can develop a trick. That's why it's called a "slow" trick.

Losers in Broken Suits

Broken suits are holdings that are missing honor cards (that is, high cards). You will be dubious of short suits that are missing honors but optimistic about long suits (seven cards or more) that have missing honors.

DUMMY
AQJ

DECLARER
87

If you finesse against the king and win with the queen, you will have no losers in this suit in your hand. The finesse, in the abstract, has a 50 percent chance of succeeding.

DUMMY
Q97

DECLARER
654

It is actually possible to win one trick in this holding, but the chances are slim (the ace and king with West or a singleton ace or king with East—very poor odds). Count this as a three-loser suit.

DUMMY
KQ87

DECLARER
VOID

From the perspective of the declarer's hand you have no losers in this suit.

DUMMY
VOID

DECLARER
KQ87

If the ace is led by your left-hand opponent and you still have a couple of trumps in dummy, you will probably have no losers in this suit. You may be able to ruff two of your losers in dummy. Opponents are not always so obliging, however, and you may not have a lot of trumps in dummy once you pull the opponents' ruffers. Conservatively estimate two or three losers unless dummy has lots of trumps.

Counting Losers—a Real Deal

West is the dealer and opened the auction 1 ♦ (see diagram following). North is in a tough spot with 12 HCP and no good bid at the one level. The hand is not worth an overcall of 2 ♣, so North passes. East passes and South keeps the bidding open with 1 ♥. You remember the lingo, right? South's 1 ♥ is a "balancing" bid.

North uses the opponent's suit to force her partner to bid again, strongly suggesting a fit in hearts. South jumps to the three level to show a full opening hand and North goes on to game.

Dlr:West
Vul:Both

```
              ♠ A 9
              ♥ K 7 3
              ♦ K J 5
              ♣ J 10 9 7 2

                   N
              W         E
                   S

              ♠ K J 2
              ♥ Q 10 9 6 5
              ♦ A 10 7
              ♣ K 8
```

West	North	East	South
1 ♦	P	P	1 ♥
P	2 ♦	P	3 ♥
P	4 ♥	All Pass	

The opening lead is the ♦3. West has led the fourth-best card from his longest suit. He could have five cards in the suit. For now leave that alone and count your losers. Examine your cards suit by suit.

DUMMY
♠ A9

DECLARER
♠ KJ2

You have one loser in this suit. You have two choices: Win two tricks with the ♠ A and ♠ K and ruff the losing ♠ 2 in dummy. Ruffing a loser in dummy is a choice method for eliminating a loser. Your second choice would be to play the ♠ A, then lead low from dummy, finessing against the ♠ Q. If East has that card, you will win two more tricks with the jack and king.

The finesse is a dangerous move. Remember that East didn't even have 6 HCP to make a response to his partner's opening bid. Who is more likely to have the ♠ Q, given that fact? One other consideration: West opened with 1 ♦, denying a five-card major. He can't have more than four spades, so it's almost sure that both opponents will have to follow when you play the third round of spades to ruff it.

DUMMY
♣ J10972

DECLARER
♣ K8

There are two losers in this suit. In isolation, you might play from dummy and put in the king, hoping that East has the ace. Don't forget that East showed a very weak hand by passing his partner's opening bid. The ♣ A is not likely to be with East. For now, count this suit as two losers. Okay, you have two potential losers in trumps, the same in clubs, and one in spades if you're not careful. That's five losers.

You are going to make one of those losers disappear immediately. That loser in spades is about to go away. Win the diamond lead in your hand and play a low spade to dummy's ace. You are winning the trick with the high card in the short hand.

Next lead a spade from dummy to the king in your hand. Dummy is now void in spades. Lead your last spade from your hand and ruff with the ♥ 3. That spade loser is gone. Good riddance. Now you are in dummy.

You still potentially have four losers—two in trumps and two in clubs. Let's tackle trumps first. You want to lead toward the ♥ K in dummy, so cross to your hand in diamonds. Lead a low trump toward the ♥ K in dummy.

You are nearly certain that West has the ♥ A. Remember, you counted the HCP in your hand and the dummy combined, and you remember that West opened the auction. All the HCP—all but two of them, anyway—are in West's hand. If he did not have the ♥ A, he wouldn't have enough points to open.

The ♥ K holds the trick and West still has the ♥ A. Lead a heart toward your hand and play the ♥ 10, hoping that this will force out the ace—put another way, hoping that East has the ♥ J. West has to play the ♥ A. You have been counting trumps, and you know that East has one trump left, but you are not on lead. West leads a diamond, you hold your breath and hope East isn't out of the suit, and when the diamond holds you are home free. You will probably have to lose two club tricks, but that's only three tricks total. You have made your game. You have earned your game bonus.

Declarer's Priorities

When playing in a trump suit, the techniques for succeeding are:

- Count the losers from the perspective of your hand. In the example deal, you started with five potential losers but made two of them disappear.
- Make a plan. You have three techniques for making losers disappear: ruffing in dummy, finessing, and establishing long suits after you pull trump. When you need to ruff losers in dummy, do that before you pull trump.
- Draw trump if you intend to attack a long suit and thereby establish long-card winners.
- When trumps are drawn, attack your longest side suit, giving up losers early to establish the suit and cash the long winners.
- Use honor cards in short side suits for transportation to achieve your plan.

Dlr:West
Vul:Both

♠ 8 6
♥ 10 6 4
♦ 6 5 4 2
♣ A Q J 3

```
       N
  W         E
       S
```

♠ Q J 10 7 5 4
♥ A 8 2
♦ J 8 7
♣ K

Contract: 2 ♠
Opening lead: ♥ Q

You are in a contract of 2 ♠. You need eight tricks. You have two losers in trumps, two in hearts, three in diamonds, and none in clubs. You have seven losers. To make your contract, you must make two of the losers disappear.

You will win the opening lead in your hand and—without delay—you will play the ♣ K from your hand, overtaking with the ace. Do you see where you are going with this? Right—you have no fast entry to dummy outside clubs, so you must seemingly "waste" a trick by playing the ace on the king. You continue with the ♣ Q and the ♣ J, pitching those losing hearts from your hand. Now, because your trumps are so good, you will lose only three diamonds and two spades. That's eight tricks for you and another success as declarer. You are getting better and better.

Dlr:South
Vul:S

♠ A Q J 5 3
♥ 9 6
♦ A K 10 9 3
♣ K

You are the dealer and you are vulnerable. You fan this hand and open 1 ♠
with these 17 HCP and two length points, one each for the fifth card in spades
and diamonds. Your partner responds 2 ♥, showing a five-card suit, and 11+
HCP. Game looks like a certainty, so you force your partner with a 3 ♦ bid.

Your partner decides her hand is worth another bid and follows with
3 ♥. You bid again, and your partner places the final contract at 6 ♠. You smile
and wait for the opening lead and give some thought to what you expect
from dummy. Six hearts cards, three-card support for your spades, and . . .
oh, well, time will tell. West leads the ♣ A and you wait for dummy.

Dlr:South
Vul:S

♠ 10 7 2
♥ A K J 7 4 2
♦ -
♣ Q 7 5 4

♠ A Q J 5 3
♥ 9 6
♦ A K 10 9 3
♣ K

You are going to lose the first trick to the ♣ A. You have three diamonds in your hand that are losers, but no heart losers. What about trumps? Well, you may have been a tad aggressive here, but it's not hopeless, so don't give up.

ALERT!

If the only solution to your problem with a hand is a particular distribution, or if one of the opponents has to have a card for you to succeed, then plan on that happening. Just believe you will succeed. Plan for success and see what happens.

You give thought to how you are going to get back and forth from the dummy to your hand. Looks like two finesses are in order—one in trumps and the other in hearts.

West wins the first trick with the ♣ A. He's pretty sure you have no more clubs, so he tries the ♥ 8 at trick two. Well, you think, should I just put in the jack? It's best not to put all your eggs in one basket, so you go up with dummy's ace, East following with the 3.

The spade finesse must work or you're history, so you try the ♠ 10 from dummy. East plays the 6. You close your eyes and play low from hand. When you look, West—bless him—has followed low.

Why was it wise to lead the ♠ 10? Since it was your intention to finesse, the ♠ 10 from dummy was equal to the ♠ Q or ♠ J in your hand. You played the 10 because you wanted to still be in dummy if the spade finesse worked (if East covers, you will win and play two more high trumps to get the kiddies off the street). Since the ♠ 10 won the trick, you lead the ♠ 7 from dummy and win in your hand with the ♠ J. Since both opponents have followed to the first two spade tricks, only ♠ K is still outstanding. Don't waste any time getting that last trump in. Go ahead and play the ace.

Now for the moment of truth. Lead the last heart from your hand and play the jack from dummy. Miraculously, it holds. There's a lot of finessing going on here. You are pleased to note, by the way, that East did follow to the second round of hearts. That means the suit split 3–2 and it's going to run as soon as you cash the king. Your three losing diamonds are going away on hearts.

The full deal:

Dlr:South
Vul:S

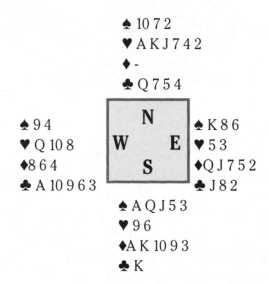

```
                    ♠ 10 7 2
                    ♥ A K J 7 4 2
                    ♦ -
                    ♣ Q 7 5 4
        ♠ 9 4            N          ♠ K 8 6
        ♥ Q 10 8      W     E       ♥ 5 3
        ♦ 8 6 4          S          ♦ Q J 7 5 2
        ♣ A 10 9 6 3                ♣ J 8 2
                    ♠ A Q J 5 3
                    ♥ 9 6
                    ♦ A K 10 9 3
                    ♣ K
```

This is not the kind of slam you should be bidding routinely. It has a very low chance of success. Still, part of the excitement of bridge is being able to land those difficult contracts that reap such huge rewards.

FACT

Using your trump cards to win tricks when a different suit is led is known as ruffing. Sometimes ruffing is referred to as "cutting." Think about why voids are suddenly valuable in a trump contract. You can immediately take a trick with a low trump card. It is more powerful than the ace of the suit led when you are void.

When playing in a trump contract, keep your options in mind. Long suits are valuable when the opponents have no trumps remaining. The race is on in a suit contract for the opponents to try to cash their winners and win tricks in their short suits using trumps. Take caution with the trump suit. Often it is wise to draw trumps immediately. If the possibility of a crossruff presents itself, remember that it's a great way to get more mileage out of those trump cards.

CHAPTER 11

Opening Leads on Defense

The opponents won the contract; it happens. Get the defense off to a good start. That is your goal when you are playing defense. The opening lead is the first salvo in the battle to win tricks. As you first start playing bridge, you will think that leading winning cards on defense is the best way. Unfortunately, it is not a good tactic against no-trump contracts unless you have both the ace and king of a suit and some lower cards to back up those honors.

Opening Leads Against No-trump Contracts

First, let's consider what you want to do in an uncontested auction. That is an auction when you and your partner have only passed. A typical auction would be:

West	North	East	South
		1NT	Pass
3NT	Pass	Pass	Pass

You know East has 15–17 HCP, and West has about 10 HCP, maybe a few more. For the purpose of playing defense with this type of auction, figure that the opener has 16 HCP, and the responder has 10 HCP. Your first consideration will be to calculate how many HCP are remaining for your partner to hold.

♠ K10764
♥ 32
♦ K9764
♣ 8

Your partner has about 8 HCP. You know this because you add the number of known HCP in each of the hands. The opponents have a combined 26 HCP, you have 6 HCP, and the remaining HCP are in your partner's hand. It's only simple arithmetic and you can do it.

FACT

When firing the opening salvo against a no-trump contract, lead the fourth-highest card from your longest suit. Although not a high card, it's an aggressive lead. Your goal is to win control of the suit led by retaining high cards in that suit. The logic is that you're trying to retain your high cards for later. When you lead your fourth-highest card, your partner will know your best suit.

In this type of auction, it is usually best to lead from your longest suit. You will consider two questions. First, what suit, and secondly, which card? A general rule when leading against a no-trump contract is to lead your fourth-best card from your longest suit. With this hand, you have two five-card suits, both spades and diamonds. Which one to choose?

Neither of the opponents has bid a major suit. West has not used the Stayman convention asking the 1NT opener for a major suit. The suggestion is that the opponents are weak in one of the two major suits. The only hope from your perspective is that the opponents' weakness is in spades. You will lead the fourth-highest card from your spade suit, specifically, the ♠ 6.

♠ 83
♥ Q1084
♦ Q1084
♣ J76

With this hand, you hold 5 HCP. Your partner should have about 9 HCP. Your only information from the auction is that your opponents have not tried to find a game contract in a major suit by using the Stayman convention. Your best bet is to lead the fourth-highest card from your major suit. Specifically, lead the ♥ 4.

Here is your hand:

♠ 5
♥ QJ104
♦ K1052
♣ AK43

Your partner has very few points. You can do the arithmetic and give your partner about 1 HCP, maybe none at all. You will probably have to win all the tricks for your side. You will start with a very aggressive lead. To figure out what you want to lead, first consider which suit you do not want to lead.

You do not want to lead a singleton against no-trump. You can eliminate the spade suit from consideration. Your club holding is very nice and will win two tricks. Save those for later and eliminate that suit from consideration. You are left with hearts or diamonds.

If you lead a diamond you would have to force out the ace, queen, and jack to win an extra trick. On the other hand, if the declarer leads the diamond suit first, she will have to allow you to win the ♦ K and maybe even the ♦ 10 before she can run the suit. She will have to give you the lead back and you can continue to attack the heart suit.

The Opponents Have Used Stayman

Stayman is a convention that is used specifically by the responder to an opening bid of 1NT. To use the Stayman convention, the responder must have at least 8 HCP and four cards in one or both of the major suits. When the opponents use Stayman, you can make inferences about their hands. Any bit of information you glean from the auction is helpful when you are considering an opening lead. Here is the auction:

West	North	East	South
	Pass	1NT	Pass
2 ♣	Pass	2 ♠	Pass
3NT	Pass	Pass	Pass

Consider your options. East has between 15 and 17 HCP. When West bid 2 ♣, he was asking his partner to bid a major suit if he had one. The 2 ♣ bid is totally artificial when they are playing Stayman.

When the opponents use a convention—in this case, Stayman—you overhear their auction. Since they are using the 2 ♣ bid as an artificial bid that says nothing about the club suit, you or your partner can use the double bid to show a natural club suit for your side. When your partner doubles an artificial 2 ♣ bid, then you should lead clubs.

Why is West using Stayman? Because West has at least one major suit with four cards and at least 8 HCP. Their goal is to find a fit in one of the major suits. West is asking the question, "Do you have a four card major?"

When East bid 2 ♠, he was saying, "I have four cards in the spades suit, and 15–17 HCP." West concludes the bidding for the opponents with a 3NT bid.

If West also had four cards in the spade suit, he would have been interested in playing in a final spade contract. What do you know? West has four cards in the heart suit and enough HCP to play in game opposite the no-trump opening bid. With that information, consider your opening lead with each of the following hands.

♠ K872
♥ Q76
♦ A10
♣ J1074

The declarer has four cards in the spade suit, and the responder (the dummy) will have four cards in the heart suit. That information eliminates either of those suits from being led. The doubleton in diamonds makes that a bad lead against no-trump, so your best choice is a club. The fourth-best card in the club suit is the ♣ 4. By the process of elimination, you have found the best lead from your perspective.

♠ KQ109
♥ K974
♦ 1097
♣ Q5

There is no sure-fire lead on this hand. Your spades are good enough to lead in spite of the auction. If you choose a spade, lead the ♠ K. Some players might lead the fourth-best heart, thereby forcing a high card to be played from dummy. A club would be a terrible lead, and the diamond might find your partner with an honor or two. Nothing is clear-cut on this hand; sometimes you have to make a guess.

♠ KQJ93
♥ A5
♦ 942
♣ 942

Your spade suit is good enough to lead. Lead the ♠ K. Sometimes your suit is good enough to lead even though you know the opponents have your suit. Your suit is better than their suit any day.

Leads Against Competitive No-trump Contracts

In a competitive auction when your partner has bid, there are rules you should consider. You have options and you are considering them in light of the information from the auction. Your first option is to lead your partner's suit. This is often a very productive lead. Your partner has bid the suit for a reason, and you must oblige and lead the suit.

Productive Leads

Productive leads in your partner's suit against no-trump contracts are:

- When holding two cards in your partner's suit, lead the higher of the two.
- When holding three low cards, lead the middle card.
- When holding touching honors, lead the higher of the honor cards.
- When holding four cards with an honor card, lead the fourth best.
- When holding three cards and two of them are touching honors, lead the higher of the two honors.

The only reason you won't lead your partner's suit is when you have a significant suit of your own. Your suit should be five cards long and headed by a couple of honors. Only then will you lead your suit in preference to your partner's suit.

But you won't lead your suit if the opponents have bid that suit. Your suit must be solid, very solid, if you intend to lead your suit when the opponents have bid that suit.

Dlr:West
Vul:Both

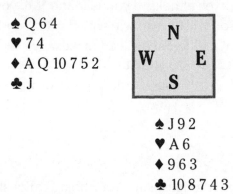

♠ Q 6 4
♥ 7 4
♦ A Q 10 7 5 2
♣ J

♠ J 9 2
♥ A 6
♦ 9 6 3
♣ 10 8 7 4 3

East is the declarer. In this auction your partner has bid hearts. The West hand is the dummy. The opponents bought the contract for 3NT (you will see that 3NT is not a good contract, but that's not the point). Lead the ♥ A, win the trick, and then lead the ♥ 6. You are leading the ♥ A so that your partner can win the next trick in hearts.

Dlr:West
Vul:Both

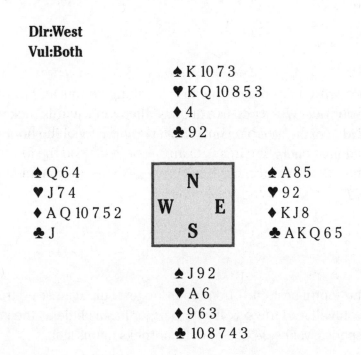

♠ K 10 7 3
♥ K Q 10 8 5 3
♦ 4
♣ 9 2

♠ Q 6 4
♥ J 7 4
♦ A Q 10 7 5 2
♣ J

♠ A 8 5
♥ 9 2
♦ K J 8
♣ A K Q 6 5

♠ J 9 2
♥ A 6
♦ 9 6 3
♣ 10 8 7 4 3

Your partner is delighted to see the ♥ A. When you continue the suit, your partner will win and runs six tricks. If you lead any other suit, the opponents will take the first twelve tricks. If you lead the ♥ 6, your partner will win and return a heart. You will have to win with the ♥ A, and your side will win only two tricks. What a difference a lead makes.

♠ 85
♥ AJ107
♦ K10974
♣ 73

In this case, lead your own longest suit. Your heart cards should win tricks when the opponents lead that suit, and you can continue to lead diamonds. Start out with the ♦ 7. Each and every time you get in—that is, when you win a trick—lead diamonds back. Your low diamonds should eventually win a trick or two.

♠ QJ9
♥ J4
♦ AK642
♣ 732

Lead the ♦ A on this hand. You have touching honors and most of the points for your side. When you see dummy after you win this trick you will have some idea of the lie of the suit. When you have touching honors, lead the higher of the honors.

♠ AQ962
♥ 764
♦ 76
♣ K64

Lead the fourth-best card from your longest suit against no-trump. In this case, you will lead the ♠ 6. If your partner has as little as the jack and two small spades, your side could win four tricks in this suit.

♠ 6532
♥ KQJ10
♦ 10853
♣ 9

Your only hope for winning tricks with this hand is to lead the top of a sequence, or touching honors. Lead the ♥ K. If your partner can win a trick she will lead back a heart, and your hand will produce three tricks for your side.

♠ KJ1093
♥ 74
♦ K83
♣ QJ10

The declarer bid spades during the auction. Do not lead that suit. Instead, lead the ♣ Q. Your intent is to play a waiting game and let the declarer lead the spades later and wake up with a big surprise. You have the benefit of attacking the club suit and waiting to spring the trap on the hapless declarer.

What Not to Lead Against No-trump

There are leads you should never make against a no-trump contract. Do not lead a suit that was bid by either of the opponents. You are literally playing into their hand if you do. (Bridge is the origin of that little cliché.) You will be giving tricks away. Leave that suit for the declarer to lead during the play. Let the declarer find out that you have honor cards in her suit.

Never, never, lead a singleton against a no-trump contract. All you are doing is helping the declarer set up a long suit. There is no hand in bridge that is worthy of a singleton lead against a no-trump contract unless your partner has bid the suit strongly. In that case, if you do not have a suit of your own, lead the singleton. Otherwise, avoid leading a singleton.

Your order of preference for leading against a no-trump contract in a competitive auction is to lead your partner's suit, or lead a suit of your own. If you were in the auction, and you bid a suit and your partner raised the suit, then, by all means, lead that suit.

A mystery unfolds for your partner when you lead the fourth-best card in your longest suit. With a simple application of arithmetic your partner will immediately know how many cards you hold in the suit. Your partner can see dummy, discern the number of cards in your hand, and instantly know how many cards are in the declarer's hand. This is called the Rule of Eleven (see page 186).

Defeating no-trump contracts takes partnership cooperation. If you lead from your longest suit and your partner wins a trick later in the play, you should expect your partner to return your suit if she can. You must do the same. If your partner leads a suit, you should look to return it later in the play. Never lead an honor card unless your partner has bid the suit, or you have touching honors. Then and only then is leading an honor a good idea.

When the opponent has bid your suit, and your partner has not bid, then lead from a worthless three-card holding. In this case lead the top of nothing.

If you have a four-card suit with broken sequences, such as KJ108, you want to lead the jack. The jack has a better chance of forcing out an ace than does the 8. If you have a broken sequence with the two cards higher than the 9 or 10, then lead the 9 or 10.

If you remember nothing more than the three most important options against a no-trump contract then you will do just fine:

1. First, lead your partner's suit.
2. Second, lead the fourth-best from your longest suit.
3. Third, lead the unbid suit. In such a case, the opponents have gotten to 3NT and have not bid hearts, and you have four of them. Lead a heart.

When looking at a hand and deciding what to lead, it is often good to consider what not to lead. By eliminating the worst leads immediately, the right lead will be easier to find.

CHAPTER 12

Leading Against Suit Contracts

Either lead, follow, or get out of the way. When defending in bridge, you will, at times, do each. You have to lead when the player on your right is declarer. Sometimes when defending, you'll just have to follow suit because you can do nothing to stop the opponents. Other times, you'll waste high cards to get out of your partner's way. Before you can lead, you have to have some vague idea of where you're going.

Your First Thoughts

Everything about defending is based on partnership cooperation. Seldom can one defender defeat the contract. As partners, you'll conspire, coax, and cajole your way to winning enough tricks to set the contract. On a good day, you'll do exactly that. On others, you won't give away anything the opponents do not deserve. And occasionally, you'll make mistakes that give the opponents a bountiful score.

It is important for you and partner to be on the same page. The cards will communicate for you. Choosing the right card in the appropriate situation will pave the way to victory.

How many tricks do you need to defeat the contract? That's a great place to start. If the opponents are in a contract of 4 ♠, you need to win four tricks to set the contract. Have that thought foremost in your mind when you consider an opening lead. Some leads are aggressive, attacking leads meant to win tricks by hitting the declarer in a weak spot. In general, it is best to be at least mildly aggressive in choosing the opening lead. This is your chance to pierce the declarer's armor. If you go passive every time, declarers will have lots of opportunities to develop their own tricks before you can secure enough for your side to defeat them.

Seldom can you defeat a contract all by yourself. Remember, there are thirteen soldiers in your partner's hand ready and willing to play in concert to defeat the contract. The declarer will do all he can to win tricks. You and your partner must stand in the way. Your partner is your ally in the effort and she is ready to help if she can.

FACT

The opening lead is an event. Defeating a contract is a process. As your skill develops, you'll see how the declarer has made tricks disappear that you thought you should've won.

Once you know how many tricks you need, next imagine how many HCP your partner holds. It's just a bit of arithmetic. The auction will help.

Next, consider how many sure tricks your side can win. Look at your hand and try to imagine how many tricks you can develop for your side as the play progresses. Imagine a way to win tricks for your side with the HCP in your partner's hand.

Where can you get additional tricks? This skill will develop. What is the declarer trying to do? This is best answered when you see the dummy. Look at the dummy and count entries, sure winners, and HCP. Do some arithmetic and approximate your partner's HCP.

The Worst Possible Leads

There are few absolutes in bridge, but there's a general rule about leading a suit headed by an unsupported ace against a suit contract. "Unsupported," means a suit such as ♥ A543. You can take this one to the bank: DO NOT lead low from this holding against a suit contract. That's as bad an opening lead as you will find. If the king is on your right, you may well be giving the declarer a trick he could never get on his own. You might also find the declarer or dummy with a singleton king in the suit and end up taking no tricks at all.

ALERT!

Eliminate the worst possible leads from your bridge play and watch your scores improve. These are bad leads because they give something to the declarer unearned. Remember, your worst possible move is to underlead an ace against a suit contract. Next worse is leading the ace in a suit without the king.

Also bad is leading the ace from that same holding. Aces are meant to take kings. If you start with an unsupported ace in a side suit against a suit contract, you are likely to fetch a bunch of low cards. You weren't dealt that ace to take 2s and 3s. It was meant to capture honors. Your partner might have the king in the suit, but so what? All you are doing is helping the declarer set up his "slow" tricks in that suit.

There will be times when the lead of an unsupported ace is okay, such as when you have a lot of cards in that suit (for example, AJ108765), and reason to believe your partner is short. If you lead the ace and find your partner with a singleton, you can give her a ruff. That's not going to happen often, however, when you have only four or five in your suit.

Another dreadful opening is the lead of a singleton or doubleton without reason, especially a doubleton. You will find many bridge players automatically lead a singleton or the top card of a doubleton. There are times when this can be very productive, but in many cases, it is not a good thing. You are likely to be helping the declarer set up a long suit. You may be picking off an honor in your partner's hand. You will learn when a short suit lead can be good. In summary on this point, give careful thought to any lead from a singleton or doubleton. Consider every possible alternative to leading a short suit. This lead is often misused, but when it's right it works.

A singleton can be an attractive lead when you know you are going to get in with trumps and your partner has some reasonable shot at getting in to give you a ruff. In that case, you lead the singleton, win a trump trick, and return to your partner's hand in another suit so she can return the suit of your void.

It's a rare day when you can get a ruff with a singleton trump, but it does happen, particularly when your partner has bid your singleton. On that occasion she is more likely to have the ace, so she can give you a ruff right away. If she doesn't, the declarer will win and start playing trumps—there goes your ruffer!

When you find that your partner is consistently making leads that you know are counterproductive, you will have to be tactful. Suggest that one day you and partner will agree not to lead from a doubleton unless your side has bid it. Using this approach you will be able to gain your partner's confidence and establish rapport.

A dismal lead is a singleton in a suit that the opponents have bid unless you are totally confident that your partner has the ace. You are most certainly helping the declarer when you lead a singleton in a suit that has been bid by the opponents. Experienced declarers can spot these singleton leads right off the bat and play the hand as though they can see all the cards.

When a suit has been bid by dummy, avoid leading that suit unless you have a powerful holding. Stay away from any suit that has been bid twice by the dummy or declarer. This admonition is important because the dummy will often have a five-card suit, and you will be helping the declarer set up the suit.

Avoid leading a suit when you have the jack but no supporting cards (10 and 9, for example). It's an especially bad lead to start with the jack from a doubleton in a suit that your partner has not bid. The same can be said of leading the queen from a queen doubleton. These are destructive leads unless your partner has bid the suit. Remember, the lead of a jack is not an attack. Similarly, the lead of a queen should never be seen. If the jack or the queen is part of a three-card sequence, then there is hope.

Sometimes you will have to lead an ace because you have no other choice. If you're dealt all the aces, something's got to give. Better to lead one of them than to underlead one. Your partner will understand when the deal is over and you show him you had no choice.

With all the prohibitions in mind you may think that finding a good lead is next to impossible. Actually, with experience you will find yourself the envy of the table for finding the lead that sets the opponents.

Good Leads Against Suit Contracts

Choosing the card to lead is qualified by your holding in the suit, or by the auction, and more often than not, by both. Occasionally you will have to consider a lead that is totally unorthodox or that you have been warned about. If you are looking for one of the rules to break about bad leads, just know that leading the ace in a suit can occasionally work at least as well as any of the leads listed in the first part of this chapter. Still, there's a better lead than the ace most of the time.

While it is the worst play to underlead an ace, underleading a king can be a very good lead. It may go against your intuition, but there's nothing inherently wrong about leading away from a king. It's an aggressive lead, but bridge is a game for aggressive tendencies. You may sacrifice a trick now and then by leading aggressively, but you will earn a reputation as a tough and fearless defender. Players will be eager to sit across the table from you.

One of the best possible leads is a card in a suit that your partner has bid. Keep in mind that the quality of your partner's suit may be tempered by when it was mentioned in the auction. If you opened and your partner responded with a suit of her own it may only be a four-card suit and not have prime quality. If your partner opened the auction with a major, you have confidence that it is at least five cards long. Factor that information into your decision.

Leading Your Partner's Suit

When leading your partner's suit you will lead low when you hold three or four cards to an honor. When holding touching honors, such as J–10 or Q–J, you will lead the higher of the honors. Now, your partner will know that your low lead denies touching honors. This is knowledge you gather by what did not happen. Your partner does not lead the higher of touching honors in a suit; therefore, your partner does not have touching honors.

If your partner overcalled the suit, it is most assuredly a good suit for you to lead. If your partner responded to your takeout double, remember that you have forced your partner to bid, and it may not be a good suit to lead. When leading your partner's suit, follow these criteria. Lead the card listed in **bold**.

Partner's Cards	Your Cards
7**6**	764**2**
65	7654**2**
A**K**5	**10**94
KQ5	K**J**104
QJ5	K**10**94
J109	Q**10**94
KQ109	

If your partner has overcalled in the suit, some of these holdings will be rare. After all, your partner is supposed to have some "stuff" in his suit when he voluntarily enters the bidding. Nevertheless, you may see some of these from time to time.

Use the same lead structure when you lead any suit against a suit contract. For the time being, you may have to refer to this chart as you advance, but when you insist that your partner follow the same guidelines you can easily communicate a lot of information on the opening lead.

When leading your partner's suit use these guidelines:

- If you have the ace, lead it. Even if partner has bid the suit, you don't want to underlead an ace against a suit contract. Your partner won't know you're holding the ace when you lead low, and this can lead to disaster.
- If you have three cards and one of them is higher than the 10, lead the low card.
- If you supported the suit, lead high with three or more cards if you have no face card in the suit.
- If you did not support the suit and you have three or more cards, lead low. If you lead high, your partner may think you have a doubleton.
- If you have touching honors, lead the higher card.
- If you have four or more cards and an honor, lead the fourth best (except for the ace).

Looking at this list you will find that leading the highest card in your partner's suit is bad bridge and not recommended with the exception of a doubleton or a hand with touching honors.

Leading an unbid suit, which is a suit that has not been mentioned in the auction, is often a good lead. Consider this lead, but temper your judgment with the facts from the auction. Did your partner have an opportunity to over-call in the unbid suit—especially at the one level, where it is much safer—but did not? The suit may be weak, but certainly explore the possibility in your mind. Do not lead from AQx or AQJ ("x" represents any card of 9 or lower). Leads from these holdings are costly. Eliminate this suit from contention.

When to Lead Trump

Your opponents will usually have most of the cards in the trump suit they contract. Remember, especially with major suits, the opponents are very likely to have at least eight trumps between them. If they control the trump suit, then why should you consider leading trump? One key consideration is the possibility that the opponents will use those trumps to ruff losers in a hand that is short in some other suit.

When you play trumps, the declarer often has to play two of them at once. Sometimes, a trump lead is the only thing to keep the declarer from taking all the tricks. If you lead trumps, especially in cases where the declarer has a 4–4 fit, you force him to play two trumps on one trick, cutting down on the possibility of his making his trumps separately. If you know you are getting in later and can lead trumps a second time, this is often devastating to the declarer's game plan.

Don't take it as a guarantee that a trump lead will be good for the defense. It many instances, a trump lead is a passive defense.

The auction will often tell you when a trump lead will be at best ineffective, at worst disastrous.

West	North	East	South
	Pass	1 ♥	Pass
1 ♠	Pass	2 ♥	Pass
2 ♠	Pass	3 ♠	Pass
4 ♠	All Pass		

Without even creating a hand for you to consider, the auction tells you that the dummy opened the auction and rebid hearts. You can expect the declarer to try to establish those long hearts as winning tricks as soon as he pulls your trump. If you lead trump you will be doing him a favor. You need to get some tricks going in clubs or diamonds before the declarer pulls your trumps and starts working on hearts (he might not even need to if the hearts are good enough). This situation occurs frequently when the opener becomes dummy.

FACT

When leading trump, it's usually best to lead low, even with a sequence such as J10x. The danger of starting with the jack in that sequence is that your partner might have a singleton queen, in which case your lead could surrender a trick. With J109, of course, the jack is okay.

Another opportunity to lead trump occurs when the opponents find a secondary fit.

West	North	East	South
		1 ♣	Pass
1 ♦	Pass	1 ♥	Pass
2 ♥	Pass	3 ♥	Pass
4 ♥	All Pass		

Your hand:

♠ 984
♥ 10
♦ AQ53
♣ 87432

You are North and have a singleton heart. Lead it. The opponents have stumbled into a game contract. Note that the opponents probably each have four cards in trump and therefore, so does your partner. Your hand is relatively weak, so your partner has some values. If he can get in again and play another trump, the declarer will be gasping for air. He may try to crossruff, but your trump lead has started the defense off in a way to thwart that idea.

Another great opportunity for a trump lead is when the opponents have intentionally overbid to keep you and partner from playing the contract. In other words, they have "sacrificed," hoping their minus score will be less than what you would have earned for your contract. On these occasions, you and partner will have the majority of the HCP and the opponents will be hoping to hold down the damage by ruffing some of your big cards. Often, one of the opponents will be short in your suit and will be hoping to make low trumps by ruffing. You can counter this strategy by leading trumps at every opportunity—and you will have opportunities when they're sacrificing.

Advanced Opening Leads

A slightly more advanced method of leading is to lead either the third- or fifth-highest card from a suit rather than the fourth best. The advantage of this type of leading system is that your partner can get a count of the hand faster.

Your partner can tell from the auction or the spot you lead if it is third- or fifth-highest and she can easily discern the distribution of the entire suit from the opening lead. There are a number of books that discuss these types of leads. Make a note as you advance in bridge to get more information about these leads.

Another gadget to add to your arsenal is called "coded 9s and 10s." When you play these leads, the lead of any 9 or 10 tells your partner instantly that you have led from either of two holdings. You will have two cards higher ranking than the card led or you will have none. The opening lead of a 9 or 10 specifically says, "I have zero or two higher-ranking cards!"

This can be helpful to you because of information given, but the same information is available to the declarer. Keep this in mind if you and your partner agree to make these leads. For example, if your partner leads the 9 and the dummy hits with low cards and you hold, say, the queen in the suit, you know that the declarer has the jack. Your partner's suit is headed by the 10–9 or the K–10–9 or A–10–9. With A–J–10 or K–J–10, your partner would lead the 10. The declarer therefore has A–K–J or A–J. In either case, you must play the queen. If you get in again, you may have to guess whether your partner started with a good holding in the suit or with 10–9 and nothing else.

All in all, it's best to use standard leads, at least in the beginning of your progress to competence as a bridge player.

CHAPTER 13

Defensive Card Play

Good bidding might make for good bridge, but smart card play will bring you victory. Defensive card play relies on good communication between partners and the ability to anticipate your opponents' next move. This chapter will look at different ways to protect yourself during the play of hands.

Your Partner Makes the Opening Lead

You see the opening lead on the table. You are in the third seat playing a card after the dummy. You will need to communicate to your partner just what you think about the tabled lead. How will you do this? A cheer? A grimace? Not in bridge. You will let your partner know how you feel about the lead by signaling with a card—not in the manner you play the card but by the card itself.

Dlr:West
Vul:None

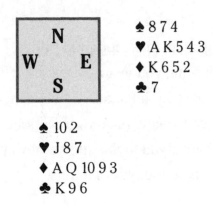

	♠ 8 7 4	
	♥ A K 5 4 3	
	♦ K 6 5 2	
	♣ 7	

♠ 10 2
♥ J 8 7
♦ A Q 10 9 3
♣ K 9 6

The opening lead is the ♠ K.

West	North	East	South
1 ♣	1 ♠	2 ♥	Pass
3 ♣	Pass	3 ♦	Pass
3NT	All Pass		

This deal was played at a tournament a number of times. At bridge tournaments, the deals move from table to table to be played over and over by different partnerships each time. Scores come from comparisons, not total points. It's a great way to play. (More about that later.) Imagine you are playing at the tournament, and the opponents reach a contract of 3NT. You must first consider the possibilities. Your side will need five tricks to defeat this contract. Since your partner led the ♠ K, she could have the queen to go with it—or the ace and the jack.

Here is the chart for preferred opening leads against no-trump (in each case, the preferred card for the opening lead is in **bold**):

76	**7**643
764	**7**6543
A**K**J4	A**Q**J3
A**J**109	A**10**93
KQJ4	**K**Q109
QJ104	**Q**1094
J1094	**10**943
AK**7**64	

You know from your partner's overcall in spades and her lead of the ♠ K that it's a good bet she has the ace (and probably the jack as well), but she might have just the queen. No matter what partner has to go with the king, you don't want her to continue the suit. If your partner has the A–K–J, continuing the suit will give the declarer a trick with the queen. If it's K–Q and the declarer ducks, your partner might lead into the A–J if you signal encouragement. You want to tell partner not to play any more spades for now. Don't worry. Partner will continue the suit if she started with K–Q–J or A–K–Q.

FACT

When you like the opening lead and wish a continuation of the suit, you will play a high card on the opening lead. When you do not want a continuation, or if you have nothing in the suit that is advantageous to your side, you will play a low card on the opening lead.

You will play your lowest spade. In this case it is the 2. Your partner now has a decision to make. She knows you do not want a continuation of the spade suit. She will recall the auction and realize that declarer has bid clubs twice. A switch to that suit would be unproductive. She is looking at the dummy and can see the hearts suit headed by the ace and king.

No shift to hearts. That leaves diamonds. Your partner brilliantly plays ♦ J at trick two.

Now, you have some thinking to do. Look at the diamond suit. You have five cards in the suit, and there are four in dummy. You can account for a total of nine cards. Dummy plays a low card and you let the ♦ J win the trick.

Your partner now leads the ♦ 8. The dummy again plays a small card. What to do? If you let the ♦ 8 win the trick, your partner must have another card in the suit to lead again. If that is the case, there is no problem.

But the ♦ 8 may be the last card she holds in the suit. If that is the case, you must overtake the ♦ 8 with the 9. You win the ♦ 9 and low and behold, the declarer plays the ♠ 6.

Does your partner have another diamond? Count the suit. You have seen diamonds played two times. On the first trick, four diamonds were played. On the second diamond trick, three diamonds were played. That is a total of seven cards played.

There are two more diamonds in the dummy, and you have three. You can account for twelve of the thirteen diamonds and you know the declarer is now void in the suit. You know you are going to set the contract and you want to win two more diamond tricks. If you cash the ♦ A, the ♦ K will be good in dummy. You have a plan.

You return the ♠ 10. You are pretty sure at this point that your partner has the ♠ A. If the declarer had it, he probably would have won it right away so as not to give your partner a chance to switch suits—and the declarer's clubs are probably running, so why hold up? So your partner wins with the ♠ K and returns her last diamond. Dummy again plays low, you win with the ♦ 10, and cash the ace, capturing the ♦ K. You win another trick with your last diamond. Your side will win a total of five diamonds and two spades, setting the contract two tricks.

You have used the spade suit as a means of transportation from your hand to your partner's hand. By doing this, you have made it possible for your partner to lead diamonds three times, thereby capturing the ♦ K and winning five tricks in that suit.

At another table, four other players played the exact same hand and the auction went differently with the final contract of 5 ♣ by East-West.

West	North	East	South
1 ♣	1 ♠	2 ♥	Pass
3 ♣	Pass	3 ♦	Pass
5 ♣	All Pass		

The ♠ K is again led. You must send a signal to your partner. You are giving attitude and count. You would like to give positive attitude, and you would like your partner to know you have two cards in the suit. You want her to continue leading spades. Why? Your partner should have five or six cards in the suit for her overcall. You see three spades in the dummy, and you have two. That leaves two or three spades in the declarer's hand. First you will tell your partner how many cards you have in the suit by playing a high card first, and a low card second.

Your partner can see the cards in her hand, and can add the five cards in the dummy to determine how many cards are in the declarer's hand. If your partner has six cards in the suit, then the declarer has only two. You won't be able to successfully ruff the third card in the suit. If your partner has five cards in the suit, then you will be able to ruff the third card in the suit and win the trick. Your partner will know that the declarer has three cards in the suit. Your first job is to tell your partner that you have two cards in the suit. She will be able to see that the third trick can be ruffed in your hand. She will continue with the ace.

When you play a high card first and a lower card on the next trick, you're telling your partner that you want her to continue because you can ruff or have something good in the suit. When you play low first and then a higher card later, you're telling your partner you don't want a continuation—that you have an odd number of cards or you have nothing in the suit and no doubleton. In a situation where you want to give information about count, high-low equals an even number, low-high an odd number.

When the contract was played in 3NT, the defenders wanted to play so that North could lead diamonds three times, allowing South to capture the

♦ K and win a fifth trick in the suit. The signal was a low spade on the opening lead to discourage the continuation.

In the other case when the suit was played in 5 ♣, the goal was to encourage a continuation of spades to allow South to ruff the third spade and then cash the ♦ A to set the contract two tricks.

When Your Partner Leads a Low Card

Sometimes your partner will lead a low card in a suit. What information can you glean from the lead? If you are defending against a no-trump contract, your conclusions are quite simple—your partner probably has led from a suit that is at least four cards long.

There is a little arithmetic ploy you can engage to figure something quite interesting. Here is how it works. Take the value of the card led when you know your partner has led the fourth-best card from her longest suit. For this example, the card is the 8. Subtract the value of that card from the number eleven. The result is the number three. That value tells you the number of higher cards in the remaining three hands—dummy, yours, and declarer's. You can see your hand and dummy, so subtract the number of cards you can see. The remaining cards are in the declarer's hand.

Dlr:West
Vul:None

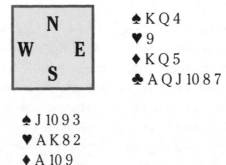

♠ K Q 4
♥ 9
♦ K Q 5
♣ A Q J 10 8 7

♠ J 10 9 3
♥ A K 8 2
♦ A 10 9
♣ K 6

West	North	East	South
Pass	Pass	1 ♣	Dbl
1 ♦	Pass	3 ♣	Pass
3NT	All Pass		

Opening Lead: ♥ 5

Okay, let's try this out in a real example. The contract and the hands are from a real game. Let's not criticize the auction or even consider if it is the best contract. Your partner has led the ♥ 5. Apply our little arithmetic formula and see what you can discover.

The ♥ 5 must be the fourth-best card in your partner's suit. Take the value of the card, 5, and subtract that value from the number eleven. The result is six. That is the number we are going to consider.

Answer the question, how many cards can you see that are higher ranking than the five? One higher-ranking card is the ♥ 9 in the dummy. You can also see three cards in your hand that are higher ranking than the ♥ 5, specifically, the ace, king, and the 8. You see four cards higher ranking than the ♥ 5—one in dummy and three in your hand. Therefore, the declarer has only two cards higher ranking than the ♥ 5.

You win the trick with the ♥ K and play the ♥ A, winning the second trick in hearts. The declarer follows with the 4 on the first trick and the jack on the second. Your partner played her ♥ 3 on the second trick. You now know how many hearts were in each hand.

Since your partner led her fourth-best heart on the opening lead and then played a lower card on the second heart trick, you know she began with five cards in the suit. Therefore, the declarer has only one heart card left in his hand, and your partner has three more. You lead another heart to the third trick, allowing the declarer to win, and then you just sit back and wait for the roof to fall in on the declarer.

The full deal:

```
                    ♠ 7 6 2
                    ♥ 10 7 6 5 3
                    ♦ 7 2
                    ♣ 9 5 2
    ♠ A 8 5                          ♠ K Q 4
    ♥ Q J 4          ┌─────────┐     ♥ 9
    ♦ J 8 6 4 3      │   N     │     ♦ K Q 5
    ♣ 4 3            │ W   E   │     ♣ A Q J 10 8 7
                     │   S     │
                     └─────────┘
                    ♠ J 10 9 3
                    ♥ A K 8 2
                    ♦ A 10 9
                    ♣ K 6
```

The Rule of Eleven

The Rule of Eleven works for the declarer as well as the defenders. To make it work, just subtract the value of your partner's lead from the number eleven. Look for the number of cards you can see in your hand and the dummy that are higher than the opening lead. Subtract that from your result, and you know the number of cards that the declarer (or the partner of the opening leader) holds that are higher than the opening lead. Comes in handy when you are figuring how to defend—or play.

ALERT!

When playing to the opening lead by your partner, evaluate what cards your partner holds in the suit. If the lead is from fourth best, then play your highest card. If your partner is leading from a sequence, then give attitude by following with the highest cards you can afford to play if you like the lead. If you don't want a continuation of the suit, play a low card on the opening lead.

Playing Second

When you are defending and playing second the situation changes. In one case, the lead has come from the dummy and you are sitting to the right of the declarer. In the other case, you are playing after the declarer and before the dummy. In either case your card is played second. As a general rule, second hand should play low. There are many exceptions, but content yourself to follow this rule right now.

On defense, a general rule is to lead through strength and up to weakness. If the dummy is on your left, it's better to play whatever suit might be strong. Similarly, when the dummy is on your right, you want to lead to weakness. The idea is that your partner may have some strength in that suit, so you want to play through whatever the declarer might have.

There will be occasions when it is obvious that second-hand low is wrong. For example, the opponents are in slam and you are looking at the ace of trumps, and the declarer leads a card from his hand and you have the ace in that suit. Your partner won't understand if you play second-hand low because you heard of that rule, and as a result your partner's singleton in that suit gets away from you. It's a no-brainer to take the ace.

CHAPTER 14

Bidding at the Two Level and Higher

If you want to earn the respect of your peers at the bridge table, you must assert your rights. Principal among them is the right to make life difficult for your opponents. That doesn't mean you should be mean to them or unpleasant. Bridge is a friendly, social game.

Weak Two-Bids

The idea of making your opponents' lives difficult, in general, means that you will learn to take your tricks when you are the declarer, and when you are defending. Being difficult also means that you will be an active bidder.

Take Up Their Space

One of the best ways to be a challenging, respected opponent is to take up the opponents' bidding space. What does that mean? Well, let's compare a couple of auctions. Say this is your hand:

♠ A2

♥ AQ63

♦ AJ

♣ K9732

Assume the dealer is on your left. You have a pretty decent hand there. In fact, you are looking forward to a nice, straightforward auction. You don't really expect your partner to open the bidding, considering that you have 17 HCP, but if she does, all the better. Your plan is to open 1 ♣. If your partner responds 1 ♥, you will like that a lot. You can show your strength by raising your partner's heart suit to the three level. If your partner bids 1 ♠ over your 1 ♣, you have enough strength to say 2 ♥, describing this hand: intermediate strength, longer clubs than hearts, real interest in a game contract unless your partner is dead minimum for her response.

Now what if the dealer bids 2 ♠? Your partner passes and your right-hand opponent bids 3 ♠.

What's going on here? Welcome to the world of modern bridge.

No Longer Strong

You learned earlier in this book that opening bids at the two level were strong and showed lots of tricks. There's no reason why you can't agree with your partner that all your opening bids at the two level are strong, but the truth is that most modern bridge players have left that bidding system behind.

If you ever play at a bridge club or on the Internet, virtually everyone you play against will be using weak two-bids. Chances are that even your neighbors who learned bridge last year are using this modern system.

You may ask why. There's a good reason: frequency. The more you play bridge the more you will see that the strong hands are relatively rare, while the weaker ones come up often.

Before we get into the rudiments of weak two-bids, let's go back to that nice hand you held earlier—the one you were contemplating so pleasantly until the opponents ruined your reverie. Here it is again for convenience, plus the auction:

♠ A2
♥ AQ63
♦ AJ
♣ K9732

West	North	East	South
2 ♠	Pass	3 ♠	?

Now how do you like your situation? Do you really want to bid that club suit, with only one honor card, at the four level? If you do, you might catch your partner with this hand:

♠ 105
♥ 10542
♦ 106432
♣ J4

You can count on playing 4 ♣ doubled and going down a lot. If you pass, your partner might turn up with:

♠ 5
♥ K54
♦ K5432
♣ A1086

You can just about take a slam in clubs to the bank. So what do you do? Most players would probably double, knowing that a big penalty was a possibility if their partner bids the wrong suit. Remember, your double in this situation is for takeout. Your partner is almost certainly short in spades—the opponents are bidding and raising the suit, after all—but if she has a weak hand or length in diamonds, it could get ugly.

The bottom line is that you were put in a difficult position because the auction was at a high level before it got to you.

FACT

In bridge parlance, a "pre-empt" is usually thought of as a weak bid that takes up a lot of bidding space. After all, if your opponent opens 3 ♥ ahead of you, it's no longer possible for you to bid 1 ♠. It's a pre-emptive action designed to hinder your communication with your partner. Strictly speaking, strong bids at high levels are also pre-emptive.

Weak Twos Defined

To start off with, there are only three suits you can use for your weak two-bids: spades, hearts, and diamonds. You still need a way of showing those monster hands when they come up, and that's with a bid of 2 ♣. More on that later.

For now, consider that there are basically two ways to play weak two-bids, defined as disciplined and undisciplined.

Weak two-bids are almost always made on six-card suits and have a limited number of HCP. You and your partner can agree on a range, but it's usually something like 5–10 or 6–11 and never an opening bid. In fact, that's one of the beauties of the weak two-bid: It's very descriptive.

In the undisciplined style, which is not recommended, any six-card suit with the requisite number of HCP is suitable for a weak two-bid. This approach is of questionable value because it puts too much pressure on the partnership. There will be times when your partner opens a weak two-bid and you have a pretty good hand yourself. You may be interested in game but concerned about the trump suit. If your partner could have as much as AKQ in the suit or as little as six to the jack and nothing else, you will never know what to do. Bridge is hard enough without having to guess in these situations.

A Matter of Style

So let's go with the disciplined approach. One way of defining it is to say that you should have two of the top three honors in your suit if you open 2 ♦, 2 ♥, or 2 ♠. That might be a little restrictive, but if you and partner are comfortable with it, then it's right for you.

Another way of playing disciplined weak two-bids is to say that the opener will always have at least 5 HCP in the suit. That means that your suit will always be headed by no worse than the KQ or AJ. This will help your partner evaluate the prospects, particularly if she is looking at one of the honors in your suit herself. For example, if you open 2 ♠ and your partner holds the ace in the suit, she will know you have at least the KQ in spades. She will easily be able to envision taking six tricks with your suit. This could be very important in helping her determine what to do next.

Inside and Outside

In general, the five-points-in-the-suit requirement will also help you with the rest of the hand as well. Remember that you should have no more than one ace or king *outside* your long suit—that is, in other suits. This is because your partner, with a really good fit in your long suit, might decide to "sacrifice" against the opponents' game contract. You remember the description of sacrifice from an earlier chapter: You are deliberately overbidding in hopes that the penalty your side suffers will be less than if you let the opponents play their game contract unimpeded.

ALERT!

If you "sacrifice" by deliberately overbidding because you think the penalty will be less than letting the opponents play their game contract, then find out that they couldn't make their contract after all, you have just perpetrated a "phantom sacrifice." You got a big minus score for nothing.

If partner opens a weak two-bid and has an ace and a king on the side, in addition to the good suit she promises according to your agreements, you might deliberately bid too high and then find out that the opponents' contract wasn't going to make after all because of all the stuff your partner had "outside" her suit.

So here are the parameters for your weak two-bids:

- Six-card suit
- Restriction on HCP: usually 5–10 or 6–11
- At least 5 HCP in the long suit
- No more than one defensive trick (ace or king) outside the long suit

Responding to Weak Twos

The weak two-bid can be a powerful weapon for you in your eternal quest to be an active bidder. The best way to decide what to do when your partner opens a weak two-bid—and here's where the disciplined style becomes so valuable—is to count tricks. Say this is your hand:

♠ 6
♥ AJ54
♦ KQ5432
♣ A7

Your partner opens 2 ♥, which you play as 5–10 HCP. What's your plan? Does your intuition tell you to bid more hearts? If so, you are showing promise as a bridge player and a tough opponent.

What? You say your partner might have only 5 HCP? What about all that stuff in the earlier chapters about having to have 25 or 26 HCP to bid a game? There are exceptions, especially when you and partner have lots of trumps and shortness in one or both hands.

What does your partner have in the heart suit? At least the KQ, so you know this suit is going to be worth six tricks for you. Your diamond holding will produce at least one trick, and partner is likely to be short in diamonds because you have six of them. You have only one spade, so the opponents can't take any more than one because your trumps will be there to ruff spades. If your partner has something like three low spades, you can ruff two of them in dummy. That's two tricks right there, plus at least one trick in diamonds and the sure trick of the ♣ A.

So, let's take stock here: There are six heart tricks in your partner's hand and a good chance for two spade ruffs in dummy (you can pull trumps and still probably have two left). That's eight. There is one trick in diamonds and one trick in clubs—and that's if your partner has only KQ in hearts and nothing else in her hand. She could actually have the ♠ A or the ♣ K.

This whole thing is looking really good for a straight shot to 4 ♥.

> When you and your partner agree to bid a certain way it is absolutely essential to refrain from violating those agreements. Your partner will appreciate you and cherish you if you always "have your bids." He will also try to emulate you and always "have his bids."

Asking for Help

You won't always have a great hand or so many trumps between your hand and your partner's. You should still count tricks, however, no matter what you decide to do. Say your partner opens 2 ♠ and this is what you're looking at:

♠ KQ4
♥ J43
♦ A7654
♣ A10

If you and your partner are playing your weak two-bids in the disciplined style, you know you have at least eight tricks—six in spades, plus your two minor-suit aces. You're progressing well as a bridge analyst, so you remember that 3NT takes only nine tricks. That rates to be easier than trying for ten tricks in spades, and you've figured that out already.

You're too sharp to overlook that potential critical weakness in hearts, so you're starting to think game is out of the question. Maybe you should just pass. Is there anything you can do?

You bet, and here's something new for you to put in your arsenal of weapons at the bridge table. When your partner opens a weak two-bid and the next hand passes, you can use 2NT to find out more about your partner's hand. In this sense, 2NT is not a "natural" bid—it's not meant to be the final resting place for your side. It is also "forcing," meaning your partner may not pass under penalty of severe damage to partnership harmony.

So what does 2NT mean? It says, "Do you have an ace or king over there outside of your long suit? If so, bid it."

Remember, your partner isn't required to have more than 5 HCP in her long suit, but she could easily have an ace or king in another suit to go with it.

So when your partner opens 2 ♠ and you hold a hand like this, what do you do? Bid 2NT, hoping your partner will show her side values—known in bridge lingo as a "feature"—in hearts. If so, you will bid 3NT, which has excellent chances of making and will actually be foolproof if your partner's "feature" in hearts is the ace. You will take six spade tricks and three aces.

When you open a weak two-bid, there is only one bid short of game that your partner can pass and that's a single raise of her suit. For example, if your partner opens 2 ♥ and you bid 2 ♠, she must bid again, raising spades if possible or rebidding her hearts without spade support. If you bid 3 ♥, however, you're just trying to get in the opponents' way. Your partner can and should pass that bid.

If your partner shows a feature in clubs or diamonds—the king in either case, since you have the ace in both suits—it's probably best just to bid 3 ♠. In the language of bridge this is a "sign-off"—telling your partner that you don't want to go any higher. You asked a question and got an answer you didn't like.

So what does your partner bid with no feature at all? She goes back to the original suit, in this case spades. If you bid 2NT and your partner bids 3 ♠, she is saying she has no ace or king outside her long suit. That makes your next decision easy—you just pass and hope you didn't get the partnership too high.

ALERT!

If you want to know more after your partner opens a weak two-bid, you can bid 2NT, asking your partner if she has a "feature"—an ace or king outside of her long suit. In this setting 2NT becomes an "artificial" bid and cannot be passed. The opener bids the suit with the feature or returns to the long suit, indicating no feature in the hand. Some partnerships agree that the opener won't show a feature if the hand is a minimum.

The Strong Two-Bid

If 2 ♦, 2 ♥, and 2 ♠ are weak bids, what if you're dealt a hand such as this?

♠ AKQ10643
♥ A6
♦ KQ
♣ A10

As you learn more and more bridge language, you will understand that this hand is a "rock crusher." It's the kind of hand you dream of if you're playing for money.

You don't want to start this one out with 2 ♠ or even 3 ♠, which is usually even weaker than a weak two-bid but with a longer suit. So if 2 ♠ isn't strong, what can you do?

The answer is that you open the bidding with 2 ♣ —that's your artificial catch-all bid for all your strong hands (except for 2NT, which is narrowly defined). An artificial bid is any bid that doesn't indicate anything about the particular suit named. In other words, when you open 2 ♣, it doesn't say anything about clubs—only that you have a very strong balanced hand or any other big hand with a long, strong suit.

A 2 ♣ bid is one that cannot be passed unless the player in the next seat takes some action (in this modern world of active bidders, you can count on it). Your plan as the 2 ♣ opener is to listen to your partner's response and describe your hand further.

Responding to 2 ♣

Your first responsibility as responder when your partner opens 2 ♣ is to describe your hand. In general, you won't have a lot of strength, but you might have a decent suit you can tell your partner about. Your most common response, however, is likely to be 2 ♦, a "negative" response—negative in the sense that you don't have a lot of help for your partner. Here are the responses to a 2 ♣ opener:

- **2 ♦**—a weak hand (0–5) or a hand without a good suit
- **2 ♥**—at least five hearts with at least two of the top three honors in hearts
- **2 ♠**—at least five spades with at least two of the top three honors in spades
- **2NT**—a balanced hand with modest strength (usually 8–10 HCP) but no long suit
- **3 ♣**—at least five clubs with at least two of the top three honors in clubs
- **3 ♦**—at least five diamonds with at least two of the top three honors in diamonds

Note that the 2 ♦ bid does not necessarily indicate a poor hand. It says only that you don't have a five-card suit with two of the top three honors. The reason it's important to restrict these responses is that the 2 ♣ opener may have a fit for the responder's suit, but if the suit is of poor quality, such as Q7654, the opener will be poorly placed to decide on the final contract. If the opener knows it's a suit headed by honors, she will have a much better idea of how to proceed.

Say the opener holds:

♠ AK
♥ J32
♦ KQJ1095
♣ AK

That's a 2 ♣ opener for sure—21 HCP, great diamond suit. If the responder bids 2 ♥, the opener will really be excited if their agreement is that 2 ♥ shows at least five hearts and two of the top three honors in the suit. The opener can easily envision game in hearts—and there might be a slam.

On the other hand, if 2 ♥ could be bid on Q7654, there might be three or four losers in that suit. That's why it's important to have these handy agreements in place. It's not too taxing on the memory, right? Five-card suit, two of the top three honors. Piece of cake.

Opening at Higher Levels

You're now an expert—or close, anyway—on two-level openers, weak ones and the strong one. So what does it show when you open at the three level or higher?

In the modern game of bridge, three-level opening bids are reserved pretty much for long suits and weak hands. A typical opening bid of 3 ♦, for example, would look like this:

♠ 4
♥ Q3
♦ QJ109843
♣ 654

Is that scary to you? You have only 5 HCP, after all, and you voluntarily jacked yourself up to the three level. But what if your opponents double?

Well, they might double, but if you always play it safe, you'll lose a lot more than you win. Remember, it's a bidder's game and it pays to put pressure on the opponents whenever you can. One way of doing that is to jump the level of the bidding way on up there when you have a reasonable long suit.

Trumps Equal Tricks

Note that the diamond suit had a sequence from the queen to the 8. That means that if you get to play diamonds, that suit is going to take a lot of tricks. It also means that neither opponent will have a terribly robust holding in the suit, making it more difficult for them to nail you with a double.

Don't forget, too, that if the HCP are distributed relatively evenly among the other three hands, your partner will have some goods to help you out. So don't shy away from your right to eat up the opponents' bidding space just because you are weak. Heck, you're *supposed* to be weak.

It's fair to have a better suit than QJ10, etc. You can do it with KQJ10, AKJ, AQJ . . . whatever, as long as your suit will be a source of tricks if it's trumps—and you don't have a lot of high cards outside your suit.

Position Counts

Believe it or not, the best place to go sailing out there with a weak bid at a high level is in the third seat. The next best spot is first seat. Can you figure out why?

In the third seat, you know you're not robbing bidding space from your partner because she already said she didn't have a great hand when she passed as dealer. Your right-hand opponent isn't loaded either. So what does that mean? Yep, the fellow sitting there licking his lips has the balance of power, so you want to take away as much bidding space as you can.

In fourth seat, it's very rare to show a weak hand with a long suit. In such a case, you would simply pass the hand out and start over. If you're weak and partner can't open, how much can you make, after all? Just pass it out and avoid a minus score.

Defense Against Pre-empts

When the opponents put it to you with a pre-emptive action, sometimes you have to stick your neck out. You'll be doubled now and then, but it cannot be overemphasized that bridge is a bidder's game.

There are risks associated with passing as well. Say the dealer opens a weak two-bid in hearts and you are next to speak. You could pass with a marginal hand and be sure to avoid a big set, but you already know that your right-hand opponent is weak, so that leaves more points for your partner, right? It's true that your left-hand opponent could have a strong hand, but it's just as likely that your partner has some goods—enough, maybe, to combine with your hand to make a game.

The Rule of Eight

Here's a tool that will help you make your decisions when you're under pressure after your right-hand opponent opens the bidding at the two or three level. It's called the Rule of Eight.

Here's how it works: In general, you should consider that whenever your right-hand opponent opens with a pre-empt, particularly a weak two-bid, your partner will have roughly 8 HCP. Sometimes she will have more, sometimes less, but on average she will have about 8 HCP.

When you consider whether to bid or pass, ask yourself if you would feel comfortable bidding if you knew your partner had the "expected" hand. For example, the dealer opens 2 ♦ and you are looking at the following hand:

♠ K65
♥ AJ432
♦ 54
♣ K109

Not a great hand. You certainly wouldn't open it as dealer, but you would overcall at the one level without a qualm. How about the two level? It's close, but you can't afford to sit and wait for the perfect hand—and it would probably be best to pass if the opener began with 2 ♠, forcing you to bid at the three level. Change your heart suit to AJ1098, however, and you're in the ballpark again.

At any rate, your partner might just put down the expected 8 HCP, giving you an excellent shot at your contract, say with a hand such as this:

♠ Q1097
♥ Q108
♦ 863
♣ A65

Higher Means Stronger

Generally, the higher you have to bid over the opponents' actions, the stronger your hand should be, with emphasis on the quality of the suit. You're cruisin' for a bruisin' if you routinely overcall at the two and three levels with trashy suits. In fact, if your suit is "beefy"—lots of 10s and 9s—you can have a little less in high cards. Remember, the more you have in your suit, the less the opponents have, making it tougher for them to double you.

Let's say the dealer opens the bidding with 3 ♥. What kind of hand should you have to enter the auction? Look at the three hands following and determine whether you want to get in there and bid. If so, what do you bid?

Hand 1	**Hand 2**	**Hand 3**
♠ A7	♠ AKJ642	♠ A75
♥ Q3	♥ Q1075	♥ A4
♦ QJ64	♦	♦ 3
♣ AQ765	♣ 732	♣ AK107642

With the first hand, you have 15 HCP. Not bad, but don't even think about bidding that ratty club suit at the four level. The downside (you get doubled and go down so much your minus score looks like a telephone number) is too great. The doubleton ♥ Q is also likely to be worthless after the opening 3 ♥ bid, so now you're looking at what is in reality a 13-point hand. Discretion is the better part of valor in this case. Just pass.

With the second hand, it's a very different story even though there are only 10 HCP. This hand has a lot going for it. One of the best things this hand has in its favor is the opening 3 ♥ bid by your right-hand opponent.

That may seem strange, but consider what the auction is telling you. Your right-hand opponent probably has seven hearts. You have four. There are but two left in the whole deck. At the outside, your partner has two. More likely, she has one or none. If she has but one heart, that leaves her lots of cards in the other suits, including spades. The very real possibility of a nice spade fit between you and partner exists on this hand. Get on in there and bid 3 ♠.

The third hand looks like it qualifies for a bid, don't you think? If you're thinking 4 ♣, you're on the right track because you are taking some action. But there's a better bid here. The 3NT.

Let's look at the hand a bit more closely to see why 3NT has a lot going for it. First, you have seven clubs headed by the AK. If your partner has two or three clubs, maybe even the singleton Q, that club suit is probably going to run. That's seven tricks right there. You are also blessed with two aces, and that's nine tricks.

Okay, the opener's partner might have some great holding in diamonds and run off enough tricks to beat you before you even take a trick. But who's to say your partner doesn't have a little something in diamonds, or maybe your left-hand opponent has a broken diamond suit, in which case you can bet the farm that he's going to do what every other red-blooded West would do in his situation: Lead his partner's suit. Better to lead your partner's suit than to be blamed for a disaster if you don't and leading it was right.

FACT

Whenever you have length in a suit bid on your right, it is safer to overcall because partner may well be short in that suit and is more likely to have trump support for your suit. Furthermore, if you need to use dummy's trumps to ruff losers in the your right-hand opponent's suit, he will have to follow suit while you ruff, providing you with more potential tricks. There are no guarantees, of course. Opener's partner might have those spades you want partner to put down in dummy, but remember that it's a bidder's game.

It pays to be optimistic in these situations. Bid with confidence and it's the opponents who have to sort things out and find the so-called "killing lead."

But what about bidding 4 ♣? Couldn't that be right? You bet, but if you think you have a shot at game in clubs, that would require a fit with partner in your long suit, and if you have that, you're back to your nine tricks in 3NT versus having to take eleven tricks in clubs. Which would you rather go for?

High-Level Takeout Doubles

The opponents are not always dealt the hands they need to mess up your auction, but you can be sure they will do so when they are given the chance. You must have all your weapons ready to fend them off. One of the most versatile is the takeout double. You learned about that device in Chapter 5, but it was applied to normal opening bids.

There's not much difference between doubling opening bids of 1 ♦ and 3 ♦ except that you should have a stronger hand if you're going to force your partner to bid at the three or four level.

For example, suppose the opening bid on your right is 3 ♠. If you make a takeout double, three things can happen: 1) your partner will pass because she holds length and strength in spades (this will rarely happen); 2) your partner will bid 3NT because she has modest values and one or two stoppers in spades; or 3) your partner will have to "take out" the double by bidding. Since spades is the "boss" suit, so to speak, your partner's suit bid will have to be at the four level.

So what does this mean? It means that if you make a call your partner must respond to and she has to bid that high, you better be putting down a dummy that is worthy of that level.

At the Four Level

There is one situation where a double at a high level is for penalty, and it's useful for you and your partner to discuss this. It revolves around the opening bid of 4 ♠.

For starters, let's discuss the opening bids at the four level. They usually consist of eight-card suits, but they do not advertise lots of high-card strength. If you have a hand with, say, eight hearts to the AKQJ plus a couple of aces, you should open that with 2 ♣, showing a strong hand with game or nearly game all on your own. It would be a hand like the following:

♠ A3
♥ AKJ109865
♦ 2
♣ AQ

Even if your partner is void in hearts, you will lose at most one heart, plus you have two aces, giving you nine tricks. If your partner has anything at all, 4 ♥ should be a favorite. Open 2 ♣ and rebid 4 ♥, showing this kind of hand.

Using this approach, you can distinguish hands of this type from those that are strictly pre-emptive in nature.

Rule of Two and Three

In general, your pre-emptive bids should be within two tricks of the contract when vulnerable and three tricks when not vulnerable. In other words, if you open 3 ♣ when you are not vulnerable, you should have a reasonable expectation of taking six tricks. If you are vulnerable, your trick expectation should be seven tricks.

Penalties for going down in doubled contracts not vulnerable are 100 for the first trick, 200 for the second and third tricks, and 300 for every undertrick over three. When you are vulnerable, it's 200 for the first trick, and 300 for every undertrick after that.

Therefore, if the opponents double you and beat you three tricks for minus 500 when you're not vulnerable, they can usually make a game themselves for plus 400 or 420, so the exchange is pretty close. The uncertainty you sow with the opposition makes this a worthwhile gamble. Remember, too, that your partner might have enough power for you to make game—or for her to double the opponents when they bid over your pre-empt.

Favorable versus Unfavorable

When you are vulnerable, you reach the minus 500 position at only two undertricks, so you have to be more cautious. Relating this to pre-empts at the four level, an opening bid of 4 ♥ when not vulnerable should have about seven tricks, and about eight when vulnerable.

4NT Takeout

Back to that situation where a double of a high-level bid is a penalty rather than a takeout. When an opponent opens 4 ♠, if you double for takeout, your partner is going to have to bid at the five level, simple as that. If that's the case, make use of a bid that is unlikely to be natural—4NT. It's not often you will want to play no-trump at that level.

By agreement, this bid tells the partner to bid something. Of course, abiding by the rule that the higher the bidding the more you have, a 4NT bid would have to deliver a pretty strong hand plus support for the other three suits, but at least it's descriptive.

So if 4NT tells your partner to bid something, double is not needed for that purpose. In this one instance, you can let double mean, "Partner, this guy just bid too much and I think he's going down." Usually, you will have at least one trump trick, more likely two, perhaps four of his trumps to the QJ or Q10.

The one thing your partner must remember when you double an opening bid of 4 ♠ is that it does not invite her to bid. Doubles of other four-level bids, up to 4 ♥, are for takeout.

CHAPTER 15

Advanced Bidding

You want to grow as a bridge player, and a huge part of that process will be the experience of playing bridge. Be aware that all bridge players, up to and including world champions, make mistakes every time they play. What is important about your inevitable errors is how you respond to them. If you allow your mistakes to deflate you, your progress will be delayed. If you vow to learn from your mistakes, you're on your way to success.

Basic Conventions

The American Contract Bridge League, based in Memphis, Tennessee, is the organizing body for most tournament bridge play in North America. More than 3,500 bridge clubs are affiliated with the ACBL. Among the responsibilities of the organization is the promulgation of rules about bidding conventions—which are allowed and which are not.

In bridge language, a convention is a bid or play with a defined meaning. Perhaps the most popular convention in the world today is the Blackwood convention. Some conventions are relatively simple, while some are quite convoluted. The more complex a convention, the more likely that its use will be restricted in some way—perhaps allowed only in the highest levels of the game.

One way the ACBL keeps tabs on conventions is with the "convention cards" it publishes and distributes. The organization prints and sends out millions of convention cards every year. If you play at a club or a tournament, you will have to fill out a convention card, listing the bidding agreements you and your partner have arrived at. Actually, the convention card has all of the most popular conventions already listed. You merely check off the ones you and your partner are using.

The CC, as it's known, also doubles as the method for players to keep their scores during the game. If you play bridge on the Internet, it's likely you and your partner will be playing what is known as the Standard American Yellow Card (SAYC). It is a convention card popular with less-experienced players because it contains only the basic conventions.

Stayman

There are two conventions you will want to play even if you decide you would prefer a "plain Jane" convention card with almost all natural bidding. One of those conventions is Stayman.

When your partner opens 1NT and you want to know if your side has a fit in a major suit, you bid 2 ♣. This has nothing to do with clubs (although it doesn't preclude your having several cards in clubs). It directs your partner to answer one question: Do you have a four-card major?

The bid of Stayman, with one exception, requires the responder to have at least 8 HCP. The use of Stayman does not mean that the partnership is definitely going to game, but it promises at least an invitation to that level.

Responses to Stayman

After your partner responds 2 ♣ to your 1NT opener, here are your responses:

2 ♦ = no four-card major
2 ♥ = four hearts, possibly four spades
2 ♠ = four spades but not four hearts

Why does the opener bid hearts first? It's simple. Remember, the responder promises no more than enough to invite game. So if the opener responds 2 ♥, showing four hearts and maybe four spades, the responder can bid 2 ♠ as an invitational bid with four spades. If the opener does not want to go to game, the bidding ends and the two hands are still at the two level.

Now suppose the opener bids spades first and the responder still has only the invitational hand. He would have to bid 2NT (implying four hearts, otherwise why bid Stayman?). If the opener is still minimum but has four hearts, she will have to bid at the three level when she believes the contract will play better in a suit than in no-trump. You never want to push yourself to a higher level than necessary. The opponents are already doing that, why should you?

So what kind of hand should you have to bid Stayman? See what you would do with these.

♠ AK105
♥ Q3
♦ 8753
♣ 1098

This is perfect for Stayman. If your partner bids 2 ♥, you will bid 2 ♠, showing four spades and enough to invite game. If your partner bids 2 ♦, you will show your invitational values by bidding 2NT.

♠ K4
♥ 106
♦ Q54
♣ AK5432

Unfortunately, you can't bid 2 ♣ —that would ask your partner to bid a four-card major. You have 12 HCP, plenty enough for game. Just bid 3NT. If you were thinking a better contract would be 5 ♣, you aren't far off. Those two wimpy hearts could be a problem, but in the long run you will be better off just blasting into 3NT.

Basically, if you want to use Stayman, you should have at least one four-card major and enough to invite game. If your hand is especially "square" (balanced), you usually won't use Stayman even if you have a four-card major. The following hand is an example.

♠ A1075
♥ A87
♦ 654
♣ K97

You have the flattest hand you could have, with no opportunity to ruff anything in your hand, which will be dummy if you use Stayman and find your partner with four spades. You have 11 HCP, meaning you and partner have at least 26 HCP together—enough for game. Just bid 3NT.

Stayman can also be used when the opening bid is 2NT. Instead of 2 ♣, the Stayman bid is 3 ♣. The responses are the same: 3 ♦ indicates no four-card major, while 3 ♥ and 3 ♠ show those suits.

Trash Stayman

Earlier in this chapter, you read about an exception to the rule that when your partner opens 1NT you must have at least 8 HCP to use Stayman.

The exception occurs when you have a weak hand with shortness in clubs. Look at the following hand.

♠ 10654
♥ Q765
♦ J975
♣ 2

Your partner has opened 1NT. This doesn't look good. Your hand is so weak that the opponents are probably going to pick your partner apart, especially if they have strength in clubs. This could be ugly, but what can you do?

You can bid Stayman—known in this case as "Trash Stayman" because your hand is so trashy. Your partner is restricted to 2 ♦, 2 ♥, and 2 ♠. So, whatever your partner says, even 2 ♦, which doesn't say she has diamonds, you are going to pass.

This has to be the right strategy, allowing your partner the luxury of ruffing some losing clubs in your hand, which might otherwise be completely useless. It's true, your partner might have only two diamonds, but that's unlikely. Even so, he will still be able to use your diamonds for ruffing clubs.

Blackwood

There is no doubt that the most popular convention in the world is Blackwood, the conventional bid used to discover how many aces the partnership has between the two hands. Here's how Blackwood works. During the auction, if one player bids 4NT—often by jumping to that level—it almost always asks the partner to tell how many aces she has.

When your partner bids 4NT, your obligation is to look at your hand and report on the number of aces you see. You tell your story by the bids you make.

5 ♣ = zero or four aces
5 ♦ = one ace
5 ♥ = two aces
5 ♠ = three aces

As a follow-up, 5NT asks your partner to reveal all about the kings in his hand.

6 ♣ = zero or four kings
6 ♦ = one king
6 ♥ = two kings
6 ♠ = three kings

Don't worry about the 5 ♣ and 6 ♣ responses causing confusion. Your partner will know when it's zero and when it's four (almost never).

What kind of hand should you have to use Blackwood? Well, here's a good general rule about the use of this convention: It's better used as a preventive. In other words, Blackwood comes in handiest when it helps you avoid bidding slam when the opponents have two cashing aces.

Here's an example hand:

♠ Q8762
♥ A10
♦ AK987
♣ K

You open 1 ♠, the next person passes, and your partner bids 3 ♠, showing four-card support and enough strength for game. What's your next move?

This is a good case for Blackwood. You can easily envision taking lots of tricks with this hand, but if you simply blast into 6 ♠, your partner might put down this hand.

♠ KJ103
♥ KQJ
♦ QJ10
♣ Q103

Your partner sure has her bid, but the opponents have two aces.

The way to keep that from happening is to bid 4NT over your partner's 3 ♠. If your partner shows no aces, you will sign off in 5 ♠. If your partner shows one, you might take a chance that he also has the king of your trump suit and give slam a shot. It might depend on a finesse, but that's a 50 percent proposition. Lots of slams with lower prospects have been bid. It pays to be optimistic, as long as you don't overdo it.

Do not ask for aces with the Blackwood convention unless all side suits have at most one loser. You may have a singleton, the king or the ace, any of which will prevent the opponents from cashing two quick tricks.

Intermediate Conventions

Stayman and Blackwood barely touch the surface of the gamut of conventions available for those with open minds and a desire for improvement. Of course, many of the bidding conventions created over the years are somewhat useless, even inane, such as the convention known, for a very good reason, as Byzantine Blackwood. Just trying to remember all the rules involved in this convention would give you a headache.

Transfers

When your partner opens 1NT or 2NT, most of the time her hand will be stronger than yours. That's not a big news flash if your partner's 1NT shows 15–17 and 2NT shows 20–21. The point is covered in that old defensive maxim: Lead *up to* weakness and *through* strength. When the dummy is on your right, you lead the suit in which dummy is weak, hoping to promote some high cards in that suit in your partner's hand. When the dummy is on your left, you often play the suit in which dummy has strength, again hoping this will be advantageous for your partner.

By the use of transfers, you can force the opponents to "lead up to strength" in your partner's hand, usually not to their advantage. Here is a complete deal to illustrate the point.

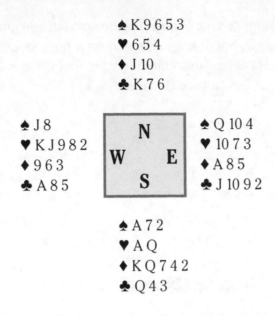

```
              ♠ K 9 6 5 3
              ♥ 6 5 4
              ♦ J 10
              ♣ K 7 6

  ♠ J 8                     ♠ Q 10 4
  ♥ K J 9 8 2       N       ♥ 10 7 3
  ♦ 9 6 3       W       E   ♦ A 8 5
  ♣ A 8 5           S       ♣ J 10 9 2

              ♠ A 7 2
              ♥ A Q
              ♦ K Q 7 4 2
              ♣ Q 4 3
```

The contract is 4 ♠. Do you see what a difference it makes if South can be declarer instead of North? If North is declarer, she will certainly get the lead of the ♣ J from that good sequence East holds. The declarer's queen will be trapped, and no matter what the declarer does, the defenders will subsequently take two club tricks, the ♦ A and one spade. That's down one.

Now look at it with South as declarer. West is in a bind. If he leads a heart, it's right into the declarer's A–Q. If he leads a club, the declarer will play low and make his queen. If West leads a diamond, it helps the declarer set up his long suit, and a neutral spade lead gives the declarer the timing to set up his diamond winners and get rid of losers from the dummy.

The declarer is obliged to bid whatever suit the responder is transferring to, making him declarer. Therefore, in nearly all cases, the strong hand will be led up to rather than through. This will keep the declarer's high cards from being picked off on the opening lead.

This type of advantage for the declarer is demonstrated over and over because of a convention most modern players use—the transfer bid.

Here's how it works. When the opener starts with 1NT and the responder has at least five cards in a major suit, she "transfers" the bid of that suit to the opener by bidding the suit directly "under" the suit she possesses. In other words, with spades, she bids 2 ♥ and with hearts she bids 2 ♦.

Versatile Transfers

Besides protecting the declarer's high cards, the transfer structure also allows for invitational bids not available without them. Without transfers, the invitational hand with a five-card major is very difficult. Simply bidding the suit at the two level is a signoff—your partner is not invited to bid again. Jumping to three of the major shows a hand good enough to be in game. There is no bid for the hand in between.

Using transfers, there is an excellent system for handling all the variations. Here it is:

After partner opens 1NT
Five or more hearts or spades and 0–7 HCP: Transfer to the major and pass.
Exactly five hearts or spades and 8–9 HCP: Transfer to the major and bid 2NT.
Six or more hearts or spades and 8–9 HCP: Transfer to the major and raise the major.
Exactly five hearts or spades and 10+ HCP: Transfer to the major and bid 3NT.
Six or more hearts or spades and 10+ HCP: Transfer to the major and raise to game in the major.

Note that when the responder bids 2NT or 3NT, the opener is free to pass without a fit (three or more cards) for the responder's major. Over a 2NT invitation, 3 ♠ by the opener shows a spade fit but not a maximum hand. Over 3NT, the opener may pass with no fit or bid game in the major.

Note also that when the responder has at least six of a major, she knows her side has at least eight of that major between them, so she is safe in not giving the opener a choice between no-trump and the major.

Minor-Suit Transfers

When you have a weak hand with a long minor after your partner opens 1NT, it's best to get to a suit contract right away. When you have a long minor and strength, you are usually going to play 3NT rather than five of a minor.

If you are using a transfer bid of 2 ♥ to show spades, then the 2 ♠ bid is not being used. Therefore, it is available for a better use.

Remember to discuss this with your partner before attempting to play it. This is the deal: When your partner opens 1NT, use the idle bid of 2 ♠ to tell partner to bid 3 ♣. You are either going to pass, holding club length, or you are going to bid 3 ♦, a signoff or "drop-dead" bid. In bridge lingo, a drop-dead bid means you most definitely do not want to hear anything more from your partner. And don't forget, when your partner opens 1NT, you are the captain. You know your hand is weak, so you know it's right to stop the auction in the lowest comfortable place.

Negative Doubles

You have been taught so far that when you double, it's serious business. In fact, a penalty double is often referred to among bridge players as a "business" double.

There's a lot more to "double" than penalty, however, and one of the most widely used conventions in the world is the so-called "negative double." The negative double, basically a takeout double, was created to solve the following problem.

Say your partner opens 1 ♣ and your right-hand opponent intervenes with a bid of 1 ♠. You have a real problem with this hand if you don't play negative doubles.

♠ 763
♥ QJ87
♦ KJ54
♣ 108

You have 7 HCP and you want to bid, but what can you say? You can't bid 1NT—no stopper in spades. You can't raise clubs—you have only two. If you bid 2 ♦ or 2 ♥ you are showing 10–11 HCP and a five-card suit. Time to try to play negative doubles.

A double in this situation would say you have support for the unbid suits and enough to respond to your partner's opener. A negative double doesn't promise a lot of HCP as would a regular takeout double of an opponent's opening bid. The negative double says only that you want to compete and you want your partner to make an intelligent bid based on the auction. Of course, a negative double doesn't preclude a big hand, but you don't promise more than about 6 HCP.

Naturally, the higher the bidding the more you should have to make a negative double. If your partner will be forced to bid at the three level, you need more than 6 or 7 HCP to get into the fray.

Besides being able to show the unbid suits, the negative double also allows you to get in there and bid your own suit even if you don't have enough high cards to do so immediately. Take this next hand for example:

♠ 654
♥ AQ1076
♦ Q98
♣ 87

Your partner opens 1 ♣ and the next player is right there with 1 ♠. You were getting ready to show your heart suit, but now you would have to bid 2 ♥. That's a no-no because it would show at least 10–11 HCP, and you don't have that much. No matter how much you are tempted to, don't fudge in this situation and bid 2 ♥ anyway. If your partner learns that she can't rely on your bids, there will be trouble.

This seems like another insoluble problem, but it's not. Using the negative double, you simply double 1 ♠, and if your partner bids 1NT, 2 ♣, or 2 ♦, you will bid 2 ♥. This tells your partner that you wanted to bid hearts the first time around because you have at least five of them but you couldn't because you were short on HCP.

When an opponent overcalls in a major after your partner opens one of a minor, a negative double by you nearly always shows the other major. If you don't have the other major, you will have a long suit you would have bid directly but for lack of sufficient high-card strength.

If your partner opens 1 ♣ or 1 ♦ and the next player bids 1 ♥, a bid of 1 ♠ by you shows five or more spades. With only four spades, you will make a negative double. Your partner will go out of her way to bid spades if she has four of them.

How High?

If you and your partner agree to play negative doubles, you must decide how high you want to go with them. That is, at what point does the double become penalty rather than takeout? On the Standard American Yellow Card, negative doubles are marked to be played "through 2 ♠." What this means is that if your partner opens and the next player bids something up to and including 2 ♠, a double by you is for takeout.

If the overcaller bids higher than 2 ♠, a double by you says a mistake has been made and you are hoping to capitalize on it by bringing in a large number. Many tournament players go higher; you and your partner should decide your own comfort level. In your early stages of bridge development, 2 ♠ is probably high enough.

You may be concerned that if you are playing negative doubles and an opponent makes a bid you know you will massacre, you now have no way to penalize the foolhardy opponent. Not true. You simply pass, and your partner will take care of you by doubling. How does he know to do this? Because he will generally be short in the overcaller's suit, which is his clue to give you a chance to get back into penalty position. If your partner doubles, ostensibly for takeout, and if you have the hand where you wanted to double for penalty right away, you simply pass—converting your partner's takeout to penalty.

Michaels Cuebid

The Michaels Cuebid, introduced in Chapter 6, is a handy weapon with which most tournament players are familiar. It is the creation of the late Mike Michaels, a Florida player and writer who could see that the traditional use for the direct cuebid—to show a powerful hand—came up too rarely to be effective.

ALERT!

A cuebid is a bid in a suit in which the bidder cannot wish to play. If your opponent opens 1 ♥ and you bid hearts at any time during the auction, it cannot indicate that you wish to play in hearts. In that sense, it is "forcing"—your partner is not allowed to pass. Cuebids may also be used at high levels to show aces. A cuebid is never an offer to play in the suit that is named.

As explained earlier, the bid of opener's suit is not meant to be natural, especially if the opening bid was a major suit. If the opener starts with one of a minor, a bid of the same minor shows at least five cards in each of the majors. If the opening bid was a major, a bid of that major shows at least five cards in the other major and an unspecified five-card minor.

The Michaels cuebid is fun to use because it is so descriptive, but resist the temptation to use it just because you have the correct distribution.

♠ J8654
♥ 105432
♦ KJ
♣ Q

This is not a good example of a Michaels cuebid of one of a minor. Most of your honor strength is in short suits. It would be much better to transfer those minor honors to your majors. Give this one a miss and pass quietly.

You must always, of course, be mindful of the vulnerability, particularly if you are using the Michaels cuebid after the opener started with a major. Remember, your partner is going to have to bid at the three level every time unless the bidding goes 1 ♥–2 ♥ and your partner has three or more spades. In all other cases, she will have to bid at the three level. If your hand looks more like what is known in some circles as a "piece of cheese," you don't want to put it down in the dummy and have your partner struggle to take tricks.

♠ 6
♥ QJ1097
♦ AJ954
♣ K9

This is a reasonable Michaels cuebid of 2 ♠ if the opener starts with 1 ♠. You have some decent spots in your long suits, so there is a measure of safety. Be prepared, however, for some calamities when your partner's hand is a terrible misfit for yours. You have no guarantees, of course, that your partner will have a fit for one of your suits, but it's certainly better to show your 5–5 hand than to overcall 2 ♥.

Do not use the Michaels cuebid unless you have two five-card suits. It is very important for your partner to be able to count on you to deliver what your bid promises. Making a Michaels cuebid with 5–4 in two suits is asking for a lot of trouble—and you will probably get it in the form of a double by one of the opponents.

Use Michaels primarily with modest hands in the 6–10 point range and with hands so good you simply want your partner to select a suit so that you can make a strong invitation to game or a direct game bid. With an intermediate hand, simply overcall in your higher-ranking suit, planning to bid the other suit (if necessary and/or practical) later.

Jump Overcalls

You have read a lot about the value of pre-emption. Here's a tip: It's not just for openers.

When you have a long suit and a weak hand, it can pay dividends to get in there and mess up your opponents' auctions.

♠ AJ87543
♥ 5
♦ Q76
♣ 93

The dealer opens 1 ♣ and you are next to speak. Do you feel a stirring in your soul—a desire to say something? If so, you're becoming a dangerous opponent. What you want to do with that hand is to bid 3 ♠. That doesn't show a great hand just because you went to the three level. You have just shown a poor hand with a long spade suit and you have made it much more difficult for the opponents to reach the correct spot. If the next player bids, it will have to be at the four level.

If your hand were slightly different, say with the ♦ A instead of the ♣ 3, you would bid 1 ♠, a constructive action. If your partner managed a raise, you might make a try for game. The point is that when you jump to 3 ♠ directly, you're telling your partner you don't have much but you want to use up some bidding space.

All jump overcalls are weak, showing long suits with no defensive tricks in other suits.

Advanced Conventions

The more you play the more you will see of the world of conventions. There will be some you don't recognize, some you don't like, but many you do. The language of bidding is intricate. Nuances abound. Sometimes you will gain information from what is not bid, just as Sherlock Holmes solved a case from the failure of a dog to bark in the night. Study the conventions so you are prepared for what comes along.

The Unusual No-trump

You have learned so far that no-trump bids show strength and a balanced pattern. There are times when the language of bidding will turn that concept on its head. To wit: the unusual no-trump. It's called unusual because the normal meaning of a no-trump bid is so different from what you have when you bid "unusually."

When an opponent opens the bidding and you chime in with a bid of 2NT, you are sending your partner a special message. Depending on the opening, you are telling your partner that you have a distributional two-suited hand with the two *lowest* unbid suits.

If the opening bid is one of a major, 2NT shows at least 5–5 in the minors and about 6–10 HCP.

If the opening bid is 1 ♣, 2NT shows diamonds and hearts, 6–10 HCP.

If the opening bid is 1 ♦, 2NT shows clubs and hearts, 6–10 HCP.

This is another descriptive bid, meant to help your side find a good fit while taking up bidding space from the opponents. If you are a passed hand, you don't need to go to the two level to express your distribution.

West	North	East	South
			Pass
1 ♥	Pass	1 ♠	1NT

This shows the minor suits, at least 5–5. This is logical because you can't have 15–17 HCP. You are a passed hand.

The unusual 2NT is like the Michaels cuebid except that your partner will always have to bid at the three level, so be careful not to use this convention with two lousy suits. It's best if your high-card strength is in your long suits. Be especially careful when you are vulnerable. Those penalty points mount up.

Defenses to 1NT

When an opponent opens 1NT, his side has a tremendous advantage. The partner of the 1NT opener knows right away how many HCP the partnership holds—within 3 HCP, anyway—and that the opener has at least two cards in each suit. This can be extremely helpful knowledge if the bidding heats up. What can you do to turn a bit of the advantage to your side?

When an opponent opens 1NT, you will frequently have a shortage of weapons. There's a very good chance the opposition will have more than half the HCP in the deck, sometimes substantially more.

Your best chance for fighting against that strength is to rely on a big trump fit. If you have a great fit with your partner in some suit and shortness in one or both hands, you can fight against their strength very effectively.

So how do you find out about a potential trump fit with your partner?

There are an endless number of conventions designed to combat the advantage gained by the other side when they open 1NT. Most of them revolve around methods to show single suits of at least six cards—and two-suited hands.

D.O.N.T.

One of the most popular conventions for combating the 1NT opener is called D.O.N.T., for **D**isturb **O**pponents' **N**o-**T**rump. It was devised by Marty Bergen, a ten-time national champion and a very creative bidder. Although retired from the tournament scene, he is a prolific author and a busy teacher in Florida.

The appeal of D.O.N.T. for many players is its simplicity and the opportunities it gives you to get into the auction. Don't be afraid to bid just because your right-hand opponent opened 1NT. If you have "shape"—a couple of long suits and some shortness—you and a partner can still compete.

Here's how D.O.N.T. works:

Double = a hand with a six-card or longer suit, usually not spades
2 ♣ = clubs and a higher-ranking suit
2 ♦ = diamonds and a major
2 ♥ = hearts and spades
2 ♠ = at least six spades

If your partner doubles to show one suit, your duty is to find out what that suit is. The way to do that is to bid 2 ♣. That doesn't mean you like clubs. It's just the cheapest bid at your disposal. If your partner's long suit is clubs, she will pass. Otherwise, she will bid her long suit and you will usually pass. When one of the opponents opens 1NT, you won't be making game very often, so just take it easy. Even if you like your partner's suit, just be happy that you found a fit. Simply say "pass."

If your partner makes a bid showing two suits, and you have at least three cards in the suit that your partner bids, pass. If you have two or fewer cards, simply bid the next suit up to tell your partner to try again. If your partner bids 2 ♣ and you have a poor holding in that suit, bid 2 ♦. That doesn't say you have lots of diamonds, it just says that you probably like your partner's other suit better than clubs. If your partner's other suit is diamonds, she will pass. If not, she'll bid her other suit.

If your partner bids 2 ♦ and you don't like that suit, bid 2 ♥. If your partner's second suit is hearts, she will pass. If not, she will bid 2 ♠.

Here are some hands to test your savvy at D.O.N.T.

♠ 98
♥ AJ1095
♦ A10762
♣ 5

This is perfect for a bid of 2 ♦, showing diamonds and a major.

♠ Q5
♥ J1042
♦ J9874
♣ 105

Don't bother. You have only nine cards in your two suits, neither of which is worth mentioning.

There will be times when you have really outstanding "shape"—such as six of one suit and five of another. If you're lucky enough to find yourself in that situation, you will need fewer high-card points than you would if you were bidding with only nine cards in your two long suits. As a famous tournament player once said, "With six-five, come alive!" That means just one thing—bid!

CHAPTER 16

Take Your Tricks

There's a saying in bridge that in some cases, you must settle for the best result possible rather than the best possible result. That means that sometimes, thanks to those meddlesome opponents, you won't be able to get to the ideal contract. You'll have to settle for the best contract you can manage under the circumstances. At any rate, while good bidding is the essence of successful bridge, it profits you little if your skill at taking tricks is less than it should be.

Second-Hand Play

Bridge players tend to put things into aphorisms with singsong lilts, making them easy to remember. One of the most well known is "eight ever, nine never." This is in reference to a nine-card holding in a suit missing the queen. To wit:

DUMMY

♠ AJ43

DECLARER

♠ K765

If you need four tricks from this suit, your best percentage play in most cases is to play the king and then low from your hand, putting in the jack if West plays low. Add another card to the mix and the situation changes.

DUMMY

♠ AJ43

DECLARER

♠ K8765

Now, conventional wisdom is that you should play the king, then low to the *ace* in a manner that is known in bridge vernacular as "playing for the drop." In other words, you are counting on West to play the queen on the second round of the suit—or for East to "drop" the queen when you play the ace from the dummy. This gives you about a 53 percent chance of success.

That is the origin of "eight ever"—always finesse when you have eight cards—and "nine never"—don't finesse when you have nine. Play your top cards and watch the queen "drop."

FACT

There is a common situation when the queen of a suit is missing and it must be "picked up" or found—it's called a two-way finesse. Such a situation exists when the two hands possess at least the ace, king, jack, and 10, divided in some way between the two hands: for example, AJ7 opposite K104. The declarer may finesse either of his opponents for the queen. The two-way finesse can also be referred to as a "two-way guess."

It's okay to adhere to "eight-ever, nine-never" early on in your bridge development. Just be aware that you will eventually learn to rely on yourself to spot clues to the correct plays rather than depending on a rigid formula.

Go Low

Another ditty is "second-hand low, third-hand high." This works best when you are starting out and need some handy, easy-to-remember reminders of what to do.

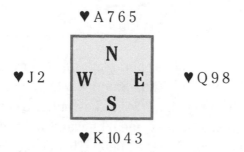

♥ A 7 6 5

♥ J 2   ♥ Q 9 8

♥ K 10 4 3

Look at this suit. South is on play and leads the 3 from hand. You are West and must play next. You are "second hand." It probably would never occur to you to play the jack—and that's good. There is no reason for you to play the jack and every reason to play the 2.

Look what happens if you play the jack. The declarer covers with the ace in dummy and all of a sudden has no losers in the suit. Why? Because she can play her next heart from the dummy, and when your partner plays the 9, cover with the 10. You will have to follow helplessly with the 2. The king will capture your partner's queen and the declarer will thank you for your generosity.

If you play the 2, the declarer can put up the ace in the dummy and play another one, but if she puts in the 10, you will win your jack. If South plays the king, it will capture your jack, but your partner's queen will then be high.

When playing second to a trick, it is seldom correct to play an honor when it is "unsupported"—that is, not backed by a touching honor—unless it is the only card in the suit you possess. For example, playing the jack from J4 or the queen from Q4 when the declarer leads to a suit with a higher honor might allow the declarer to finesse against any honors your partner might hold.

Play from Equals

Let's take a break from second-hand low for a second to discuss the cards you play from "equals." Equals? What does that mean? Well, let's look at a suit, spades for example:

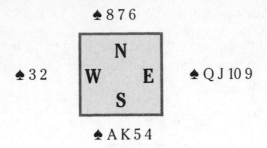

Say South is the declarer and plays the ♠ 6 from the dummy. You are East here. If you play the 9 and South wants to win the trick, he will have to play the ace or king, right? South has only two cards higher than the 9 in his hand, so he has to play one if he wants the trick. Can you see, therefore, that the 9 is "equal" to the queen. The 9 will force the ace or king just as well as the queen would. Let's let South trade the ♠ 4 for the ♠ 9. Now which card must East play to force a high card from South's hand? Right, the 10. Still, the 10 is equal to the queen.

Why is this important to know? Well, here's another general rule about playing your cards: You almost always play low from equals. That is, you play the lowest card in a sequence such as in the example. What difference does it make? A lot, as you shall see.

Important Information

Say you are on defense against a no-trump contract, and your partner has led the ♦ 4 (you remember—fourth from your longest and strongest, another aphorism).

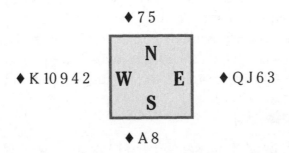

You are East and can see your partner's ♦ 4 on the table (your partner is the dummy). The 5 is played from the dummy and now it's your turn. You are going to play one of your face cards. Does it matter which one you play? It matters very much.

If you play the jack and South wins the ace, it sends a very clear message to your partner—that you have the queen. How? Think about it. If South had the ace and queen, why would he win the ace when the queen would do? Of course, he wouldn't. So when the jack drives out the ace, West can draw only one conclusion—South doesn't have the queen. West can't see it in his hand or in dummy, so it must be in your hand.

West now knows that your side can take a lot of tricks in diamonds if he can just get in. Is it really that bad if you play the queen? You bet it is. If you play the queen, you are denying the jack. West will therefore think the declarer started with something like AJ8 instead of the A8 he actually has. West might get in and, fearful of giving South a trick with the jack by playing the king, go messing around trying to get you in the lead so you can play a diamond back.

Splitting Honors

Now that you know about playing the lowest card from equals, you are ready for some exceptions to the second-hand low rule. In the following sequences, you are West.

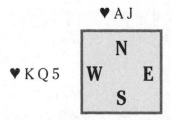

♥ A J

♥ K Q 5

N W E S

Declarer is on lead (playing South) and plays the ♥ 6. It's your turn. Now what? If you have "second-hand low" going through your head, you might play the 5, giving the declarer a chance to make a trick where none was available. You must be alert and put the ♥ Q out there, forcing the ace from dummy. Later, your king will capture the jack. This is known as "splitting" your honors, playing the lowest in sequence to force out a higher card.

Don't forget that you must play the queen. If you play the king, your partner may think the declarer has the queen, and there could be an accident.

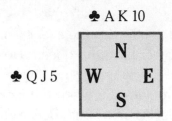

♣ A K 10

♣ Q J 5

This is a tricky situation. If the declarer can easily get back to her hand, you may give the show away if you play the jack. The declarer won't have a difficult time figuring out why you played the jack. If she can get back to her hand, she will be able to play low to the 10 the next time clubs are led. If this situation is near the end of the play, however, and the declarer is known not to have any way back to her hand, you must play the jack or the declarer can get away with no losers in the suit by putting in the 10.

Don't Duck the Setting Trick

Do not duck the setting trick. What does that mean? Well, here's an example:

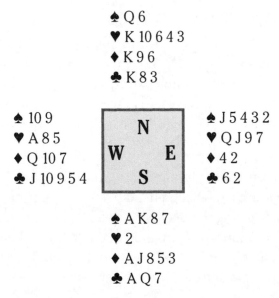

♠ Q 6
♥ K 10 6 4 3
♦ K 9 6
♣ K 8 3

♠ 10 9
♥ A 8 5
♦ Q 10 7
♣ J 10 9 5 4

♠ J 5 4 3 2
♥ Q J 9 7
♦ 4 2
♣ 6 2

♠ A K 8 7
♥ 2
♦ A J 8 5 3
♣ A Q 7

You hold the West hand. The opponents, for better or worse, have arrived in 6 ♦. If you look at all four hands, you will say that the diamond slam is not such a good one, but over the years bridge players have bid literally millions of slams with worse prospects—and many of them have come home because of inattention by the defenders.

Say you lead the ♣ J against the slam and dummy comes down. The declarer wins with the ♣ A. Let's just look at those two hands while you contemplate the situation.

These are the cards that are left.

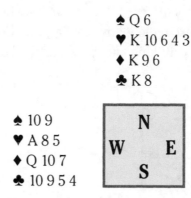

           ♠ Q 6
           ♥ K 10 6 4 3
           ♦ K 9 6
           ♣ K 8

♠ 10 9
♥ A 8 5
♦ Q 10 7
♣ 10 9 5 4

If you're living up to your potential as a bridge player, you will have noticed that the declarer has at least one loser in the diamond suit. Since it's the trump suit, this is an unavoidable loser.

If the declarer plays the king from dummy and then another one to the jack, you will win your queen. If the declarer leads a low diamond from his hand toward the K9 in the dummy, you will be smart enough to play the 10, forcing the king and assuring you of a winner in the diamond suit.

It's your turn to play. Don't even think about second-hand low. That ♥ A sitting in your hand is the setting trick. If you play that card right now, the declarer will go down because of the unavoidable loser in diamonds. If you play low, what do you think the declarer will do? He's going to put up the king and come waltzing home with that slam that he wasn't supposed to make. Don't let that happen.

Third-Hand Play

It's a common fault of new players to be offended when their partner leads a suit in which they have a single honor. For example, the contract is 3NT and the partner leads a low card in a suit in which the third hand has K432. The dummy has only a couple of low cards. Now third hand is annoyed that her king is getting picked off. It's not uncommon to see the player in third seat play a low card, holding on to that king for dear life. That's just wrong.

When your partner makes her opening lead, you should be pleased that you have something to contribute to the cause of the defense. Suppose all you had was the 5432 instead of the K432? Won't that king help your partner's hand if you play it? You are East in the following diagram. Consider the effect of playing low versus playing your king after your partner leads the suit.

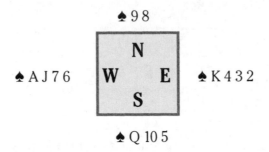

♠ 9 8

W ♠ A J 7 6   E ♠ K 4 3 2

♠ Q 10 5

Your partner leads the ♠ 6 against 3NT. If you get stingy with that king, the declarer will win a trick he isn't entitled to. If you play the king, not only will it win but you will still be on lead to play another spade through the declarer's Q10 to your partner's AJ. You will take four spade tricks.

In general, it's best to play the highest card in the suit your partner leads—remembering that when holding a sequence of cards your proper play is the lowest of "equals."

When Not to Play High

Before you start becoming annoyed about all the exceptions to all these rules, remember that experience and common sense will help you work out most of them. These seemingly complicated ideas will become second nature to you.

Your partner leads the ♦ 6 against 3NT. Dummy comes down and it's your turn to play:

♠ Q 5 4

♠ K 10 8

We've learned about third-hand high, so your correct play is the king, right? Not quite. Let's think about what your partner has led from and what the declarer might hold. Using the Rule of Eleven, which you learned earlier in this book, you know that there are five cards higher than the ♦ 6 outside your partner's hand. Dummy has one—the queen—and you have three: the king, 10, and 8. That's four. Therefore the declarer has one card higher than the 6. What is that card? Does it matter? . . .Yep, it does.

Say your partner has led from four spades to the jack. That means the declarer has the ace—but it's the only card higher than the 6 in her hand. If you play the 10—the proper card in this case—it will drive out the ace. You will be poised later over the queen in the dummy to assure that her highness takes no trick. You don't want to play the 8 because if your partner has led from the AJ, the declarer might make a trick with the 9. That would be embarrassing!

If you simply recite, "Second hand low, third hand high," and make that your mantra, you will play the king, and the declarer will be able to take two tricks in the suit.

Suppose your partner's opening lead was from the AJ. If you put in the 10, it will hold. Then you can play the king and another spade to your partner's ace and you will take four tricks in the suit.

If your partner's lead was from AJ and you play the king, your king will win, but when you play the suit back, your partner will have to play his ace in front of the dummy's queen, and the queen will turn into a trick.

Opening Leads

The fact that defenders have the first shot is an advantage to them, a good thing—at least from the defenders' point of view—since the declarer has the advantage of being able to see all the assets between his hand and the dummy. He knows what he has to work with and will take care to hide key assets when he can to keep the defenders in the dark.

Defenders, of course, can also see the dummy, but in general they are not as aware of their combined strengths as the declarer is of his.

As a defender, you have a target of the number of tricks you are trying to take. If the declarer is in a game contract in a major, he must take 10 tricks. Your goal as a defender is to get four tricks, leaving him at least one short.

If the contract is 3 ♦, you and your partner must do your best to take five tricks. It pays to keep your goal in mind at all times. In a sense, it's a race. In 3 ♦, for example, the declarer is trying to get nine tricks before you and your partner get five. First one to his or her goal is the winner.

When to Be Aggressive

In general, it's best to be aggressive on opening lead because in the race we just talked about, there is a key element called "tempo." In many contracts, the declarer will have to work to establish tricks to cover for some weak spots she might have. Here's a simple example.

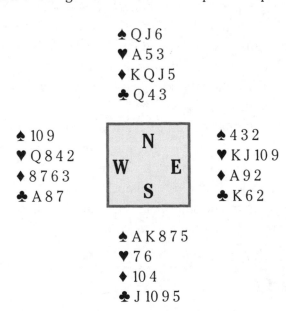

```
                    ♠ Q J 6
                    ♥ A 5 3
                    ♦ K Q J 5
                    ♣ Q 4 3

  ♠ 10 9                              ♠ 4 3 2
  ♥ Q 8 4 2         N                ♥ K J 10 9
  ♦ 8 7 6 3      W     E             ♦ A 9 2
  ♣ A 8 7           S                ♣ K 6 2

                    ♠ A K 8 7 5
                    ♥ 7 6
                    ♦ 10 4
                    ♣ J 10 9 5
```

The declarer, South, reaches 4 ♠, making West (you) the opening leader. With that West hand, the opening lead possibilities run the gamut from super-aggressive to totally passive. Let's look at the possibilities.

You could lead a spade—that's passive. Passive leads are meant to avoid giving up tricks. A passive lead is usually from a suit containing no honor cards. A passive lead may also be a trump, since the declaring side usually has most of the strength in that suit. Passive leads can be effective on occasion, but as a regular diet they will leave the defenders starving for tricks.

Hold On to Your Aces

You could lead a diamond but that's also passive. So how about the ♣ A? That's super-aggressive, not usually warranted or very effective. It's rarely correct to go banging down your aces. Do you think the opponents will voluntarily play their high cards under your aces when you just slap them on the table at trick one? They won't.

On this deal, that leaves you with a heart lead, a moderately aggressive lead aimed at promoting some tricks for the defense. It's true, you could give up a trick if the declarer has the ♥ AKJ, but it's an acceptable risk if the upside is defeating the contract.

Look what happens when you lead a heart. The declarer is, in the language of bridge, "a tempo behind." If you had led a spade or a diamond, the declarer would have "time" to draw trumps and knock out the ♦ A, giving her three winners in the suit. On one of those winners, she would be able to throw away that losing heart in her hand.

The only thing left for the declarer to do then would be to establish her club tricks and score up her game. If you lead a heart, however, you have pierced the declarer's armor on the opening shot. You have established a heart trick for your side with the opening lead. Say the declarer wins the ♥ A at trick one and pulls trumps. When she plays on diamonds, your partner will win the ace, cash the ♥ K. That's two tricks in the bank with two club tricks to come.

When Passive Is Best

You will find that in the long run, it's better to lead "from something" than "from nothing." That means that it's better to lead away from strength than from weakness. For one thing, if you have led from a poor holding and your partner gets in a couple of times during the defense, she will be very frustrated if she wastes time leading back your suit in hopes of promoting a trick or two when in fact there was never a chance of that at all.

ALERT!

It's good to be aggressive on opening lead, but remember that it's almost always a poor idea to lead an ace without the king unless your partner has bid the suit at some point in the auction—and you never, ever lead low from an ace against a suit contract, even in your partner's suit.

Remember, when you have a sequence such as QJ10, it's not considered aggressive to lead that suit—it's normal. It's when you have an honor holding that isn't supported by touching cards that it's considered aggressive to lead that suit, such as Q1054 or KJ63.

Having said all that, there are definitely times when it pays to go passive. The most common situation is when your partner is known to have a poor hand, perhaps even no high-card points at all.

Say you are looking at the following:

♠ K6
♥ AJ109
♦ AJ43
♣ 987

You are West and you hear the following auction:

West	North	East	South
			2NT
Pass	3NT	All Pass	

South's 2NT bid announces 20–21 HCP and a balanced hand. North will have at least 6 HCP to raise to game. That means that North and South between them have 26 HCP. Look at your hand. You have 13 HCP.

There are only 40 HCP in the deck, and you know where at least 39 of them are, so your partner has at most one jack. That's not going to be any help at all for you.

Normally that heart suit would be ideal for the opening lead—leading the jack from a holding of AJ109 would be considered perfectly normal—but on this bidding, it's too likely to give away a trick. With all the defensive HCP in your hand, the declarer may have a tough time bringing in nine tricks. If you make an aggressive lead here, you supply her with a potentially crucial trick.

Another time when conventional wisdom tells you to take care at opening lead is when the opponents have bid a grand slam. You need only one trick to defeat this contract, and sometimes the declarer will need only one trick to fulfill hers, so if you give away a trick on opening lead you may be surrendering trick number thirteen right off the bat.

For instance, if you lead a low card from a suit such as J654, you might well be leading into the declarer's AKQ10, or perhaps the declarer will have the AKQ2 in hand and the 1098 in dummy. If the declarer needs that extra trick you have just given away, you'll have a major headache.

Leading from a queen is no better. You might be taking away a guess for the declarer if she needs an extra trick in that suit—and it's unlikely if the opponents have gotten that high in the bidding that your side has substantial assets anyway.

Of course, if you have some sequence to lead from—such as J1098—it's a different matter, but leave the aggressive leads for another time.

Listening to the Auction

The language of bidding is meant to convey information. That's how partners find out their best contract and how high they should go in the auction. At the same time, the opponents are listening—or they should be—and they are privy to the same information. On many occasions, they can use that information to ferret out the best opening lead, best for you meaning the most damaging to the declarer.

One of the most common ways that "listening to the auction" can help you is when the declarer has bid two suits and his partner has preferred the first one. Here's an example:

West	North	East	South
			1 ♠
Pass	1NT	Pass	2 ♥
Pass	2 ♠	All Pass	

Suppose this is your hand:

♠ 43
♥ KJ109
♦ J1098
♣ K54

Normally, that ♦ J stands out as the opening lead because you have such a good sequence. You dream of finding the king in dummy and your partner with the ace and queen. You might start off with the first three tricks.

Cut Down the Ruffs

That heart suit is also tough looking, and your right-hand opponent, the declarer, has announced that she has at least four of them. You have the declarer's suit under control for sure, but let's look at what you know about the dummy.

For starters, North (the dummy) bid 1NT after his partner opened 1 ♠. That means the dummy probably has no more than two spades. If he had more, he would have raised spades. When South showed her second suit, the dummy went back to the first one. There's a good chance the dummy will have a doubleton heart to go with the doubleton spade. The dummy's hand could easily be:

♠ J5
♥ 86
♦ AK432
♣ 8752

If you start with the ♦ J, the declarer will win with the ace and play a heart to the ace and another heart. If you don't play a trump right away, there's a good chance the declarer will get to ruff both of her heart losers in dummy.

Do you see where this is going? You have strength in the declarer's second suit and you have a means of keeping her from getting rid of those losers by ruffing them. If you start with a trump, you can win the second round of hearts and play another trump, eliminating spades from the dummy and keeping the declarer from using them to ruff hearts. This might or might not defeat the contract, but it will certainly save at least one trick.

Attack Small Slams

You were told earlier that when the opponents bid a grand slam, that is one occasion that usually calls for a passive lead if you don't have a sequence such as KQJ or QJ10.

The philosophy of leading against small slams is the exact opposite. The reason: Many small slams are bid because of the likelihood that a long side suit in one of the hands will produce a lot of tricks. When the side suit is not headed by all three top honors (AKQ), it is often necessary to develop that suit by knocking out a high card held by the defenders.

Even if you have an ace and the opponents have bid to a grand slam, be careful about leading it unless you are certain that the opponents have had an "accident" in the bidding. It would be devastating if you led the ♣ A against 7 ♠ only to find that the dummy had the ♣ KQJ765 and the declarer a void in the suit.

Here's a good "listening to the auction" case to study:

West	North	East	South
			1 ♠
Pass	2 ♦	Pass	2 ♠
Pass	4 ♠	Pass	4NT
P	5 ♦	Pass	6 ♠
All Pass			

You are West. Your hand is:

♠ 98
♥ K8732
♦ A6
♣ 10986

The opponents have had a strong auction to the small slam. They need twelve tricks to make their contract. What do you know about the entire deal?

You know that North's bidding shows spade support and a good diamond suit—in bridge parlance, the diamond suit is a "source of tricks." Now, you know the diamond suit is not running yet because you have the ace. So what can you do about it? What's your plan?

Get Yours First

You know that if you start out passively, the declarer will pull trumps and start working on the diamonds, which will eventually produce four or five tricks. There's probably not much you can do about the establishment of the diamond suit, so what you must do is try to build a trick for your side before the declarer has a chance to go after the diamonds.

Are you closer to making your decision about your opening lead? You should be.

Ask yourself: What is our best chance for developing a trick for our side before the declarer starts working on the diamonds?

A club could work out, but the declarer didn't get excited until he heard about his partner's great diamonds and trump support, then he launched into Blackwood and sailed into the slam. He is probably pretty well heeled in clubs. The declarer almost surely has the ♥ A—he wouldn't bid Blackwood with two or more quick losers in the suit—and is counting on dummy to have an entry to diamonds once they're set up. That puts the ♣ A in dummy, so the declarer almost surely has a strong holding in that suit. Even if your partner has the queen and jack of clubs, you don't have "time" to get that suit going. The declarer will be drawing trumps and playing on diamonds any second now.

That leaves you with only one choice: a heart. Oh, but what if you lead right into the ♥ AQ in your partner's hand? You are still virtually certain to take your ♦ A anyway, and you will have taken your best shot at building a trick for your side. Leading into the ♥ AQ is not likely to be the difference maker. It would mean only that the slam was unbeatable.

What you are hoping for is that your partner has the ♥ Q so that the declarer will have to play his ace, leaving him at least one loser in hearts when you come in with your ♦ A. You hope the entire deal looks like this:

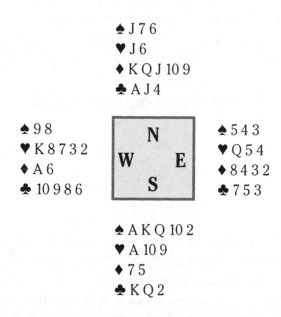

```
                    ♠ J 7 6
                    ♥ J 6
                    ♦ K Q J 10 9
                    ♣ A J 4

    ♠ 9 8                           ♠ 5 4 3
    ♥ K 8 7 3 2        N            ♥ Q 5 4
    ♦ A 6          W       E        ♦ 8 4 3 2
    ♣ 10 9 8 6         S            ♣ 7 5 3

                    ♠ A K Q 10 2
                    ♥ A 10 9
                    ♦ 7 5
                    ♣ K Q 2
```

You can see the devastating effect of your heart lead. Your partner will play the queen, knocking out the ace. When the declarer plays on diamonds—he has no choice and can do no more than hope for a miracle or a huge mistake by you—you will win the ace and cash your ♥ K.

What happens without a heart lead? The declarer wins, pulls trumps, and plays a diamond. After you take your ace, the declarer will have three discards coming—remember, he has only two diamonds and dummy has five really luscious ones. Those diamonds will be used to get rid of the ♥ 109. He won't even need the third discard because his hand will be high and he will make the slam.

Your Partner Can Help

There will be many occasions when you will find yourself on lead with no obvious choice for your first shot. You might have no honor to lead from—or you might have virtually identical holdings in two or more suits. Is there a way to find guidance? Yes, if you continue to practice listening to the bidding.

West	North	East	South
	1 ♥	Pass	1NT
All Pass			

You find yourself on lead with the following hand:

♠ K95
♥ J874
♦ J75
♣ J96

You don't want to lead a heart—that's the dummy's five-card suit—so your choices are from the ♠ K or one of your minor-suit jacks. Is there a clue to help you decide which suit to lead?

Clearly, if the opponents have stopped in 1NT, they don't have a lot of extra high-card strength. Your hand is not particularly robust, either, so that means that your partner has a few high cards over there. Yet she took no action. She could have bid spades at the one level, but she passed. That should dissuade you from leading a spade from a three-card holding. You might only be helping the declarer.

What about minors, then? Well, your partner might well have a five-card minor but not enough strength to have bid at the two level. Remember, if you enter the auction at the two level, you must have a suit good enough to keep from getting killed if the opponents double you. If you lead a diamond or a club, you might hit your partner's suit. It's a better chance than trying a spade.

CHAPTER 17

Advanced Play

The plays described in this chapter are within the ability of any bridge player with a desire to improve. One of the beauties of bridge is that no matter who your opponent is, a world champion or a neophyte, if you make the correct play he or she can do no more than follow suit. All it takes is a bit of work, concentration, and confidence when the time comes.

Counting

The ability to count is the most underrated of the skills that new players should work to acquire. Learning to count can help you avoid countless mistakes. When counting becomes so automatic that you don't even have to think about it, you are on your way as a bridge player.

You are already counting by adding up your HCP to determine whether you should open the bidding. You are counting HCP to decide if your hand is strong enough to bid at the two level over your partner's opening one-bid. You have already started learning to count in your handling of trumps. When you and your partner have an eight-card trump fit, you have learned to observe the opponents when you are pulling their trumps as you play the contract. You know that if you have four trumps in your hand and four trumps in dummy, and both opponents follow to the first two rounds of the suit, there is only one trump outstanding.

You also know that the trump suit in this case is divided 3–2. If one opponent shows out on the second round of trumps, you know that the suit is divided 4–1.

Counting High-Card Points

Whenever you are a defender and dummy comes down, add your HCP to the HCP in dummy. In each case, the bidding has done 1NT by South, 3NT by North. Your partner has made the opening lead and the dummy has hit the table. Your partner's lead is the ♠ 10.

Dummy	Your Hand
♠ A42	♠ 65
♥ KJ3	♥ A95
♦ Q96	♦ K10843
♣ 10732	♣ 852

What do you know about this deal? South opened 1NT, showing 15–17 HCP. The dummy has an ace, king, queen, and a jack. That's 10 HCP. That's at least 25 HCP between the two hands, maybe 27. You have 7 HCP, leaving your partner with how many? Well, 25 plus 7 equals 32, which means your partner could have as many as 8 HCP. She might have only 6 HCP, though. You can't be certain right away.

You may ask how this could be useful to you? Your partner has led the ♠ 10, probably the highest card he has in the suit. That means the declarer has the ♠ KQJ. The declarer wins with the jack and cashes the ♣ AKQ, dropping your partner's jack, and continues with a club to the 10 (you throw a heart) in dummy. The declarer then plays a low heart from dummy. You play low and the declarer wins the queen. A heart comes back to dummy's jack and you win the ace.

Let's take stock here. What have you seen so far? The declarer showed up with the ♠ KQJ, the ♣ AKQ, and the ♥ Q. That's 17 HCP right there. She doesn't have another face card in her hand. What does that mean for you? Look at the diamonds. You have counted the declarer's points and know that she cannot have even the jack in that suit, so your partner is marked with the ace and the jack.

You play a low diamond over to your partner's known ace, and he returns the jack, trapping dummy's queen. The contract is down. If you had not been counting, you might have been afraid to lead away from your king, thinking it would allow the declarer to get a trick with the queen she might not get on her own.

FACT

When an opponent opens 1NT or 2NT, showing a narrow limit of high-card points, your job of counting high-card points is easier because players rarely fail to adhere to the HCP requirements for no-trump openers. Opening bids in suits, on the other hand, may be based in part on distributional values—plus they have a wider range in HCP to start with.

Playing Detective

Enough cannot be said about the necessity to try to guess which opponent has a queen—that's when you have the so-called two-way finesse.

If you become an automatic counter, you will see that many times the search for the queen won't be a guess. You will know for certain who has it. This deal is a good example, starting with the bidding. You are South.

West	North	East	South
Pass	Pass	Pass	1 ♠
Pass	2 ♠	Pass	3 ♠
All Pass			

No need to comment on your optimistic game try of 3 ♠. The fact is, you are in 3 ♠ and must figure out how to take nine tricks with the following cards:

Dummy	**Your Hand**
♠ KJ7	♠ A10986
♥ Q104	♥ 765
♦ K82	♦ A7
♣ 10986	♣ KQJ

Things don't start off very well for you. West plays the ♥ K, followed by the ♥ A and a third heart, which East ruffs. East then returns a club to your King and West's ace. A club is returned and you win in your hand.

You have lost the first four tricks and cannot afford another loser. You have no more losers in clubs and none in diamonds, but what about trumps? Looking at your hand and the dummy, you can finesse against the ♠ Q either way—through West or through East. Which way should you go? Is this one of those famous two-way guesses?

Take your adventures in counting in small steps. Don't expect everything to fall into place at once. Start by counting only the trump suit. Once that becomes second nature, add a second suit. Make it your habit to add your HCP to the dummy's whenever you are a defender. Be diligent and don't be discouraged if you count wrong sometimes. Practice is the key.

It's not a guess if you consider what has transpired so far. West has shown up with the ♥ AK and the ♣ A. That's 11 HCP. If he had the ♠ Q, that would make 13 HCP, right? Do you remember the auction? West was dealer and he passed. Would he have passed with 13 HCP? Not very likely. You can just about take it to the bank that the ♠ Q is sitting in East's hand right now. It remains only for you to play over to dummy's ♠ K and play the ♠ J, letting it ride if East plays low.

Counting Distribution

You learned previously about the most common ways in which the four suits are distributed—sometimes called "patterns." A notation such as 4-4-3-2 means that there are two four-card suits, one three-card suit, and one two-card suit. A hand like the following:

♠ QJ76
♥ 32
♦ AK6
♣ A1098

To express that hand's exact distribution, the pattern would be 4-2-3-4, but it's still two four-card suits, one three-card suit, and one two-card suit. There are thirty-nine possible distributions, all the way to 13-0-0-0 (if you ever see that one, you can be confident someone fiddled with the deck). It's best in the early stages to concentrate on the ones you will see most often.

Here's a good exercise to help you get your mind ready to assimilate information about distributions, of which there are many. This will work best with your partner.

Have your partner speak the first two or three parts of one of the patterns. For example, he would say, "Four, four, three . . ." and leave the rest to you. You would say, "Two."

Next he says, "Five, four, three . . ." You say, "One." He can even say them in a different order, such as "Two, two, five." You say, "Four."

In a way it is like flash cards. You are committing the various distributions to memory, ready to fill in the blanks without straining to think about it. When your partner is through saying them to you, you say them to him.

You will find that applying that skill can help you when you are trying to figure out an opponent's distribution.

ALERT!

The easiest hands to count are ones that are opened with pre-emptive bids at high levels. If your opponent opens 3 ♠, before anything happens you know seven of her cards. It's a lot easier to work out the rest of her hand when you start with such a big portion of it already known.

The Squeeze

More than any of the other advanced plays, the squeeze has an aura of mystery. New players are more inclined to believe that squeezes are most definitely the exclusive province of the experts. A squeeze is a play in which an opponent is forced to discard in such a way that no matter what he does, it is to his disadvantage. Look at this game (these hands are after many tricks have been played) to see how the squeeze works.

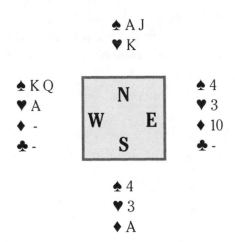

South, who has the lead, must take all the tricks. It looks as though that is impossible. Either of West's spade honors will knock out dummy's ace, and if the declarer plays the ♠ J, West will win and her ♥ A will also be good.

Look what happens, though, if South plays the ♦ A. What is West to do? She has no diamonds, so she must make a discard. No matter what West plays on the ♦ A, she is ruined. If she pitches the ♥ A, dummy's king will be good and the declarer can throw away the ♠ J. If West discards one of her spade honors, dummy's ♠ J will be good. South needs only to toss the ♥ K from dummy and play a spade to take the last two tricks.

In bridge parlance, West was "squeezed" on the play of the ♦ A. If South had not had a winner to play, there would have been no squeeze.

FACT

> The squeeze in bridge gets its name from the baseball play. Bridge great Sidney Lenz coined the phrase after noticing a squeeze at work during play. He later analyzed the play and created the name. Prior to Lenz's naming the squeeze, it was referred to as "putting the opponent to the discard."

Squeezes are so exciting and interesting that the first time you execute one, even if it's not on purpose, you might start looking for squeezes on every hand. That would be a mistake and a distraction for you and your partner.

Squeeze Requirements

There are certain conditions that must be met before a squeeze will work. First of all, you must be within one trick of your target. A squeeze won't produce two extra tricks. Let's look at that end position again with a slight change.

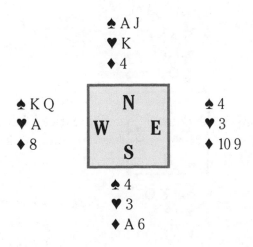

Look what happens now when South plays the ♦ A. West simply discards the ♣ 8, retaining his good spade cards and the ♥ A. Whatever South does, she will win only one more trick, and she needs three. The ♣ 8 in West's hand is known as an "idle" card. It is not needed by the defender. In the earlier diagram, West had no idle cards. He needed all three of the cards he had left to guard against North's spades and ♥ K.

Another requirement for a squeeze to operate is a "threat" card. In the first diagram, North had two threat cards—the ♥ K and the ♠ J. They were threatening to become winners because of the pressure put on West.

ALERT!

Whenever you have a long suit to run but are one trick short of your contract, it can pay off to run that suit and force the opponents to make discards. Even when a squeeze is not actually in effect, the opponents may err in the discarding, effecting what is known as a "pseudo-squeeze," one that exists only in their minds. Making a contract on a pseudo-squeeze gets the same score as a real squeeze.

The truth is that many squeezes operate without the declarer's knowledge, and in many cases all you really have to do is look for a particular card as you run a long suit. Here's an example.

♠ 10 6 4 2
♥ A K 7 6
♦ 7 5 4
♣ Q 6

♠ A K Q
♥ J 3 2
♦ A K Q J 10
♣ A

You find yourself in the great contract of 7NT. The opening lead is a low club (let's say East got to double for the lead at some point). East inserts the 9 and you win your singleton ♣ A.

Count Your Tricks

Taking stock, you have one club trick, six diamonds, three spades, and two hearts off the top. That's twelve tricks, but you need thirteen. What can you do? First, look over your assets and see if there are any potential sources of extra tricks.

You've got six tricks in diamonds but no more. No hope there. The club suit is hopeless. The ace is gone, and East is ready to pounce with that king. So what about the majors? There are definite possibilities.

You have the AKQ in your hand and four to the 10 in dummy. If you play out the top spades in your hand, maybe one of the opponents will have a singleton or doubleton jack—or maybe the suit will divide 3–3, in which case the jack will fall for sure.

There's also the remote possibility that the ♥ Q is all by itself and will fall the first time you play the suit. Since you have two stoppers in hearts, you go ahead and try that one. It doesn't cost but it might gain. You play the ♥ 2 from hand and West contributes the 9. Dummy's ace fetches the ♥ 4 from East, so that remote chance didn't work.

So you go back to spades, hoping for something good to happen there with the jack. That is much more likely than the singleton ♥ Q, but on this day you are disappointed. Both opponents follow to the top two spades, but when you pay the ♠ Q, East discards. Now what?

Well, your only hope at this point is to catch West in a squeeze between hearts and spades. You must hope that West, known to hold the ♠ J, also has the ♥ Q. You have no choice but to run your diamond winners and watch for that ♠ J. It's that simple. You cash five diamond winners, discarding a heart and the useless ♣ Q, to reach this position with one diamond to play.

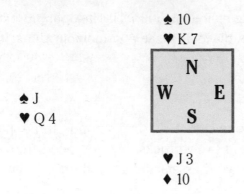

♠ 10
♥ K 7

♠ J
♥ Q 4

♥ J 3
♦ 10

When you play the winning diamond, West must make a fatal discard. Pitching the ♠ J means dummy's 10 is good, and discarding a heart means you can play low from your hand, taking the queen with the king, and returning to the ♥ J, your thirteenth trick.

Safety Plays

When you take the wheel as declarer, you have but one mission: to make your contract. All other considerations, namely overtricks, are secondary. Why it is necessary to make a statement which seems so obvious? History proves that it's not so obvious to some. Look at these two hands:

♠ 5 4 3
♥ 9 6
A K Q 5 4 3
♣ J 10

♠ A K 6
♥ A 5 4 3
♦ 6 2
♣ A 7 6 5

You are in 3NT, and West leads the ♠ Q. You win and stop to count your tricks. You have the top two spades, the ♥ A, the ♣ A, and the top three diamonds. That's seven tricks—two short of your goal. But what about that lovely diamond suit in dummy? It's really worth more tricks than just the top ones, right?

If one opponent has three diamonds and the other opponent two, the suit will "run," as bridge players say—it will be good for six tricks. So six diamonds, two spades, and one each in clubs and hearts make 10 tricks. An overtrick!

Not so fast.

What happens if you play the ♦ A, then the ♦ K and one of your opponents shows out. That means someone has four diamonds. The suit isn't running after all, but your problems are bigger than that. If you cash the ♦ Q and play another one, making the last two diamonds in dummy winners, it will all be for nothing because you won't be able to get to them.

Plan for the Worst

That dummy, with two good diamonds sitting there, is as dead as a doornail. You'll never be in dummy again. Not only that, but you have no way to develop extra tricks in the other suits, so you are headed for a minus score on a deal that should produce nine tricks most of the time.

Do you see what went wrong? You failed to plan for a potential bad break. It's true that the odds favor a 3–2 split in diamonds, but you should assume the worst and plan accordingly. You may give up an overtrick now and then, but that's a small price to pay for assuming that, whenever the contract can be made, you will make it.

So what's the solution? You must win the opening spade lead and play a low diamond from your hand, playing low from dummy. One of your opponents will win the trick, but you are in control if both follow.

Remember, if both follow, that means the diamonds were no worse than 4–1, meaning the ♦ AKQ will pick up all the rest of the opponents' cards in that suit and you will still be dummy to cash the last two.

Now you will have five diamonds, two spades, and two aces for nine tricks and your game. Let the other guys worry about overtricks. You prefer the safety play that sees you home when the breaks are bad.

Outnumber Them

Here's another safety play. Say you have no losers in any other suit and clubs are trumps. You must avoid two losers. Assume you have taken the opening lead in dummy and want to draw trumps right away. How do you play? Look at the cards you and your partner share:

DUMMY
♣ 972

DECLARER
♣ AJ106543

You have ten cards in your suit between the two hands, missing the king and the queen. Obviously you cannot take more than six tricks, but what is the best chance to do so?

There are three cards missing, so any time the suit breaks 2–1, you can bang down the ace and simply play another one and the rest of your clubs will be good. It doesn't matter who has what, as long as the suit breaks 2–1.

But what if clubs break 3–0? Now, if you bang down the ace, the ♣ KQ will be good and you will lose two tricks instead of just one. What can you do? How about a safety play?

On this deal, if you lead a low club from dummy and East follows low, you simply put in the 10. If that loses to the king or queen, no problem. As long as East followed, that means the suit has split 2–1, so the ace will capture the last outstanding card as soon as you get back in. If East plays a face card in clubs, you win the ace and play the jack to drive out the last club. If East had all three clubs, your safety play was necessary. Playing the ace first would have cost you the contract—a loss you could have prevented.

This works when you have ten cards between the two hands. With nine cards, if the 10 lost the first time, your best bet is to return to dummy and play low to the jack, unless East plays the other honor.

If East shows out when you play a club from dummy—oh, well. That's life. West has ♣ KQ8 and you will lose two tricks. You did the best you could.

Looking for His Honor

There are many varieties of safety plays, and many of them involve playing low on the first round of a suit to maintain communication in the event of a bad break. Here's one where you play a high card first. Again, you can afford one loser in the suit but not two:

> **DUMMY**
> ♦ 987
>
> **DECLARER**
> ♦ AQ10654

If you need six tricks from this suit, your best bet is to play a diamond to the queen, hoping that East has the doubleton king or three to the king without the jack. In the latter case, when you play the queen, West will have to play the jack and you will be able to finesse again with the 10 on the second round of the suit.

If you can afford one loser, you must start with the ace. That may seem esoteric, but it really is not.

You are missing the ♦ KJ32. Say you play low, East follows with the 2, and you play the queen, losing to the king. Now you go back to dummy and play another diamond. This time, East follows with the 3. Do you play the ace, hoping to drop the jack in the West hand—or do you put in the 10, finessing against East's jack?

Trying to guess in these situations will drive you mad, and if you guess you will be wrong part of the time. You will hate yourself when you should have played the ace and caught West's jack—or when you should have finessed against the jack with East.

Now see the benefit of playing the ace first. There are four possible cards West can play: the king, jack, 3, or 2. Say West plays the 2 first and East plays the 3. Now you go to dummy and play another diamond toward your hand. If East has a diamond left, it will be a face card.

If he puts in the jack, you simply cover with the queen. If West wins the king, all the rest of your diamonds will be good. If East plays the jack and you cover with the queen and West shows out, East will have only the king left—and he can do what he wants with it; it's the only trick he will take. If East plays the king and West shows out, East will have only the jack left, and you will pull that soon with your queen.

On occasion, West will drop a face card under your ace, and you know you will have no more than one loser. In fact, if West drops the king, you will have no losers. You will simply go to dummy and play a diamond, finessing against East's jack. Aren't you clever? You just picked up the whole diamond suit, while a player with lesser skill than you might have lost the finesse to a singleton king, then played the ace, hoping the jack would fall.

On those occasions when West has three or four diamonds to the king-jack, you can console yourself with the knowledge that there was nothing you could do about it. Even the greatest player who ever lived would lose two tricks in that case.

Endplays

Just as there are many variations of safety plays, there are also many variations of endplays. The name is evocative of the timing of the plays. They usually come near the end when the players have few cards left, although some endplays can be executed early in the deal.

The essence of the endplay, however, is that an opponent is forced to play a card that can only be to your advantage. Endplays usually involve the elimination of one or more side suits, taking away from the opponent what are known as "out cards"—cards in a suit that, if played, wouldn't yield a benefit to the declarer.

Here is a classic endplay situation:

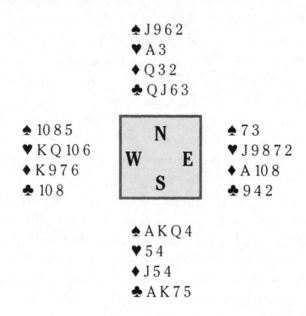

You are in 4 ♠, playing as South-North. West leads the ♥ K. You win the ace and look over your prospects. You have no losers in spades or clubs, just one in hearts (and nowhere to put it because all your suits are the same length) and the situation in diamonds is not so good. You have very poor cards to back up your ♦ Q and ♦ J. You will almost certainly lose three tricks if you play the suit yourself. Is there any way to get the opponents to play the suit?

Take Away Exit Cards

Follow along now. You win the opening heart lead with the ace and pull trumps in three rounds. Next you cash your club winners to arrive at this position:

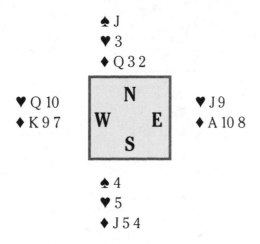

Neither opponent has a black card left in his hand. All you have to do is put your ♥ 5 on the table and three diamond losers turn into two.

Do you see what happened? Whichever opponent wins the heart trick, he must play a diamond or a heart. If he plays a diamond, you must make at least one diamond trick. That is, if the opponents break diamonds, you hold your losers in the suit to the ace and king. Sketch the diamonds in all four hands out on paper and play it out.

If either opponent decides not to break diamonds, then she must play a heart, with equally good results for you. Remember that you are void in hearts in both hands. So if either opponent plays a heart, you can ruff in one hand and discard a heart from the other, leaving you with only two diamond losers in that hand.

It wouldn't have worked if you hadn't taken all the opponents' "out cards" from them by playing out your clubs after you pulled trumps. It was okay to play four rounds of clubs, but you didn't want to play four rounds of trumps, because then you wouldn't have had the opportunity to take advantage if an opponent played a heart.

Here is another endplay situation, this time involving trumps.

♠ 10 9 8 6
♥ Q 4
♦ K Q J 3
♣ J 6 5

♠ A K 7 4 3
♥ J 5
♦ 10 9 8 2
♣ A Q

West	North	East	South
1NT	Pass	2 ♥	2 ♠
Pass	3 ♠	All Pass	

Your partner may have been a bit exuberant in raising you to 3 ♠, but you can discuss the bidding with him later. For now, you must do your best to concentrate on the task at hand: taking nine tricks in spades.

West leads the ♥ K and continues with the ♥ A. She then plays the ♦ A and another diamond. It's time to take stock.

What does the bidding tell you? Well, you know that West opened the bidding with 1NT, so she has 15–17 HCP. So far, she has showed up with the ♥ AK (7 HCP) and the ♦ A (4 HCP) for a total of 11 HCP. Between your hand and dummy are 23 HCP. That means there are 17 HCP held by the opponents. West has at least 15 of them, so East will have 2 HCP at the most.

Looks like the prospects are pretty good. If the spades are divided 2–2, you can pull them and lose at most one club. If spades don't divide well, are there any other chances?

First let's see how the trumps go.

You cash the ♠ A and follow with the king. West plays the jack and East, the rat, tosses a heart. So much for 2–2 trumps. You have a certain loser in trumps. Guess you'll have to turn to the club finesse, right?

When dummy and declarer are void in the same suit, with trumps in each hand, and an opponent leads the suit of which both hands are void, the declarer gains an advantage known as the "ruff and discard" or "ruff and sluff." The declarer can ruff in one hand and discard from another suit in the other hand. This is almost always to the declarer's advantage, and frequently the product of an endplay.

Some other player might be looking at clubs for an extra trick, but not a counter like you. You now know of 14 HCP by the declarer: ♠ QJ, ♥ AK, and ♦ A. That's 14 HCP. Is there another jack somewhere for West to get her total up to 15? Nope, you know where all four jacks started off. How about queens? You know about all of them as well.

So if East has the ♣ K, that means West opened 1NT with 14 HCP. Is that logical? Not really. Players don't usually mess around with the point count when they open 1NT. It's bad for your partner's morale if you do that.

So West has to have the ♣ K to have her 1NT opener. That means that if you play a club to queen, you are giving up completely on any chance of making this contract. It doesn't look good, but what other choice do you have?

Well, there's always the endplay.

A holding such as A–Q or K–J is known as a "tenace" in bridge parlance. The A–Q is considered a major tenace, K–J a minor tenace. More broadly, a tenace can be any two cards in the same suit not in sequence.

Simply play a diamond to dummy, noting that West discards. Now play a spade, happily giving up the trick to West, who will then find herself with no choice but to hand you your contract on a silver platter.

Executing an endplay successfully can be just as satisfying for you as it is frustrating for the opponents, but the good sports will congratulate you for your astute maneuvering. The better ones will want to play *with* you next time instead of against you.

CHAPTER 18

The Next Step: Duplicate Bridge

You know that in your next game you'll have a partner and two opponents, that you'll deal out the cards, conduct an auction, fight it out with the opponents for your tricks, then toss the cards in a pile to be shuffled so you can start the next deal. However, there is a completely different way of playing bridge—a style that many players find infinitely more satisfying. Welcome to the world of duplicate.

Duplicate Basics

In the twenty-first century, everyone plays contract bridge. You may play bridge for money, known as "rubber bridge." You may prefer to play only at home with the neighbors. This is usually called "party bridge." If you discover duplicate at a club or a tournament, that may be your preference. No matter which way of playing bridge you prefer, however, each is a form of contract bridge. Many people who are unfamiliar with duplicate bridge believe it is different from contract bridge. The method of scoring and the strategies are different, but it's still contract bridge.

Who Plays Duplicate?

Anyone with a bit of a competitive streak is a natural for duplicate. The mechanics of duplicate will be explained later in this chapter. For now, it's important to know that duplicate is a more competitive game than party bridge, but don't make the mistake of assuming there is no social element to duplicate.

On the contrary, bridge clubs are typically the most social of gathering places, and many people enter the duplicate arena with a desire to make new friends and find new partners as much as they do for the competition.

FACT

Duplicate bridge is so called because the deals are played over and over. Hands are not thrown in and shuffled each time they are bid and played. The deals are preserved in special trays and moved from table to table to be played up to thirteen times in one session.

The 170,000 members of the American Contract Bridge League, which is the sanctioning body for tournaments in North America, run the gamut of occupations and experience levels. The ACBL conducts three major tournaments each year—in the spring, summer, and fall—and you can find players who are just starting out playing at the same tournament as world champions. They don't play against each other, of course, because there are games for all levels of players.

Besides running those three big tournaments each year—they go on for eleven days—the ACBL also sanctions more than 1,000 tournaments of various levels and sizes. Just about anywhere you live, there will be several tournaments a year within easy driving distance of your home. If you live in a large metropolitan area, there may be several tournaments a year right where you live.

How It Works

As noted before, in other forms of bridge, when you finish play, the cards are thrown back in a pile and someone picks them up to shuffle so the game can continue. The deal that was just played is gone forever. In duplicate, it doesn't happen that way. A duplicate game starts with two or three trays on the table, each of them numbered. In each tray—more commonly known as a "board"—there are four slots, one each for North, South, East, and West. In each slot, or pocket, there are thirteen cards. To get the game going, the cards are removed from the slots, shuffled together, and dealt, but the cards are not thrown to each person at the table as you would do if you were playing at home. Instead, you deal out the cards in four piles right in front of you. When you are finished, you take the piles, each with thirteen cards, and slip them into the slots in the board. When all the dealing is done, you are ready to play.

When you play duplicate, your true opponents are not the players you are sitting with at the table. Your true opponents are the pairs who are playing the same direction you are. If you are East-West, your scores will be compared to the other East-West pairs, even though you are playing against North-South players during the session. It is the East-West pairs whose scores you want to beat.

You noticed when you started out that you were sitting in one of the compass directions. You will keep that seat throughout the session. If you are playing East-West with your partner, you will be moving from table to table throughout the session. If you are North-South, you get to stay at the table where you started.

Each table in a duplicate game has a place card on it, also with a number. With a ten-table game, the tables would be numbered one through ten. The number of the table you start at is your number for the entire session. If you are playing East-West and start out at table one, you are pair number one. You will see why this is important as the game of duplicate is explained further.

Don't Mix 'Em

In duplicate, the cards are not mixed together the way you learned to do it for contract bridge. When you play a card in duplicate, you place it on the table in front of you, and it stays there. When the next player sees that you have played, she places the card she wishes to play on the table in front of her. As declarer, you would call a card for dummy to play, and your partner would pick that card up and place it in front of her. Finally, the last person to play would place a card on the table, completing the trick.

You and the opponents continue this way until all thirteen tricks have been played. The cards are never mixed together.

So how do you keep track of which tricks you won and which tricks you lost?

It's easy: If you win the trick, you place it down on the table in a vertical position—that is, straight up. If you lose the trick, you place the card horizontally. Each player does this throughout the deal.

When the deal is complete, you determine how many tricks you took, make sure everyone is in agreement on that issue, then each player picks up the thirteen cards in front of him or her and replaces the cards in the correct slot in the board. If you are East, you return your cards to the East slot. Each board, besides having a number, also has the compass directions on the top of the tray to assist players.

All this may sound complicated and difficult, but in no time at all you will find that it is second nature. You won't even have to think about what you're doing after only two or three deals.

The Lure of Masterpoints

A common question asked by non-bridge players of those who play at duplicate clubs or at tournaments is: What do you get if you win?

The answer is usually mystifying: masterpoints. What are they? Can you spend them at the supermarket or turn them in for valuable prizes?

No, but tens of thousands of people lust after them just the same. In fact, the masterpoint is the stock in trade of the ACBL, the world's largest bridge organization, and its cousin, the American Bridge Association. Most bridge organizations in foreign countries reward their members' bridge achievements with masterpoints.

A masterpoint is a measure of achievement in bridge competition. Bridge clubs might have a jackpot of a few dollars, but there are no cash prizes for winning, nor are there at tournaments, even large ones. The currency is masterpoints.

One of the ACBL's principal duties is to award and keep track of the masterpoints awarded to each and every member. This is done by player numbers. Whenever you play at a bridge club or enter a tournament, your player number—unique to you—is entered so that if you do well, you will receive proper credit.

Scoring Differences

It is vital that you keep your cards from getting mixed up with other players' cards because of the way the scoring is done in duplicate.

Take that same 4 ♥ contract. If you bid and make it, you get your 120 as in regular bridge, but you also get a bonus tacked on right away: 300 if you are not vulnerable, 500 if you are. So your score for that one deal would be 420. If you happened to make an overtrick you would get the 150 plus your bonus, 450 or 650 depending on your vulnerability.

With part scores, it's a different matter. Say you bid 2 ♠ and make it on the nose. You would get your 60—two times 30 for two tricks over the basic six—but you would also get a bonus of 50 points for making your contract. Your total would be 110.

Say you had a bidding mishap and stopped in 2 ♠ when you should have been in four. You must bid your game to get credit for it, but you do get plus 120 for the tricks and the bonus of 50 for making your contract. That's plus 170.

If you bid to game, you get the game bonus but not the 50-point bonus for making your contract.

There are slam bonuses as well (higher if you are vulnerable) and a special bonus of 50 points if you make a doubled contract. The various scores are usually on the back of that table card mentioned earlier—the one with the number on it and the compass directions.

Pairing Up

Most of the duplicate games you will find at clubs, and the majority of the games you will experience at tournaments, are pairs games. That is, the contestants are all divided up into partnerships or pairs. It's you and your partner against everyone else.

In a regular bridge game, scoring is on "total points." In duplicate, all the pairs are competing for a commodity known as "matchpoints." From start to finish in a duplicate game, the North player fills out score tickets that reflect what happened on that particular round. Most duplicate games are played with two or three deals per round.

ALERT!

The highest plus score available in duplicate bridge is for the contract of 1NT redoubled, scoring all thirteen tricks—3,160. The highest minus score also involves the taking of all thirteen tricks by the defense in a redoubled contract—7,600.

When the auction is completed, the North player writes down the contract and who is playing it, such as 3NT by West. When the play on that deal is completed, North will record the result. If 3NT is successful, East-West will get a plus score. If 3NT fails, North-South will get the plus.

After each round is completed, the director picks up the score slips and punches the information into a computer equipped with software especially designed for bridge games.

When all play is completed and all the scores from all the tables have been entered into the computer, the director pushes the button to score it all and the software spits out the final product: all the scores of all the pairs in the game. The East-West pairs are ranked together, as are the North-South pairs.

Comparisons

You might think all these scores you've been getting have been piling up in the computer and are ready to come tumbling out, with your minus scores subtracted, of course. But, it doesn't work that way.

Your score will be based on comparisons: how you and your partner did on each deal compared to the results achieved by all the other pairs who played the same deals. Let's look at a typical deal from a typical game.

Let's say there were ten tables in play. In most ten-table games, there would be three boards per round and a total of nine rounds. What follows is the story of Board 1.

Duplicate Game

Contract	Pair	Score	Matchpoints
4 ♠	1N-S	+420	3
4 ♠	10N-S	+420	3
4 ♠	9N-S	+450	6.5
3NT	8N-S	+430	5
3 ♠	7N-S	+170	1
4 ♠ X	6N-S	+590	8
5 ♠	5N-S	-50	0
4 ♠	4N-S	+420	3
4 ♠	3N-S	+450	6.5

Here's how matchpoints work. If you and your partner are playing North-South, you will get your score by comparing how you did on each of the deals to the score achieved by each of the other North-South pairs. For each pair you beat, you received one matchpoint. You received ½ matchpoint for all pairs you tie.

Looking at the chart more closely, here's what happened. Starting with the top score of plus 590, North-South Pair 6 got to the game, and for some reason one of the players of the East-West pair thought it was a poor contract, thus the double (as noted by X). In duplicate, when you play a doubled contract, you get double your regular score plus 50 for making a doubled contract, plus the game bonus.

So on that score, it would be 240 (double the usual 120), plus 50 for making a doubled contract, plus the non-vulnerable game bonus of plus 300. Add them up and you have plus 590.

FACT

When you make a doubled contract, you received a bonus of 50 points to go with the other scores. In bridge parlance, the 50-point bonus is often articulated this way after the other scores have been noted: ". . . and 50 for the insult."

Going back to the chart explaining Board 1, North-South Pair 6 scored plus 590. That was better than eight other scores on that board, so their matchpoint score was 8.

Looking further, we see that Pairs 3 and 9 managed to take eleven tricks in 4 ♠ and thus recorded plus 450: five tricks over the basic six at 30 points per trick, plus the 300 point bonus for bidding game. Plus 450 was better than six other scores, but two pairs achieved the score, so they received an additional ½ matchpoint for the tie. Thus their scores were 6.5.

North-South Pair 8 arrived at the unusual contract of 3NT and they took the same 10 tricks as most of the other pairs in spade contracts, but the extra 10 points for the first trick in no-trump gave them an edge. At plus 430, they score better than five other pairs, so their matchpoint score is a 5.

You can see that three pairs played in 4 ♠ and made it on the nose for plus 420. They were better than the plus 170 and the minus 50, and they each received an extra point for tying two other pairs, so their score was 3.

Now we come to the pair who had a bidding misunderstanding and stopped short of game at 3 ♠. They made ten tricks, but since they didn't bid the game, they don't get the game bonus. Their score of plus 170 was better than only one other pair—the minus 50—so they receive only one matchpoint.

Pity North-South Pair 5. They got too high, bidding up to 5 ♠, and the opponents took three tricks. For minus 50, they got no matchpoints because their score was not higher than any other pair's. They received what is known in the duplicate world as a "zero" or a "goose egg." Conversely, the pair who were doubled in 4 ♠ and made it, got what is known as a "top"—the top score available.

Minus Can Be Good

You will note that you don't have to have a plus score in duplicate to score a lot of matchpoints. Suppose, for example, that you open 1NT, everyone passes and after the opening lead, dummy comes down with almost nothing. You know you have no chance to make your contract, but if you can hold the minus score to a smaller number than the other pairs playing the same hand you are holding now, you can get a good score.

Say in this 1NT contract you are really clever and manage to go down only two tricks for minus 100, while at every other table the declarers went down at least three, sometimes more. In that event, with the lowest minus score, you would receive the same top as if you had actually made your contract.

In duplicate, the margin of the excess is not important. What is important is to have the highest plus score or the lowest minus. In other words, if you are playing North-South and make plus 110 for bidding and making 2 ♠ while every other North-South pair gets plus 100 for beating their opponents in some contract, you will score the same top as if you egged your opponents into bidding to some high contract and then doubled them and collected plus 1,400.

How much you beat the other scores by is not important. It's important only that you beat them or have a lower minus.

In each duplicate game, the top matchpoint score will be one less than the number of times the deal is played. In the ten-table game there would be nine rounds, so each board was played nine times. That means the best score available was eight. Each pair has eight comparisons to make. An average score is half of the maximum—in this case four.

Why Duplicate?

When you play rubber or party bridge, you are at the mercy of the cards. If you are dealt good cards, you are a favorite to win. If you are dealt poor cards, your chances of coming out ahead are slim to none.

In duplicate, you don't need good cards to win. As explained, what you need is larger plus scores or lower minus scores. You will probably never go through a game with no plus scores or no minuses, either, but in theory you could have all minuses and still win—as long as your minuses were low enough.

Duplicate is so fascinating because from the very beginning, you have a basis of comparison and, more important, a way to measure your progress.

Say you look at the score sheet at the end of the game and note on one particular board that you got plus 110 for bidding and making 2 ♠ on the nose. You see that it was a poor score because most of the other declarers scored plus 140 for making nine tricks in a spade contract. Perhaps you will go find the board and take out all the hands—they are still there, just as they were during the play—and look at the full deal to see how you should have played to earn that overtrick. Already, you are progressing as a player.

Get the Hand Records

At most tournaments, there are hand records available after each session with all of the cards from all of the deals played that day, right there waiting for you to go over them to see how you might have bid or played better.

The hand records are a great way for you and your partner to review each deal, finding weaknesses in your bidding system or your defensive play. You might take a deal you had difficulty with and ask a more experienced player what you should have done differently or how you might have played better. Perhaps the experienced player will tell you about a new way of bidding that would solve your problem.

At many duplicate tournaments, there are lectures by famous players, who usually stay and answer questions. Most professional players are approachable and more than willing to help someone who is just starting out.

Duplicate Strategies

There was a deal in Chapter 17 about safeguarding your contract with a strategy called the "safety play." The two hands are repeated for convenience.

♠ 5 4 3
♥ 9 6
♦ A K Q 5 4 3
♣ J 10

♠ A K 6
♥ A 5 4 3
♦ 6 2
♣ A 7 6 5

In the discussion of this contract (3NT by South), it was noted that if you play the diamonds from the top and the suit splits 4–1 instead of the expected 3–2, you will go down. You can guarantee your contract any time diamonds split no worse than 4–1 by simply playing a low diamond from both hands on the first round of the suit.

That's useful to know, but mostly irrelevant in a pair game. There are two reasons: (1) the likelihood that the five diamonds held by the opponents will split 3–2 and (2) the importance of overtricks in a game scored by matchpoints.

When "Safe" Isn't

When you hold eight cards in a suit, the opponents hold five. The suit will split 3–2 nearly 68 percent of the time. It will split 4–1 28 percent of the time. A 5–0 split is not factored in because in this example it will mean that the contract cannot be made.

If you take the safety play, you will score plus 400, which will be a great score 28 percent of the time because the other declarers will be playing diamonds from the top and going down when the suit splits 4–1. More than two-thirds of the time, however, your plus 400 will compare poorly with the other declarers because they will be scoring plus 430 with six diamond tricks, the top two spades, and the ♥ A and ♣ A. You will receive a near-bottom score for plus 400.

In Good Company

It is true that you will risk your contract by ignoring the safety play, but you must consider that the other declarers will be doing the same thing, and when the diamond suit breaks poorly they will be minus the same as you are. In fact, it's conceivable that on this deal minus 50 could be an average score. True, you will get a top on the occasions when the safety play comes in handy, but you will be close to a bottom more than twice as often.

Unlike total points scoring, overtricks are very important in a game scored by matchpoints. One tiny overtrick can be worth a mountain of matchpoints, as seen in previous examples.

When to Play Safe

In normal contracts such as the one in the example, you should not consider safety plays. There are occasions, however, when playing safe to make your contract is the only way to go.

A prime example would be when you are in a doubled contract. Let's change this example contract around a bit:

♠ A K 6 2
♥ 8 6 2
♦ 5 4
♣ A J 10 3

♠ 5 4
♥ A 4 3
♦ A K Q 10 7 6
♣ 7 6

West	North	East	South
	1 ♣	1 ♥	2 ♦
Pass	2 ♥	Dbl	2NT
Pass	3NT	Dbl	All Pass

Your partner's 2 ♥ bid was checking to see if you had a stopper in hearts. East doubled that bid to confirm with his partner that he wanted a heart lead. You showed your stopper by bidding 2NT and your partner went to game. East was not convinced that you can make nine tricks, so he doubled.

West led the ♥ 9, and East played the jack. You played low, and East continued with the ♥ K. You played low again, and West showed out. East played a third round of hearts, knocking out your only stopper in the suit. Now what?

Clearly, you can make ten tricks if the diamond suit splits normally, but what if East has four to the jack? If you play the suit from the top, on the fourth round East will get in and cash a bunch of hearts to defeat you in a doubled contract.

It isn't any better if West has four diamonds to the jack. Say you play the suit from the top and give a diamond to West. She won't have any more hearts to play to East, but you won't have any way to your hand to enjoy those now-good diamonds. Your ♥ A is gone, remember.

The solution? Go to dummy with a spade and play a diamond to your 10. Assuming East follows, West can win the jack if she has it but she has no heart to play to her partner. You can win the return and play that low diamond in dummy to your hand, racking up your nine tricks and a doubled contract. For the record, making 3NT doubled is 550—750 if you are vulnerable.

Either score will be a clear top. If you made the overtrick, you would have scored plus 650 or plus 950, but you don't need the overtrick in this case because of the foolish double by East.

APPENDIX A

Bridge Resources

Bridge-Related Websites

American Bridge Association
www.ababridge.org

The American Contract Bridge League
World's largest bridge organization. Myriad features, information, bridge news, tournament calendars, and free "Learn to Play Bridge" software.
www.acbl.org

Baron Barclay Bridge Supply
World's largest bridge supply house.
www.baronbarclay.com

BridgeBase
Free site with a wide variety of information, tutorials, quizzes.
www.bridgebase.com

Bridge blog list
List of numerous blogs by well-known experts and aspiring players. Wide variety of topics.
www.clairebridge.com/blogs.htm

Canadian Bridge Federation
www.cbf.ca

ECats Bridge
From Great Britain, lots of information about bridge.
www.ecatsbridge.com

Great Bridge Links
Canadian site with dozens of links.
www.greatbridgelinks.com

Karen's Bridge Library
Comprehensive list of bridge books for advanced players.
www.kwbridge.com

World Bridge Federation
Umbrella organization for nearly 100 bridge groups throughout the world. Puts on all world championships, promotes bridge.
www.worldbridge.org

Personal Websites

Phillip Alder
Syndicated columnist and teacher.
www.phillipalderbridge.com

Larry Cohen
Top player and author.
www.larryco.com

Jeff Hand
National champion and teacher.
www.realbridgehands.com

Eddie Kantar
Another well-known name in bridge.
www.kantarbridge.com

Mike Lawrence
One of bridge's most popular authors.
www.michaelslawrence.com

Migry Zur Campanile
Editor of *Israeli Bridge* magazine. U.S. national champion who now resides in America.
www.migry.com

Online Bridge Play

Bridge Base Online
By far the largest online service. Games around the clock, including dozens of ACBL masterpoint games weekly.
www.bridgebase.com

OKbridge
Also has many ACBL masterpoint games.
www.okbridge.com

Swan Games
Some ACBL masterpoint games.
www.swangames.com

Bridge Magazines

The Bridge Bulletin
Included with membership in the ACBL. Articles on improving bidding and play, tournament schedules, tournament reports, personalities, features on new players.

Bridge Today Weekly Bridge Quiz
E-mailed fifty times a year in .pdf format.

The Bridge World
Venerable publication more for experienced players and experts. Can be esoteric. Challenge the Champs (bidding contest) and Master Solvers (bidding problems) each month.

Recommended Books

American Contract Bridge League. *Laws of Duplicate Bridge*. ACBL, 2008.

Bergen, Marty. *More Points, Schmoints!* Bergen Books, 1999.

Bergen, Marty. *Points, Schmoints!* Bergen Books, 1995.

Berkowitz, David, and Brent Manley. *Precision Today*. DBM Publications, 2002.

Bird, David. *Saints and Sinners*. Master Point Press, 2007.

Blackwood, Easley. *Card Play Fundamentals*. Devyn Press, 1986.

Grant, Audrey. *Introduction to Bridge Bidding*. The Club Series. American Contract Bridge League, 1994.

Grant, Audrey. *Introduction to Bridge: Play of the Hand*. The Diamond Series. American Contract Bridge League, 1999.

Hamman, Robert, and Brent Manley. *At the Table: My Life and Times*. DBM Publications, 1996.

Hardy, Max. *The Problems with Major Suit Raises and How to Fix Them*. Devyn Press, 1998.

Hardy, Max. *Two over One Game Force*. Hardy, 2006.

Horton, Mark. *The Mammoth Book of Bridge*. Carroll & Graf, 2000.

Kantar, Edwin B. *Introduction to Declarer's Play*. Wilshire Books, 1990.

Kantar, Edwin B. *Roman Key Card Blackwood*. Robert Hale Limited, 2001.

Kantar, Edwin B. *Take Your Tricks*. 2nd Edition. Squeeze Books, 2008.

Kantar, Edwin B. *Test Your Bridge Play*. Wilshire, 1981.

Kelsey, Hugh. *Killing Defence at Bridge*. Houghton Mifflin, 1994.

Kelsey, Hugh. *Simple Squeezes*. Houghton Mifflin, 1995.

Klinger, Ron. *Playing to Win at Contract Bridge*. Orion, 1999.

Lawrence, Michael. *The Complete Book on Balancing in Contract Bridge*. Max Hardy, 1981.

Lawrence, Michael. *The Complete Book on Hand Evaluation in Contract Bridge*. Devyn Press, 1993.

Lawrence, Michael. *How to Play Card Combinations*. Devyn Press, 1989.

Lawrence, Michael. *How to Read Your Opponents' Cards*. Devyn Press, 1991.

Lawrence, Michael. *Mike Lawrence's Workbook on the Two Over One System*. Baron Barclay Bridge, 2006.

Lawrence, Michael. *Passed Hand Bidding*. 2nd edition. Lawrence & Leong, 1993.

Love, Clyde. *Bridge Squeezes Complete*. Dover, 1968.

Mahmood, Zia. *Bridge My Way*. Granovetter, 1992.

Manley, Brent. *The Tao of Bridge*. Adams Media, 2005.

Mollo, Victor. *I Challenge You*. Fireside, 1988.

Mollo, Victor, and Nico Gardener. *Card Play Technique*. Batsford, 1955; reissue, 2002.

Root, William. *The ABCs of Bridge*. Three Rivers Press, 1998.

Roth, Alvin. *Picture Bidding*. Granovetter, 1992.

Seagram, Barbara, and Marc Smith. *Bridge: 25 Ways to Compete in the Bidding*. Master Point Press, 2000.

Sheinwold, Alfred. *Five Weeks to Winning Bridge*. Permabooks, 1962; reissue, Pocket Books, 1996.

Simon, S. J. *Why You Lose at Bridge*. Pomona Press, 2008.

Sontag, Alan. *The Bridge Bum*. Master Point Press, 2003.

Stewart, Frank. *Better Bridge for the Advancing Player*. Prentice Hall, 1984.

Stewart, Frank. *Frank Stewart's World of Bridge*. Squeeze Books, 2008.

Stewart, Frank. *My Bridge and Yours*. Stewart, 1992.

Wolff, Robert. *The Lone Wolff* (autobiography). Master Point Press, 2008.

Glossary

ABA:
American Bridge Association, based in Atlanta. Membership of about 5,000.

ACBL:
American Contract Bridge League, based in Memphis. World's largest bridge organization at approximately 170,000 members.

advance:
The first move made by the partner of a player who overcalls. The player who makes that first move is called the "advancer."

arrangement:
The method of separating one's cards, usually in alternating black and red suits.

artificial bid:
A bid that does not denote a holding designated by that bid.

asking bid:
A bid that requests information from the partner of the player using the bid. Examples are Stayman and Blackwood.

attack:
Usually associated with opening leads, an attack implies an aggressive position, which incurs some risk.

attitude:
On defense, one player's position regarding a play by his or her partner. This is expressed by the cards played, never by facial expression, gesture, comment, or in any physical way.

auction:
The process of deciding on the final contract via the bidding.

auction bridge:
The predecessor to contract bridge.

average:
In duplicate, exactly half of the maximum score attainable.

avoidance:
The process of keeping one's opponents off lead, usually to prevent a play through a particular card, such as a king.

balance:
Action aimed at keeping the auction from dying at a low level, usually based on the assumption that high-card points are fairly evenly divided between the two sides.

balanced hand:
A hand with no singleton and no more than one doubleton. There are three balanced patterns: 4-3-3-3, 4-4-3-2, or 5-3-3-2.

bid:
A call that offers to win a certain number of tricks in the denomination named.

bidder:
A player who makes a bid.

bidding space:
The amount of "space" in terms of bids which can no longer be made. All bids must be higher than previous bids. An opening bid at the three level uses "space" by precluding all bids at the one and two levels.

Biritch:
A Russian card game from which the name of the game of bridge is said to have been derived.

Blackwood:
A bid, usually of 4NT, requesting that the bidder's partner indicate in steps how many aces she holds in her hand.

blank:
Another way of denoting a void—no cards in the suit.

board:
In duplicate, a reference to the tray used to hold the hands and which moves from table to table during a game.

book:
The first six tricks won in the play of any contract. These tricks do not count in the score.

bottom:
In duplicate, the lowest possible score on a deal—a zero.

break:
The layout of opposing cards in a suit. Five outstanding cards rate to "break" 3–2 most of the time.

bridge whist:
The forerunner of auction bridge.

broken sequence:
A combination of at least three high cards with two of them in sequence, such as AQJ or KJ10.

buy:
Being successful in a competitive auction, as in, "He bought the contract for 3 ♠."

call:
Any bid, pass, double, or redouble. All bids are calls, but not all calls are bids.

captain:
In a team event, the player designated to turn in scores and to determine who plays.

captaincy:
A principle that states that the first player to make a limit bid cedes captaincy to her partner. Once one player has limited her hand during the auction, the other player is presumed to know how high the two hands should go. His decisions must be respected.

cash:
To play a winning card.

cash in:
To take tricks by playing winning cards one after another, usually as a last chance. Also articulated as "cash out."

cheapest bid:
The bid that takes up the least amount of space from the previous bid, as 1NT after 1 ♠, or 2 ♦ after 2 ♣.

claim:
To shorten play, usually by declarer, when it is clear the defenders can take no more tricks. It is sporting to claim rather than play on when there is no point to it, but claiming can be dangerous if not accurate. Best avoided by new players.

clear a suit:
In no-trump play, to force out high cards held by the opponents so that the remaining cards in the suit are good.

club:
The lowest-ranking suit (♣). Also, a place where bridge is played.

coffeehousing:
To indulge in unethical actions intended to mislead the opponents, usually by mannerism.

come-on:
Usually a signal accomplished by a sequence of card plays that indicates a desire for a suit to be continued (see **echo** and **high-low**).

comparison:

The method of determining scores in duplicate bridge (see **IMP** and **matchpoint**).

compass points:

The positions of the four players, particularly at duplicate. East-West always play as partners, as do North-South.

contract:

The designation of the target number of tricks for the declaring side in a particular denomination.

convention:

A call or play with a particular meaning, such as Blackwood 4NT or fourth-best opening leads.

convention card:

In duplicate, a preprinted card that is filled out according to a partnership's agreements as to conventions, bidding system, and defensive carding.

count:

To keep track of high-card points and cards in the four suits.

crossruff:

To use trumps in each hand to ruff losing cards from the other hand.

cuebid:

A forcing bid that normally is not offered as a possibility for play, especially the bid of an opponent's suit. A cuebid often indicates a control, such as an ace or void, in a suit.

deal:

To distribute all fifty-two cards, and the entire deck once the cards have been dealt. A hand is thirteen cards, a deal is fifty-two cards.

dealer:

The player who distributes the cards.

deception:

The deliberate attempt to mislead an opponent, usually by the declarer, but only by the card played, not by the manner in which it is played (as with a hesitation aimed to deceive).

declarer:

The player who was first to name the denomination of the final contract. The declarer controls the plays made by the dummy.

defeat:

To prevent the declarer from making his or her contract.

defender:

Either opponent when the other side has won the contract.

defense:

The process of attempting to prevent the declarer from winning enough tricks to make his or her contract. Defense is said to be the most difficult part of the game of bridge.

defensive bidding:

The actions taken by partners after the opponents have opened the bidding. Also known as "competitive bidding."

diamond:

The second-lowest suit in rank (♦).

director:

In duplicate, the person who runs the game, usually entering scores and ruling on irregularities, such as leads out of turn.

distribution:

How the cards are dispersed in a given suit among the four hands.

double:

A call that increases the scoring value of contracts that are made—or of penalties for defeated contracts.

double finesse:
A finesse against two honors, such as playing the 10 when leading up to the AQ10, hoping the king and jack are both on the left.

double raise:
Skipping a level of bidding in the process of raising, as in 1 ♣—P—3 ♣.

down:
Unsuccessful in an attempt at a contract, as in, "I was down two in 3 ♥."

draw trumps:
To play high trumps in an attempt to remove them from the opponents' hands.

drop-dead bid:
A bid that strongly suggests to your partner that there should be no more bidding.

duck:
To deliberately play a low card without attempting to win a trick, usually to maintain communication between hands or to deceive the declarer or a defender about the location of a particular card.

dummy:
The declarer's partner, and the cards held by the declarer's partner. The dummy is always exposed after the opening lead has been made.

dummy play:
Bridge parlance for the way in which the declarer manages the cards.

duplicate bridge:
The form of bridge in which scores are determined by comparisons after deals have been played again and again.

echo:
A signal accomplished by the play of a high card in a suit, followed by a low card (see **high-low**).

This usually indicates interest in a continuation of the suit or of a doubleton.

empty:
A term usually indicating a lack of good spot cards to go with an honor, as in a suit such as A432 being called "ace empty fourth."

endplay:
The process of forcing an opponent to make a play to his disadvantage, such as leading away from a king into an AQ.

entry:
A means of moving from one hand to the other.

equals:
Cards in a sequence. For example, the jack is equal to the queen in a holding of QJ.

establish:
To make a suit or a card good, as in playing the queen, then the jack in a suit to make the 10 good.

ethics:
A philosophy that winning at bridge should be accomplished by fair play.

face card:
A king, queen, or jack.

falsecard:
The act of playing a card intended to deceive an opponent. The card itself.

final bid:
The last bid in an auction, followed by three consecutive passes.

finesse:
An attempt to win a trick with a lower-ranking card by taking advantage of the position of a higher-ranking card, as in leading to the Kx, hoping the ace is on the left.

first hand:
The dealer.

five-card majors:
The bidding system which requires that an opening bid of 1 ♥ or 1 ♠ indicates at least five cards in the suit. This is the basis for the Standard American bidding system.

flat:
Another way of saying extremely balanced distribution of a single hand, usually 4-3-3-3.

follow suit:
The requirement that one must play a card of a suit led if possible.

forcing:
Any action, including pass, that requires further action by the player's partner.

four-card majors:
A bidding system of decreasing popularity in North America that permits opening bids of one of a major with only four cards. The British Acol system is based on four-card majors and a 1NT opening of 12–14 HCP.

free bid:
A bid made when the obligation to bid with minimum values has been removed by an intervening action by an opponent.

gadget:
Colloquialism for a convention.

game bid:
A bid of 3NT, 4 ♥, 4 ♠, 5 ♣, or 5 ♦.

game force:
A bid indicating sufficient strength that neither partner is allowed to pass until a game contract has been reached.

garbage:
A poor hand or a hand with unsupported queens and jacks, which usually do not pull their full weight.

Gerber:
Another ace-asking convention, usually 4 ♣, with responses the same as Blackwood (in steps). Used over no-trump openings.

good cards:
Cards that have been established in play and can be cashed.

grand slam:
A contract at the seven level, requiring that declarer take all thirteen tricks.

half trick:
The proposition that a particular holding will win a trick half the time, as with Kx in a suit, considered one-half trick, or AQ, considered a trick and a half.

hand records:
A complete record of the deals played in a session, almost always available at ACBL tournaments.

heart:
The second-highest-ranking suit and the symbol of the suit (♥).

high card:
Ace, king, queen, or jack. These have numeric values—4, 3, 2, and 1, respectively—to enable players to evaluate their hands for opening and responding purposes.

high-low:
A method of playing one's cards to indicate distribution and/or "attitude" about a particular suit. If you play the 9 followed by the 3 under your partner's king and ace, you are indicating you want that suit continued.

hold up:
To delay taking a high card, usually to disrupt communication between opposing hands or to maintain control of an opponent's suit.

holding:
The cards dealt in a particular suit or hand, as in, "What was your heart holding?"

honor:
Ace, king, queen, jack, or 10.

hook:
Bridge lingo for a finesse: "I made the slam by taking the heart hook."

huddle:
A noticeable pause in the bidding or play. To be avoided if possible because of information that can be conveyed by the break.

illegal call:
A call—bid, pass, double, redouble—out of rotation or of insufficient level, as 2 ♣ over 2 ♦.

IMP:
International Match Point, a method of scoring team events.

impropriety:
An action that violates the standards of ethical conduct, such as a grimace or gesture which indicates to the player's partner unhappiness with a bid or play.

inference:
What is learned about your partner's hand or the opponents' hands during the bidding and play.

insufficient bid:
A bid that is not higher than the previous bid.

insult:
The penalty paid when an opponent makes a doubled contract (50 points). If the successful contract is redoubled, the penalty is 100 points.

interior sequence:
Cards in a sequence such as AJ109 or Q1098. The J109 and 1098 are considered interior sequences.

invitation:
A bid that invites game or slam but does not commit the partnership to either.

jack:
The fourth-ranking card in a suit.

jump bid:
A bid that raises the suit at least one level higher than a simple raise: 1 ♠—P—3 ♠.

jump overcall:
A bid after an opponent has opened that is at least one level higher than necessary. This is usually a weak bid.

jump shift:
A response that jumps the bidding into a new suit: 1 ♦—P—2 ♥.

kibitz:
The act of watching play. A spectator is known as a kibitzer.

king:
The second-highest-ranking card in a suit.

knockout teams:
A team event, usually played with extended matches, in which the losers are eliminated.

Laws of Contract Bridge:
The set of rules by which the game of bridge is played. A slightly different set of rules are used for duplicate play.

lay down:
To put the dummy down.

laydown:
Descriptive term for a contract that appears to be so ironclad that the declarer can claim almost as soon as the opening lead is made.

lead:
The first card played after the auction is completed. The player to the left of the declarer makes the opening lead.

lead direction:
A call, usually a double, to indicate a strong holding in a suit and the desire for your partner to lead that suit if the opponents win the auction.

lead up to:
To play a card toward a stronger holding, as from the declarer's hand to the dummy.

Life Master:
The rank to which most members of the American Contract Bridge League aspire.

limit bid:
A bid that is narrowly defined in terms of high-card points.

loser:
A card that cannot win a trick.

major:
Either of the major suits: hearts or spades.

make:
The action of dealing the cards, as in "make the boards," or to be successful in one's contracts, as in "she made 4 ♥."

master card:
The highest unplayed card of a suit.

masterpoint:
A measure of achievement in competition. Awarded to bridge competitors by most bridge organizations, including the ABA and ACBL.

matchpoint:
The means of scoring duplicate bridge pairs contests. Players earn matchpoints on every deal by comparing their scores on those deals to the scores achieved by other pairs playing the same deals.

mirror distribution:
A condition that exists when both partners have the same number of cards in each of the four suits.

misfit:
Two hands with long suits opposite shortness in those suits in the other hand.

mixed pairs:
A duplicate contest in which all partnerships must be of one man and one woman.

negative double:
A double in competition (after an overcall) that is for takeout rather than penalty.

north:
The player who sits opposite South.

North American Bridge Championships:
One of three major tournaments put on by the American Contract Bridge League in the spring, summer, and fall. The NABC lasts for eleven days and includes contests for every level, from beginners to world champions.

no-trump:
A denomination in the bidding with no trump suit.

not vulnerable:
A condition that exposes a partnership to lower risk but also lower rewards for game and slam contracts.

odds:
Mathematical probabilities, usually regarding suit distribution.

offside:
A term indicating a card is not finesseable, as with the king "behind" the AQ and therefore offside.

one no-trump:
A bid usually indicating 15 to 17 high-card points. As a response to an opening bid, 1NT usually shows a lack of trump support and a limited range of HCP, typically 6–9.

opponent:
A member of the opposing side.

over:
One's position at the table with respect to one's right-hand opponent.

overbid:
To bid too much.

overcall:
To enter the auction with a bid after an opponent has opened the bidding.

overruff:
To make a trump trick by ruffing with a higher card than an opponent has ruffed.

overtrick:
A trick in excess of that needed to make one's contract.

pair:
Two players in partnership.

pairs game:
A game scored by matchpoints.

par:
The condition that exists when both sides have done as well as possible on a particular deal.

partial:
Colloquial for part score.

partner:
The person on the other side of the table from you.

pass:
A call that names no denomination and indicates no desire to double or redouble at that turn.

pass out:
Four consecutive passes in an auction.

pass-out seat:
The position of the player whose pass will end the auction.

passive:
Usually applied to defensive action, a nonaggressive, safe action.

penalty:
The score awarded to defenders when a doubled or redoubled contract has been defeated. Also, the action taken by a director when a player has committed an irregularity, such as revoking.

penalty card:
A card played in error and prematurely exposed. It usually stays face up on the table.

penalty double:
A call aimed at increasing the penalty for an unsuccessful contract.

penalty pass:
A call that converts a takeout double into a penalty double, as with 1 ♥—Double—All Pass. The double of 1 ♥ was for takeout. Fourth hand's pass makes it a penalty double.

pianola:
A contract so ironclad that it is said to "play itself."

pickup slip:
The score slips used in duplicate pairs games.

pip:
The symbol indicating a suit: ♠, ♥, ♦, or ♣.

pitch:
Another way of saying "discard."

plain suit:
In a trump contract, any suit that is not trump.

pointed suit:
A spade or diamond.

powerhouse:
A very strong hand in terms of high-card points or a long, strong suit.

pre-emptive bid:
A bid that consumes a large amount of bidding space, usually with a long suit but not much high-card strength, particularly outside the long suit.

primary honors:
Aces and kings.

private scorecard:
The preprinted convention card provided at ACBL games. The card includes space for scores on the other side.

psychic bid:
A call, almost always a bid, that significantly mis-states the high-card strength or the suit length held. Not recommended.

push:
In a team game, a score comparison with no difference or a difference of only 10 points. A tie.

quack:
The queen and jack together, usually in a useless holding.

queen:
The third-ranking card in a suit.

quick trick:
A holding that will win a trick without the need for establishment. AK together are considered two quick tricks, AQ one and a half, A or KQ together one, and Kx a half.

raise:
A bid that indicates support for your partner's suit.

rebid:
Opener's second bid.

redouble:
A call following a double that further increases the penalty for an unsuccessful contract, or the reward for making it.

renege:
To fail to follow suit when it is possible to do so. More properly known as "revoke."

reopen:
Another term for "balancing."

respond:
To make a bid after your partner has bid or made a takeout double.

responder:
The partner of a player who has made a bid or takeout double.

reverse:
A rebid by the opener showing extra strength because the responder, in order to go back to the opener's first suit, must do so at the three level. Example: 1 ♦—P—1 ♠—P; 2 ♥.

review:
A summary of the bidding, starting with the opener.

rock:
A very strong hand; short for "rock crusher."

rotation:
The clockwise order in which calls and plays occur.

rounded suit:
A heart or club.

rubber bridge:
As opposed to duplicate, the style of bridge where the cards are not preserved for play at other tables. A rubber of bridge is complete when one side wins two games.

ruff:
To win a trick with a trump by using it against a plain suit.

ruff and discard:
Also known as ruff and sluff, it occurs when a plain suit is led and both opposing hands are void in that suit, affording the declarer the opportunity to ruff in one hand and discard from another plain suit in the other hand.

Rule of Eleven:
The mathematical rule applied to fourth-best opening leads, allowing the declarer and the partner of the opening leader to determine how many cards are held in the other hands based on the number of the card led.

Rule of Twenty:
A general guideline for opening bids, stating that if the high-card points and length of the two longest suits equal twenty, an otherwise subminimum hand may be opened.

sacrifice:
To deliberately overbid, expecting to be doubled, in hopes that the penalty suffered will be less than the value of the opponent's contract.

scoring table:
List of the various scores for contracts, undoubled, doubled, and redoubled, vulnerable and not vulnerable, all the way from 1 ♣ through 7NT.

seat:
A player's position at the table: North, South, East, or West.

section:
In a duplicate game, a group of tables designated by a letter, such as "Section A."

sequence:
Two or more cards in order: KQ, J10, 987, etc.

short hand:
Usually indicating a hand with fewer trumps than partner's hand.

shuffle:
To mix up the cards preparatory to dealing.

side suit:
A secondary suit in one's hand.

simple finesse:
A play designed to surround a single card in an opponent's hand.

single raise:
A raise of a suit to a minimum level, as 1 ♣—P—2 ♣.

singleton:
One card in a suit.

slam:
A contract requiring the declarer to take twelve tricks (small slam) or thirteen tricks (grand slam).

spade:
The highest-ranking suit (♠).

spot card:
Any non-face card: 10 through 2.

squeeze:
A play that produces an extra trick by forcing an opponent to choose between discards, all of which are bad for the defense.

standard American:
A bidding system based on five-card major openings.

Stayman:
A convention used after a 1NT or 2NT opening to determine whether the opener has a four-card major.

stiff:
Colloquial term for a singleton.

stopper:
Cards in a suit sufficient to keep the opponents from taking all the tricks in that suit.

Swiss teams:
A form of duplicate in which teams of four compete in head-to-head matches, with comparisons converted to International Match Points for ranking purposes.

takeout double:
A double not intended for penalty, usually of an opening bid and indicating approximately opening-hand values and support for the unbid suits.

tenace:
Two cards not in sequence, such as AQ or KJ.

third hand:
The third player to bid in the auction or to make a play.

threat card:
Required for the successful operation of a squeeze.

throw-in play:
An endplay in which an opponent is put into the lead to his disadvantage.

top:
In duplicate, the highest score to be achieved on a deal.

trick:
Four cards played in rotation.

trump:
The suit designated by the auction.

trump support:
Three or more cards when the opening bid has been in a major, or if any suit has been over-called. For minor-suit openings, trump support is usually at least four cards.

two-bid:
Any opening bid at the two level.

two over one response:
A response to an opening bid at the two level, as 1 ♠—P—2 ♣.

two-suiter:
Usually a hand with two suits of at least five cards. Also sometimes applied to hands with 5–4 in two suits.

unbid suit:
Any suit not mentioned in the auction.

underlead:
To lead away from, as to lead the 2 from K542.

unfavorable vulnerability:
A condition existing when one side is vulnerable and the other is not. The vulnerable side is said to be at "unfavorable."

up the line:
Bidding at the cheapest level possible.

void:
No cards in a suit.

vulnerable:
A condition in bridge with greater rewards for game and slam bidding, and greater penalties for unsuccessful contracts.

whist:
A predecessor to bridge, played primarily in England.

winner:
A card that usually will win a trick.

working card:
A card is said to be working when it faces other high cards in the same suit.

yarborough:
A hand with no card higher than a 9.

zero:
In duplicate, the lowest score on a deal.

Index